M000313344

On the Origin of Hockey

Hockey on the Ice.

ON
THE ORIGIN OF HOCKEY

CARL GIDÉN
PATRICK HOUDA
JEAN-PATRICE MARTEL

HOCKEY ORIGIN PUBLISHING
STOCKHOLM AND CHAMBLY

© 2014 Carl Gidén, Patrick Houda and Jean-Patrice Martel

Printed and bound in Canada.

18   17   16   15   14   1   2   3   4   5

ISBN 978-0-9937998-0-8
Library and Archives Canada Cataloguing in Publication data is available
upon request.

Hockey Origin Publishing
ontheoriginofhockey@gmail.com

To all people searching for the truth

Contents

Acknowledgments

THE AUTHORS WOULD LIKE to acknowledge the contributions of the following people to their project:

Mike Barford, for his help in finding and identifying the various editions of *The Boy's Own Book,* especially the 1868 edition, which provided the spark that got this book project going.

The owners of the Blyberg-Lefever Collection, for kindly providing us with good-quality reproductions of the Le Petit engraving, and for the research that led to the likely identification of its artist (Benedictus Antonio Van Assen).

Bill Fitsell, founding president of the Society for International Hockey Research (SIHR), for always having the piece of information that we were looking for, and so generously providing it within hours and sometimes minutes of the request, and perhaps more importantly, for his encouraging words and interest in our research, and for creating SIHR in the first place.

Martin Harris for providing key illustrations found in the book as well as the sets of NSA rules from 1883.

Hugh Dan MacLennan for his knowledge of shinty and hurling, particularly for several of the early shinty references, and more generally for helping us understand the evolution of those games through his books and the personal exchanges of research findings.

Kevin Shea for knowing so much about hockey books and for being so generously willing to provide excellent advice.

James Milks for his work on the Hockey Origins database and for being so tolerant of our sometimes strange requests.

We wish to thank the members of the Origins of Hockey committee of SIHR and its former chair, Paul Kitchen, for providing a clear and universally accepted definition of hockey, so we didn't have to create our own.

And very special thanks to our spouses and family members for being so accepting of our passion and the long hours we dedicated to it in the last few months—as well as the last several years.

Foreword

Writing a book on the origin of hockey is just about the most exciting project that hockey researchers can endeavour to do. It is also a frightening one.

When Carl Gidén started researching the origins of European hockey more than two decades ago, he was surprised to discover that much of the "recorded" history of the sport was in fact inaccurate. Hockey history has plenty of myths about its origins that have as much bearing to the truth as the Cooperstown/Abner Doubleday story does to the origins of baseball.

Patrick Houda, who was also researching the origins of hockey, had — not surprisingly — come to a similar conclusion. It is no coincidence that, before long, they crossed paths and started teaming up for some of their projects.

Together they have produced several documents, including the online hockey timeline available to the members of the Society for International Hockey Research (SIHR) since 2010 — which has since been replaced by the Hockey Origins database. It was also these two Swedes who prepared a "who's who" of the pioneers of hockey in Canada, providing short biographies of, among others, all 18 participants in the very first game of hockey played in Montreal, on March 3, 1875.

These two guys from across the ocean have also unearthed a few gems about early instances of hockey played in Canada, notably the discovery of hockey played in Niagara Falls, Ontario, in 1839, and of what was probably a hockey-like game—using a ball and "hurlies" (sticks)—reportedly played in Pictou, Nova Scotia, in 1811.

I met Patrick at the 2008 annual general meeting of SIHR in Quebec City—a meeting I organized and which coincided with the final weekend of the International Ice Hockey Federation's World Championship tournament. I very much appreciated that Patrick did not give me a hard time when my presentation on the 1970 tournament debacle was quite critical of the Swedish hockey authorities of the time. In fact, he seemed to agree with my interpretation of the events.

I met Carl through SIHR, thanks to his work on the timeline, but our encounters so far have only been remote. The Internet does make the world smaller. By the time you read this, the three of us will have gotten together for the first time on the occasion of SIHR's AGM in Penetanguishene, Ontario, in May 2014.

Don't be surprised if some of the information in this book seems hard to believe at first. It did seem incredible to all three of us that there is so much material available about the origins of hockey that nobody seemed to be aware of before—material that tells a story so completely different from what we have read and heard about everywhere.

In this book, you will find very few references quoting other hockey historians, because we have made the choice to use, in nearly all cases, primary sources. Of course, exceptions were made for historians who were alive at the time of the events that they recorded. We have also chosen to provide, as much as possible, the full texts from the original sources, to avoid misleading the reader with truncated quotes.

The majority of these references from primary sources can be found in the SIHR Hockey Origins database mentioned earlier. Each reference provides the full text of the quote, and comes with additional information about the location of the reported event, where applicable, and mini-biographies of the people involved, where known.

So writing a book on the origin of hockey is exciting and frightening, as I mentioned earlier. Perhaps this is why Carl, Patrick and I did not set out at first to write one. Our goal was to write a paper for SIHR's *Hockey Research Journal,* highlighting some of the most important (and recent) findings about the origins of hockey.

But we quickly realized that limiting ourselves to just a subset of the subject matter would be exceedingly frustrating, as we would have found

ourselves constantly evoking available information without the space to actually provide it. So a change of plans was quickly adopted.

How was I selected from among the three of us to write the text? I don't
know for sure; all I can say is that it was the idea of Carl and Patrick, and
together they hold a majority of votes among our group... It might have
had something to do with the fact that I initially was the one pushing for
the project. It certainly is an honour that I hope I have proven worthy of.

The debate on hockey's origin is not closed—far from it. It almost certainly
will never be. But we like to think that this book will reinvigorate the debate
and give it somewhat of a fresh start, while clearing up several misconceptions
and false assumptions that have been perpetuated over several decades by
researchers who did not have at their disposal the benefit of the 21st-century
research tools now available.

Enjoy!

JEAN-PATRICE MARTEL, APRIL 25, 2014

The Birthplaces of Hockey

THE BIRTHPLACE OF HOCKEY is in Canada. We all know that. That is why, after all, Canadians are so good at the game. But the question of where exactly the game was created has been the subject of unending speculation. Ask hockey fans to identify the birthplace of hockey, and the answer you will get is likely to depend on the hometown of the person asked.

Typically, that answer will be among one of the following: Windsor, Nova Scotia; Kingston, Ontario; Halifax (or Halifax-Dartmouth), Nova Scotia; Montreal, Quebec; Deline, Northwest Territories; or (for those paying really close attention) Niagara Falls, Ontario. As you will see, a few more Canadian towns have thrown their hat into the ring, though to very little effect.

The amount of evidence provided to the public appears to depend much on the seniority of the claim; those of Deline and Niagara Falls, being based on recent research findings, lag far behind the other four, which have had books (or at least some printed publications) and, more recently, websites presenting thousands of words of arguments as to why their claim is the truly valid one.

The attentive observer, however, will eventually notice that nearly all of the evidence provided by the claimants is circumstantial, backed up by very little in the way of solid references.

Let us take a look at exactly how much documentary proof underlies each of these claims.

Windsor, Nova Scotia

The Windsor claim, championed over the years by the late Garth Vaughan—who wrote the 210-page book *The Puck Starts Here*[1] —and the late Howard Dill, is probably the best known of all birthplace claims, and the Windsor Hockey Heritage Society was able to use this notoriety to convince the Nova Scotia Ministry of Transport to erect a sign reading BIRTHPLACE OF HOCKEY at the highway exit leading to Windsor.

The claim puts the origins of hockey ca. 1800, based on a very short passage from the novel *The Attaché*, written by a Nova Scotia Supreme Court judge and author, Thomas Chandler Haliburton (1796-1865). Haliburton created the character of Samuel "Sam" Slick in 1835; Slick was featured in stories published first as newspaper sketches in *The Novascotian,* and later collected and published in *The Clockmaker* (1836); *The Attaché, or, Sam Slick in England* (published in two volumes, in 1843 and 1844); and *Sam Slick's Wise Saws and Modern Instances* (1853).

The Windsor claim points to a passage in the second volume of *The Attaché*, in which Slick is talking to Squire Poker, also a fictitious character, who acts as the narrator. Slick imagines how the reunion of Poker with an old friend might go:

> When you see him, don't the old schoolmaster rise up before you as nateral as if it was only yesterday? and the school-room, and the noisy, larkin', happy holidays, and you boys let out racin', yelpin', hollerin', and whoopin' like mad with pleasure, and the playground, and the game at bass in the fields, or hurly on the long pond on the ice, or campin' out a-night at Chester lakes to fish—catchin' no trout, gettin' wet thro' and thro' with rain like a drown'd rat,—eat up body and bones by black flies and muschetoes, returnin' tired to death, and callin' it a party of pleasure...[2]

The claimants' interpretation is that the author was reminiscing about his own early education at King's Collegiate School (known today as King's-Edgehill School) in Windsor, from which he graduated in 1810. Considering Judge Haliburton's birthdate (December 17, 1796), it would appear that the "ca. 1800" affixed to the claim is optimistic, as it presumes the author could reminisce about events that occurred when he was no older than three years and two weeks of age. A more likely estimate would be ca. 1805–1810, corresponding to the last five years of the author's stay at King's, when he was between eight and thirteen years old.

This interpretation got a boost with the finding of an anonymous letter published in the *Windsor Mail* in 1876 (exact date unknown), in which the author remembers his own years (1816–1818) at the same school:

> The Devil's Punch Bowl and Long Pond, back of the College, were favorite resorts, and we used to skate in winter, on moonlight nights, on the ponds. I recollect John Cunard (brother of Sir Samuel of steamship fame) having his front teeth knocked out with a hurley by Pete Delancey of Annapolis.[3]

Such recollections, some 60 years after the fact, must always be considered cautiously; however, John Cunard, born in 1800, would have been at least 16 at the time, which makes the story at least plausible. Hurley (or hurly) is usually the name given to the stick used in hurling, a stick-and-ball game played in Ireland.

A controversy has arisen as to exactly which pond is the "Long Pond." It appears that the body of water that is today most commonly viewed as the "Long Pond" used to be called "Steel Pond" and was mechanically enlarged (elongated?), while another nearby pond was always called "Long Pond."[4] We have not researched this extensively, as both ponds are situated in Windsor, after which the claim is named.

Pictou, Nova Scotia

There isn't really a "Pictou birthplace claim," yet two different references involving Pictou have surfaced.

The first appeared in the 1895 book *East River Sketches, Historical and Biographical: With Reminiscences of Scottish Life,* written by Rev. Robert Grant. In the book, the reverend tells the story of Hugh (The Big Deacon) McKay (1789–1869), who was known to be strongest man in the County of Pictou. As told, the story took place in 1811. Grant writes:

> When the Deacon was 22, there came to Pictou town a professed wrestler from the United States. His name was William Allan. He put up at Lorraine's hotel, and sent forth his challenge to any bluenose within 20 miles, for a trial of strength and skill. In the prosecution of his calling, the best

wrestlers about town and the West River lay prostrate on the floor. In
these extremities, after consultation held, the future Deacon is waited
on by a delegation, at his house at Riverton.

Grant goes on to describe the first meeting between McKay and Allan.
Finally, the wrestling match occurs:

> The highlander gained an easy victory, and the assembled bluenoses,
> elate with joy, and proud of their youthful hero, for farther recreation
> repaired to the ice on the harbor to skate and play ball. While thus en-
> joying themselves to their heart's content, a messenger appears in their
> midst, with a fresh challenge from the hotel—the Yankee wished to
> wrestle again.
>
> Nothing loath, skates and hurlies laid aside, there is another rush for
> the hall. The combatants assume their former position and attitude. The
> benches are more crowded than before. But the Deacon told me that,
> this time, Allan was a totally different man from what he was in the
> forenoon—acting entirely on the defensive.

Grant concludes with Allan suggesting that they call it a draw, but the
Deacon refuses to stop until Allan acknowledges that McKay is the better
man of the two. Allan made the required acknowledgement, and "the affair
ended in peace and mutual good will."[5]

Another reference from Pictou is occasionally used to bolster the Windsor
claim.[6] Following a Nova Scotia Supreme Court decision in 1829, allowing
recreational amusement on the Sabbath, an irate observer wrote to Pictou's
newspaper, the *Colonial Patriot and Miscellaneous Select.*

> Every idler who feels disposed to profane the Lord's day, may now secure
> from any consequences turn out with skates on feet, hurly in hand, and
> play the delectable *game* of break-shins without any regard to laws which
> were made solely for the 'levity of manners which prevailed in the days of
> Charles 1st,' and which are declared by our Judges to be of no validity.[7]

Fort Daer, Pembina, ~~Manitoba~~ North Dakota

This barely qualifies as a claim. It is included for completeness and because
it is a good story. At a time when the present-day province of Manitoba

was still part of Rupert's Land (owned by the Hudson's Bay Company), Scottish peer Thomas Douglas, 5th Earl of Selkirk, appointed Miles Mac-Donell (circa 1767–1828) as the first governor of Assiniboia and tasked him with leading a party of settlers to the Red River colony in 1812. On October 27, the group set up makeshift huts on the south bank of the Pembina River, near its confluence with the Red River and across from Fort Pembina. They named their settlement Fort Daer, in honour of Selkirk's son, James Dunbar, the future 6th Earl of Selkirk.

MacDonnell kept a diary, which is now held as part of the collection of the 5th Earl of Selkirk at the Archives of Manitoba. The entry for December 25, 1812, reads as follows:

> Christmas day—Play at the Hurl on the ice with the people of the 3 Forts. We all dine at Mr. Hillier's, dance to the Bag Pipe in the evening. Very pleasant party. Mr. McRae ordered the 2 men that came last with meat to go off immediately for more, they came to me and I gave them leave to stay not knowing. We had afterwards some words in consequence of Mr. McR's order. He accused me of not supporting my officers.

No skates are mentioned, and it seems unlikely that settlers would have had them, let alone that there would have been enough for everyone.

Until 1823, both Canada and the United States believed that Pembina and Fort Daer were in Canadian territory, but the survey of the 49th parallel by U. S. Army Major Stephen H. Long brought a surprise: their sites were less than three kilometres south of the border, making this birthplace claim the only one suffering from identity disorder.

Unlike Pictou, however, there is an actual "claim" for Fort Daer being hockey's birthplace, although its proponents are not particularly active. They were last heard from in 1957, in a program from a Winnipeg Warriors (Western Hockey League) game. The report does not cite its sources, and probably only had MacDonell's diary (and evidently no atlas) to go by, but it is a sufficiently interesting read to be reproduced here:

THE BIRTH OF HOCKEY

Hockey was born on Christmas Day, 1812, in a game on the ice at Red River (now Winnipeg) between Lord Selkirk's settlers and the Hudson's Bay men. Scots who knew hurley and Irishmen who knew shinny played in the game along with Moravians, French-Canadians, Orkney-men, Indians and half breeds. Any kind of rounded end stick was used, the puck was a leather ball and no one had skates. None the less it was the beginning of hockey. Dozens played the game, no holds were barred and since the fur men resented the settlers it must have been some scrimmage. "Even so, when it was ended," says Governor Macdonald [sic] in his journal, "everyone dined at Mr Hilliar's [sic] and later Danced to the Bag Pipe." The day after the New Year's more serious feuding was on again.

Deline, Northwest Territories

The Deline claim is quite recent. Only in August of 2002 did the reference underlying it come to light, thanks to the investigative work of Joseph Nieforth. The claim is based on writings by Sir John Franklin (1786–1847), a British explorer who hailed from Spilsby, Lincolnshire, and made four trips to map out the Canadian Northwest Territories—specifically to search for Northwest Passage, that elusive holy grail of shortcuts that would have greatly reduced the travel distance from Europe to the Far East.

Sir Franklin kept detailed diaries of the events of his voyages and wrote many letters to family and acquaintances, so his explorations are particularly well documented. On his second expedition, which lasted from February 16, 1825, to September 26, 1827, he made several mentions of hockey played on ice by his crew.

First, in a letter to the Scottish geologist Sir Roderick Impey Murchison, evidently written on October 21, 1825, though dated November 6:

> Until the day of before yesterday, 20th October, we had comparatively little snow, and this is the first day that our dogs have been used in dragging sledges. Four trains of two dogs each were despatched for meat this morning. We endeavour to keep ourselves in good humour, health, and spirits by an agreeable variety of useful occupation and amusement. Till the snow fell, the game of hockey, played on the ice, was the morning's sport.[8]

Then, in his diary, written in the later part of October 1825:

> We were visited on the 20th by a storm of snow, which continued, without intermission, for thirty-six hours. Although it put an end to the skating,

and the games on the ice, which had been our evenings' amusement for the preceding week...⁹

Finally, in a letter to his niece Mary Anne Kay dated November 8, 1825:

> The house was opened on the 23rd of September by a ball...I forced myself however to join in the dance with spirit, and after a time, when I have witnessed the harmony and happiness that brightened every countenance in the mixed assembly of English, Highlanders, Canadians, Esquimaux, and Indians, I was much relieved...We had but two ladies and a half, one being a little girl...I have seldom seen a finer or better behaved body of men. Our stock of wine, &c., will not allow of our having many set dances, but the men often foot it in their own houses to Wilson's pipes, and at other times they join with the officers in blind man's buff, hiding the handkerchief, and other games, in which I daresay you and the Admiral would gladly join, but since the ice has set in they have been kept in full exercise by the game of hockey...¹⁰

While sweaters proclaiming Deline as the "Birthplace of Ice Hockey in Canada" are known to exist, the primary advocate for the claim, Norman Yakeleya, the member of the Northwest Territories legislative assembly whose constituency includes Deline, did eventually scale the claim back to the more plausible proposition that the Franklin reference was "the first time the words ice and hockey were used in Canada, to say that it's ice hockey."¹¹ As we will examine later, there is a world of difference between a "first time" and a "birthplace," and the amended claim appears to err on the side of caution. Still, not only is it true that this was the first time that *ice* and *hockey* were used in Canada (that we are currently aware), but it is the oldest known contemporary reference to any hockey-like game played on ice in Canada.

Halifax-Dartmouth, Nova Scotia
This long-standing claim came to particular prominence with the 2002 publication of *Hockey's Home—Halifax-Dartmouth: The Origin of Canada's Game*,¹² a 118-page book by Martin Jones, with a foreword by none other than Paul Henderson, hero of the 1972 series between the Soviet Union

and (for the first time) the best NHL professionals, which came to be known as the "Summit Series."

The book, based partly on the work of the late Halifax-Dartmouth historian Dr. John Martin (1886–1969), supports the theory that the earliest form of hockey developed on Dartmouth's Lake Banook and, about five kilometres away, Halifax's Northwest Arm, originally called Sandwich River—possibly renamed when it was discovered that it was in fact not a river.

Jones conveniently grouped most of the contemporary evidence at his disposal at the very beginning of his book, stressing how much better documented the Halifax-Dartmouth claim was relative to the Windsor one,[13] a statement that appears to be objectively correct.

The oldest reference known to exist for the Halifax-Dartmouth claim was a poem published in the January 1827 edition of Halifax's *Acadian Magazine*:

> Now at ricket with hurlies some dozens of boys
> Chase the ball o'er the ice, with a deafening noise.
> Now some play at curling, and some with great ease
> Cut circles or figures whichever you please
> On their skates, or else letters—the true lover's knot,
> And a dozen such things which I've really forgot.[14]

"Ricket" is understood to designate a hockey-like game, while the "hurlies" are the sticks used in the game. The author of the poem does not appear to be known, so it remains to be confirmed that he/she was actually referring to an activity practised in the vicinity of Halifax or Dartmouth.

The next exhibit is the 1831 cut portrait (silhouette) of six-year-old Henry Piers, executed by Halifax artist Hankes.[15] The boy does appear to be carrying a stick resembling those used to play hockey. Martin Jones calls it a "hockey stick," though the term "hockey" would not be used in Halifax for about three more decades, so a "hurley" might have been a better term. It is impossible not to notice that the boy is on foot, not on skates.

Then, in 1842, on January 18, the Halifax *Morning Post*[16] reported on the ice condition:

> The Dartmouth Lakes were rough yesterday. Maynard's was best—but a great spot might be found almost on any of them for a game of ricket.

Hankes' silhouette of a stick-carrying boy and his parents.

By the way, there is to be a great match today, if the weather be fine—which is very doubtful.

The next quote comes from a book that appears to mix fiction and true historical events. Such sources must always be considered carefully (as with the Windsor Haliburton reference), but should not necessarily always be dismissed out of hand. The book, published in 1846 under the name Miss Grove, is entitled *Little Grace, or, Scenes in Nova Scotia*. The author was probably Anne Grove (1813–1899), who was born in Staffordshire, England, and immigrated to Philadelphia in 1832. After the death of her father, she moved to Halifax and established the Miss Grove School for Country Girls. A passage from the book describes how a boy named George went skating on the lake at Dartmouth around Christmas 1844.

> When George had been at home a week, he went with a party of boys to skate on a lake at Dartmouth . . .
>
> The lake the skaters had chosen was the same Grace had seen on the day Miss Martha had given the children the pic-nic in the woods, but it looked very different. Then she had seen a squaw paddling her canoe through the transparent water; now it seemed as solid as a rock, and parties of skaters were flying over it in all directions. Grace looked about for George, and as she did not see him, she felt sure he was with some boys whom she saw playing at hurley on the ice.[17]

On Saturday, January 22, 1853, the *Acadian Recorder* reprinted an article from *The Church Times,* itself probably reporting on events from the previous Sunday (January 9) that took place on the North West Arm (as it was then spelled):

Sabbath Desecration

> The streets of Halifax on Sundays, at the usual hours for worship are generally thronged with old and young, on their way to their respective Churches and Chapels, thus giving the appearance at all events, of reverence for the day of God.
>
> Not so was it in the vicinity of the Town, on Sunday last. The Lake above Mr. Hostermau's, was literally covered with skaters, with their hurlies, and the small spots of ice available on the N. W. Arm were similarly occupied, to the great peril of those upon it.
>
> The road leading in that direction, was filled with persons of all ages, going towards the place of sport; and we regret to add, that well dressed *females* were to be seen in the considerable numbers on the shores, enjoying the scene,—while the vile effluvia, from hundreds of cigars, polluted the pure atmosphere of heaven, for a considerable distance around. All this too, during the hours of Divine Service...[18]

A better description of the activity appears in the January 4, 1859, edition of *The British Colonist,* a Halifax newspaper:

THE YOUNG MEN OF HALIFAX

We have long held the opinion that the young men of this city are second to none in the world of energy, skill, and daring, in all manly games and exercises … Often have we been led to express the same opinion, when the bat laid aside, skates strapped on, and hurly in hand, the ball is followed over the glassy surface of the lakes, which ring to the skates' heel…[19]

The most detailed Halifax reference comes from … Boston. On November 5, 1859, a Boston *Evening Gazette* reporter described the winter sports played in Nova Scotia, and "particularly in Halifax":

In Nova Scotia the time for fun is during the months of December, January and February. The lakes are then frozen and the ground generally covered with snow, although but seldom is there snow enough before Christmas to make sleighing. Skating is the favorite pastime during December, and, indeed, all through the winter, if—as is sometimes the case—there is not a great deal of snow.

There are some excellent skaters in the Provinces, particularly in Halifax. I have seen young men who could cut their name in German text, or write the Lord's prayer with skates on the ice easier than most skaters could cut the "outside edge." I don't like to be uncharitable, but I have known some skaters who, I think, would not be able to do it without a written or printed copy before their eyes. Throwing a somersault on skates is almost an impossibility yet I once saw it done successfully.

Fancy skating is not so much practiced in Nova Scotia now as formerly; more attention is paid to games on the ice. Ricket* is the favorite pastime, and is played thus. Two rickets are formed at about the same distance, one from the other, that cricketers place their wickets. If there are many players, the rickets are further apart. A ricket consists of two stones—about as large as the cobble stones with which some of our streets have been lately paved—placed about three or four feet apart and frozen to the ice. Sides are then formed by two persons—one opposed to the other—tossing or drawing lots for first choice of partners. The one who obtains the first choice selects one from the crowd, the other party then chooses another, and so on alternately, until a sufficient number is obtained on each side. Any number can play the game, and, generally, the "more the merrier." Each ricketer is provided with a hurley (or hockey, as it is termed here,) and all being ready, a ball is thrown in the air, which is the signal to commence the play, previous to which, however, a ricket is chosen by each side and placed in charge of a man whose duty it is to prevent the ball from passing through. The game may be 10, 15 or 20, or any number agreed upon, the side counting the number first being winners. The counting consists in putting the ball through your adversary's ricket, each time counting one. From the moment the ball touches the ice, at the commencement of the game; it must not be taken in the hand until the conclusion, but must be carried or struck about the ice with the hurlies. A good player—and to be a good player he must be a good skater—will take the ball at the point of his hurley and carry it around the pond and through the crowd which surrounds him trying to take it from him, until he works it near his opponent's ricket, and "then comes the tug of war," both sides striving for the mastery. Whenever the ball is put through the ricket the shout "game ho!" resounds from shore to shore and dies away in hundreds of echoes through the hills. Ricket is the most exciting game that is played on the ice.

*Note of the Editor, Boston *Evening Gazette*... It might be well if some of our agile skaters would introduce this game. It would be a fine addition to our winter sports, and give a new zest to the delightful exercise of skating. We have sent down for a set of hurleys preparatory to its introduction.[20]

The part omitted describes (much more summarily) other activities like curling, sledding, sleighing and moose and fox hunting. Who better to report on local customs than foreigners? The same article appeared, 10 days later, in Halifax's *The British Colonist,* even including the Note of the Editor—with the mention "*Eds. Gazett.* [sic]."[21]

In 1863, one of the first covered ice rinks in Canada was erected at the Horticultural Gardens in Halifax. Dartmouth historian Martin, who made an extensive research of hockey and its origin in Nova Scotia, stated in his privately published work *The Birthplace of Hockey*[22] that the rink had been the site of indoor hockey games.

Dr. Martin noted that organized games played in the new rink in the winter of 1863 were regularly reported in the local papers, and that "Hockey must have been a game of long standing in and about Halifax, because the newspapers did not comment on anything extraordinary about the contests: which suggests that their readers were well acquainted with hockey procedure and practices. The only seeming novelty was that the game was played indoors for the first time, and necessarily limited the number of players on each side."

Unfortunately, Dr. Martin did not provide specific examples of the games played in the rink, and many of the original newspapers from those years, which were held in the archives of Nova Scotia, were destroyed in the 1960s. As a consequence, none of the game reports evoked by Dr. Martin has been uncovered yet.

An article published in the *Halifax Reporter* on January 2, 1864, contains a novelty: the use of the term "hockey on the ice" in a Canadian publication:

> If we turn towards the country, we are at once struck by the almost total absence of stone throwing boys, upon whose characteristics and mode of life we remarked in a former article. What has become of them? The nearest pond answers this question; they are playing hockey on the ice and occasionally mimicking the mistakes of such among their betters as are not quite at home upon skates…[23]

While the game is not described, it is *called* hockey, and is clearly played on the ice, with skates.

Ice hockey was apparently also played in 1867 in Halifax, according to Charles Cooper Penrose Fitzgerald (1841–1921) in his 1913 book, *Memories of the Sea*. The Irish-born Fitzgerald, a vice-admiral in the (British) Royal Navy, wrote a two-part autobiography, of which *Memories* was the first volume.

In the winter of 1866–67 he was serving as first lieutenant on the 11-gun Racer-class sloop HMS *Cordelia,* stationed at Halifax. Using his own journal to recall the events of the winter, he elaborates on how the crew was kept occupied:

> As for the officers, we thoroughly enjoyed ourselves with skating, sleighing, tobogganing, and dancing. There were several thaws during the winter,

so that we not only had skating in the covered rink, but also on one of the numerous lakes on the Dartmouth side of the harbour, and also on an arm of the sea known as the North-west arm.

The open-air skating was much more enjoyable than the rink skating, and, as most of the young ladies at Halifax were accomplished skaters, we had tea-parties on the lakes, lighting a fire and making tea on the ice, which was two or three feet thick. Ice hockey was also good fun and warm work, and the winter was, in fact, one big holiday—all beer and skittles—so that we were quite sorry when the spring came and we had to re-rig our ship and go to sea again. And, strange to say, none of us got engaged to be married, though we were all, except one, bachelors.[24]

Note that, while the text is based on a diary written in 1867, the book itself was written in 1913, which probably explains the use of the term "ice hockey," which is unlikely to have been used as far back as 1867.

That same winter of 1867, the *Halifax Evening Reporter* published a fairly detailed account of two games played simultaneously three days earlier on the North West Arm:

Skating Scribblings by Icicle

The North West Arm being rough, Maynard's Lake bleak and partly open, the 1st and 2nd Dartmouth decidedly sheely, skaters cast about for good ice, and by some unknown means the initiated were informed of there being a good surface on the almost unknown 'Oathill Lake', where our grandfathers fished fifty years ago....

On Saturday the lake was covered with skaters of both sexes, there being about 1000 there during the afternoon. In every direction pretty sylphlike forms were to be seen either cutting the 'outside edge' independently, or timidly learning to 'stroke out', aided by the strong arms of the sterner sex....

Two well contested games of 'ricket' were being played. At the upper end were a number of young men from Dartmouth and the City, playing their 'hurlies' and 'following up' the ball while the centre was occupied by a number of officers of the Garrison and Fleet, in a match game called hockey i.e. ricket.

The boundary lines of each game were not well defined, and occasionally the 'aristocratic hockey ball' would encroach on the upper game when the 'plebian hurleys' would pass it around for a time and send it back again to its select circle.

Very little science was displayed in either game, the old class of players seem to have died out, and their successors are not up in the science of leading off the ball, doubling and carrying it through.

Instead of the old styles, the game as now played is dangerous to outsiders, especially to ladies, some of whom were rather roughly treated in the scrimmage after the ball. There was no tenderness displayed in the 'United Service Game', as many sore shins can testify, and more than one poor little middy got a stretcher from their heavier antagonists of the land service.

Some small boys had the hardihood and impudence to raise their hurleys to strike the 'swell ball' as it passed them, for which the flagrant crime they were visited with condign punishment. This was not relished by the friends of the juveniles, who after their own fashion encroached upon and took partial possession of the select territory which, during infringement resulted in terrible forebodings of a conflict between both sides, but although a forest of sticks and hurleys were raised in the air, not a head was broke, or, as Pat said at Donnybrook, 'six o'clock came and no blow struck'.

However, the 'exclusives' had to abandon their game and retire from the field with their 'hot porter' apparatus, which had been well patronised during the day. To the bystanders it was great fun, and it would be hard to say which side behaved the best or the worst.

This much must be said, that if exclusive games of hockey are to be played, a crowded lake is no place for it, moreover as one said, a ricket ball on the ice is like an old hat on the road, to be hit by everybody, and as it is the established custom for everyone who chooses to take a hand in, it is next to impossible to play match games except on unfrequented ice.[25]

Again, the description is quite detailed and mentions the "science of the game" and the "old class of players," which suggests that the game had indeed been played in the region for some time. Perhaps of particular interest is the suggestion that "raising the hurley" to strike the "swell ball" was frowned upon, an apparent indication that, despite the name of the stick (hurley), the game did not resemble today's hurling in any way.

*"Curling on the Lakes, Near Halifax, Nova Scotia"; the hockey-like
activity is behind the curlers.*

The following winter, a British officer and artist, Henry Buckton Laurence
(1842-1886), was inspired by "Canadian sports and pastimes" to produce
a collection of 19 lithographs, published in London in 1870 under the full
title *Sketches of Canadian Sports and Pastimes dedicated by kind permission
HRH Lieutenant Prince Arthur of the Rifle Brigade*.[26] Laurence, who in the
winter of 1867-68 held the rank of lieutenant, drew inspiration for one of
these prints from the various activities practised on ice in Halifax. The print's
title, *Curling on the Lakes, near Halifax, Nova Scotia*, refers to the game
played in the foreground of the illustration, but many more activities are
seen in the background, including at least seven players wielding sticks and
chasing a ball (or perhaps a puck—it's hard to tell), in a game that decidedly
resembles hockey (or "ricket"). There is no information available as to exactly
which frozen body of water the scene took place on.

Shortly before the onset of the winter of 1869-70, the creation of a club
"for the prosecution of the interesting winter sport of ricket" was proposed

in the *Acadian Recorder*. The city already had two ricket clubs, so the game had seemingly started the process of becoming organized:

> A meeting will be held on Tuesday or Wednesday...for the purpose of completing the organization.
>
> There is a ricket club formed of the officers of the 78th Regiment, another by some members of the Phoenix Cricket Club and one is proposed at Dartmouth.[27]

It is not known whether the club came into existence.

Some references mentioned by Mr. Jones have been left off this list, for reasons we will discuss in chapter 14. These include an 1831 newspaper article referring to a game of "wicket" (presumably on the ice), an 1863 poem entitled "Frost" and an 1864 *Halifax Morning Sun* article entitled "A Few Hints on Skating!"

Kingston, Ontario

This might be viewed as the "historical" birthplace claim.

Kingston was the home of James Thomas Sutherland (1870–1955), one of the most famous characters in the early history of hockey in Ontario. First a player, then a coach, he returned from World War I with the rank of captain and a passion for hockey that would lead him to assume the top executive positions at the provincial level, with the Ontario Hockey Association, and then nationally, with the Canadian Amateur Hockey Association.

In 1943, when the location of an eventual Hockey Hall of Fame was being discussed, Sutherland pulled out all the stops to have his hometown selected. His efforts included the advancement of the argument that Kingston was the birthplace of hockey, a claim he'd been making since as far back as 1924, in an article entitled "Origin of Hockey" that appeared in *Hockey Year Book* by George King.

> Whatever measure of merit the claim of other places may have, I think it is generally admitted and has been substantially proven on many former occasions that the actual birthplace of organized hockey is the city of Kingston, in the year 1888.[28]

The year was incorrect—he actually meant 1886—and it is now generally accepted that organized hockey had already been played more than a decade earlier in Montreal. In fact, Sutherland would be strongly criticized by Emanuel M. Orlick (1910-2001) in *The Gazette* (Montreal) in 1943[29] for the absence of any contemporary references in his "research" into the origins of hockey. Yet, there may still have been some validity to a Kingston claim.

Sir Arthur Henry Freeling (1820-1885), 5th Baronet of Ford and Hatchings, Sussex, was born in London. He embraced a military career, and in 1839, while a first lieutenant, he was posted to Upper Canada, soon to become Canada West, where he subsequently served as adjutant to Colonel William Holloway. He was recalled to England in 1844, where he was assigned to supervise the construction of large barracks.

Freeling's diary contains a passage, part of an entry dated January 24, 1843, of particular interest to hockey birthplace researchers: "Began to skate this year, improved quickly and had great fun at hockey on the ice."[30]

Freeling's observation is usually viewed as the primary "modern" argument for the Kingston claim, though detractors are quick to point out that, as for the Deline claim, even though skating and hockey are mentioned in the same sentence, there is no evidence that both were done simultaneously.

Between 1838 and 1843, more than 40 reports of games of "shinty" appeared in various Kingston newspapers, referring to games played on ice by members of a shinty—or "camac"—club (*camac* being the Gaelic word for shinty), but among them there does not appear to be a single mention of skates. This could not, however, be verified with certainty and it would be a worthwhile project to collect all those references and examine them in detail. Below is one such report, from the Kingston *Chronicle and Gazette* in January 1840, mentioning that a game had been played on Kingston Harbour ice for the second consecutive New Year's Day:

> At the appointed hour about 300 persons, including spectators, assembled on the ice in front of the town... The ball was flung up in the air between the two adverse chieftains as the signal to commence hostilities and immediately a most vigorous contest was begun and maintained nearly three hours with unabated energy.[31]

In a second reference to early hockey (or something similar) played on ice with skates in Kingston, Captain Edwin "Ted" Horsey (1837-1908), father of the local historian Edwin Horsey, shared his recollections with a journalist from the Kingston *Daily British Whig.* It should be noted that these reminiscences, published on March 3, 1906, are often presented as being taken from a diary, as in the Canadian Amateur Hockey Association's 1942 report, *Origin of Hockey in Canada,* but there is no evidence that it was anything more than a cordial conversation between Captain Horsey and the *Whig* reporter. As it is in the CAHA report, the quote is also often, perhaps disingenuously, presented in a heavily condensed version, making it seem as though the "boys" mentioned might have been soldiers stationed in Kingston, something that is clearly disproven by the longer excerpt below. The number of players is also typically omitted, as the rather large number mentioned ("fifty or more") would appear to describe a particularly informal game, with probably very few rules:

> I have frequently heard it said that Kingston has not advanced in the last fifty or sixty years. I will give a description of the limestone city of sixty years ago, and the reader can judge whether the city has advanced or retrograded.
>
> Sixty years ago I came to Kingston from England....
>
> The common to the south side of Brock Street...was the general play ground for boys, where they flew their kites, played their games and settled their disputes. Cricket was the principal game, base ball and lacrosse had not been introduced.
>
> The boys were a pugnacious lot. They were formed into different squads or cliques and were very clannish...
>
> The boys in those days went in for swimming, sailing and skating; almost any boy in the city could swim, handle a boat and skate.
>
> Most of the boys were quite at home on skates. They could cut the figure 8 and other fancy figures, but shinny was their delight. Crowds would be placed at Shoal tower, and Point Frederick, and fifty or more players on each side would be in the game.[32]

There is not much description, but the term "shinny," like the "shinty" used in 1840, clearly designates a game at least reminiscent of hockey.

One account has been deliberately ignored. The CAHA report asserts: "The first hockey was played by the Royal Canadian Rifles, an Imperial unit, stationed in Halifax and Kingston in 1855.... The playing of hockey games as early as 1855 in Kingston is certain."[33] This contention is based on a game report mentioned by Captain Sutherland of a game played on Christmas Day, 1855, on Kingston Harbour. However, it is unambiguously established that, on that date, the harbour was not frozen. Furthermore, the game report itself has never surfaced.

Niagara Falls, Ontario

The most recent of hockey birthplace claims (it was spurred on by a 2008 finding by two of the authors) has so far failed to gain much traction among the general public, despite the fact that the account on which it is based is particularly detailed, though some of the details are rather unfortunate.

Like Sir Arthur in Kingston, Sir Richard George Augustus Levinge (1811–1884), 7th Baronet of High Park (now Knockdrin Castle) in the Irish county of Westmeath, pursued a military career and found himself headed for Saint John, New Brunswick, as a lieutenant with the left wing of the 43rd (Monmouthshire) Regiment of Foot. In December 1837, the light infantry unit was en route to Lower Canada (now Quebec) to help suppress the rebellion. The following July, the 43rd moved again, this time to the Niagara district. He would return to England in 1839.

A few years later, in 1846, he wrote the first of six books, this one recalling his memories of life in Canada: *Echoes from the Backwoods; or Sketches of Transatlantic Life.* The quote below describes the winter of 1839 (note: the racial insensitivity is vintage, and we apologize that it needs to be included here):

> During the winter, the skating on the Chippewa Creek was excellent, and added not a little to our amusement. Large parties contested games of hockey on the ice, some forty or fifty being ranged on each side.
>
> A ludicrous scene, too, was afforded by the instruction of a black corps in skating: from the peculiar formation of a negro's foot, and the length of his heel, they were constantly falling forward; it was impossible to keep them on their skates, and down they came by whole sections.
>
> They might have done admirably on snow-shoes, but it was lamentable to witness the dreadful 'headers' they suffered from the skates.[34]

The number of players (40 to 50 on each side) points to rather informal games, and also suggests that, to use 21st-century terminology, the players had better been "good without the puck," though of course it is quite possible that they were playing with a ball.

Montreal, Quebec

Montreal's claim is in an entirely different league. Few people make the argument that Montreal is the birthplace of hockey—rather, it is designated as the birthplace of *organized,* or "modern," hockey.

There is little doubt that hockey was played, on ice and most probably with skates, on March 3, 1875, in Montreal. An announcement had been made in that afternoon's *Gazette:*

> VICTORIA RINK—A game of Hockey will be played at the Victoria Skating Rink this evening, between two nines chosen from among the members. Good fun may be expected, as some of the players are reputed to be exceedingly expert at the game. Some fears have been expressed on the part of intending spectators that accidents were likely to occur through the ball flying about in too lively a manner, to the imminent danger of lookers on, but we understand that the game will be played with a flat circular piece of wood, thus preventing all danger of its leaving the surface of the ice. Subscribers will be admitted on presentation of their tickets.[35]

The next day, *The Gazette* was happy to report on the game:

> HOCKEY —At the Rink last night a very large audience gathered to witness a novel contest on the ice. The game of hockey, though much in vogue on the ice in New England and other parts of the United States, is not much known here, and in consequence the game of last evening was looked forward to with great interest. Hockey is played usually with a ball, but last night, in order that no accident should happen, a flat block of wood was used, so that it should slide along the ice without rising, and thus going among the spectators to their discomfort. The game is like Lacrosse in one sense—the block having to go through flags placed about 8 feet apart in the same manner as the rubber ball—but in the main the old country game of shinty gives the best idea of hockey. The players last night were eighteen in number—nine on each side—and were as follows:—Messrs. Torrance (captain), Meagher, Potter, Goff,

Barnston, Gardner, Griffin, Jarvis and Whiting. Creighton (captain), Campbell, Campbell, Esdaile, Joseph, Henshaw, Chapman, Powell and Clouston. The match was an interesting and well-contested affair, the efforts of the players exciting much merriment as they wheeled and dodged each other, and notwithstanding the brilliant play of Captain Torrance's team Captain Creighton's men carried the day, winning two games to the single of the Torrance nine. The game was concluded about half-past nine, and the spectators then adjourned well satisfied with the evening's entertainment.[36]

Another, only slightly less enthusiastic report appeared the same day in the *Daily Witness:*

HOCKEY IN THE VICTORIA SKATING RINK. —Last evening a game of hockey was played in the Victoria Skating Rink between two nines, Messrs Torrance (Captain), Meagher, Potter, Goff, Barnston, Gardner, Griffin, Jarvis, and Whiting; and Messrs Creighton (Captain), Campbell, Campbell, Esdaile, Joseph, Henshaw, Chapman, Powell and Clouston. The game is generally played with a large rubber ball, each side striving to knock it through the bounds of the other's field. In order to spare the heads and nerves of the spectators, last evening, a flat piece of board was used instead of a ball; it slid about between the players with great velocity; the result being that the Creighton team won two games to one for the Torrance. Owing to some boys skating about during the play, an unfortunate disagreement arose; one little boy was struck across the head, and the man who did so was afterwards called to account, a regular fight taking place in which a bench was broken and other damage caused. It was the intention of the players to have another game, but this disgraceful affair put a stopper on it.[37]

A third Montreal newspaper, the *Evening Star,* also reported on the game, in what is probably the least-known coverage of that game. It seems to be nothing more than a shortened version of *The Gazette*'s report:

An interesting game of hockey was played last evening at the Rink and witnessed by a large number of spectators. The players were 18 in number, nine on each side. The match was well contested and efforts of the players excited much merriment as they wheeled and dodged each other and notwithstanding the brilliant play of Captain Torrance's team Captain Creighton's men carried the day, with two games to a single of Captain Torrance. The game concluded about half past nine and spectators adjourned well satisfied with the evening's entertainment.[38]

A very short report of the game, focusing entirely on the unfortunate ending, appeared two days after the game, in both the Ottawa *Times* and the Kingston *Daily British Whig:*

> A disgraceful sight took place in Montreal at the Victoria Skating Rink over a game of hockey. Shins and heads were battered, benches smashed, and the lady spectators fled in confusion.[39]

As this article was published in both newspapers two days after the game, one possibility is that the *Daily Witness* report's last two sentences were extracted and slightly expanded upon, ignoring the actual hockey match. One also notes that the article does not feel the need to explain, to readers in Ottawa or Kingston, what hockey is, or how it is played on ice.

The main Montreal references are well known and have even led to a plaque being unveiled in Montreal by the International Ice Hockey Federation (IIHF) in May 2008, recognizing the Victoria Skating Rink as the site of the first organized hockey game. Such was the importance the IIHF placed upon the Victoria rink that it also instituted an annual hockey game between the champion European team and a designated NHL team, and the trophy awarded to the winner of the game was named the Victoria Cup (the event was held twice, in 2008 and 2009).

The instigator of the Montreal game—and captain of one of the teams— was James George Aylwin Creighton (1850-1930), who would continue to organize and play in games in Montreal for five years, until 1879. He left Montreal for Ottawa in 1882, where he worked as law clerk to the Canadian Senate, and eventually took part in a few games with the team that would come to be known as the Rideau Rebels.[40]

Creighton has been called the "father of organized hockey,"[41] and the IIHF recognized his contribution to the (organized) origins of the sport, also with a plaque, at the same 2008 event, and in his case in conjunction with the Historic Sites and Monuments Board of Canada, which had designated him a "person of national historic significance" earlier in the year.

The history of the Montreal game—and, most importantly, of what followed from it—is well known. Exhibition games were reported at a relatively low pace of one to three games per winter for a few years, and then a tournament was organized during Montreal's Winter Carnival starting in 1883. The tournament was held a total of five times, in addition to a "replacement" tournament held in Burlington, Vermont, in 1886, the same year that the Amateur Hockey Association of Canada (AHAC) was created. The AHAC would end up being the ancestor of all of today's ice hockey leagues in the world.

Summary

Allow us to summarize, in a table, the existing birthplace claims, together with the references that support it and some information about each: whether the reference is contemporary, the term used to identify the game, and the nationality of the author.

Claim	Date of Ref.	Contemp.?	Term	Author Nat.
Windsor	Ca. 1805–10 (*Attaché*)	No	Hurly	Canadian
	1816–18 (*Windsor Mail*)	No	Hurley*	Canadian
	Total: 2			
Pictou	1811 (*East River Sketches*)	No	Hurlies*	Canadian
	1829 (*Colonial Patriot*)	Yes	Break-shins	Canadian
	Total: 2			
Pembina	1812 (MacDonell diary)	Yes	Hurl	Scot/Canadian
Deline	1825 (Franklin letter to Murchison)	Yes	Hockey	English
	1825 (Franklin diary)	Yes	Games on the Ice	English
	1825 (Franklin letter to niece)	Yes	Hockey	English
	Total: 3			
Halifax-Dartmouth	1827 (*Acadian Magazine*)	Yes	Ricket	Canadian
	1831 (silhouette)	Yes	None	Canadian
	1842 (Halifax *Morning Post*)	Yes	Ricket	Canadian
	1844 (*Little Grace*)	Yes	Hurley on the Ice	Eng./Can.
	1853 (*Acadian Recorder*)	Yes	Hurlies*	Canadian
	1859 (*British Colonist*)	Yes	Hurly*	Canadian
	1859 (Boston *Evening Gazette*)	Yes	Ricket	U. S.?

Claim	Date of Ref.	Contemp.?	Term	Author Nat.
	1864 (*Halifax Reporter*)	Yes	Hockey on the Ice	Canadian
	1867 (*Memories of the Sea*)	Yes/No	Ice Hockey	Irish
	1867 (*Halifax Evening Reporter*)	Yes	Ricket	Canadian
	1867-68 (*Sketches*)	Yes	None	English
	1869 (*Acadian Recorder*)	Yes	Ricket	Canadian
	Total: 12			
Niagara Falls	1839 (*Echoes*)	Close	Hockey on the Ice	English
Kingston	1843 (Freeling diary)	Yes	Hockey on the Ice	English
	1846-47 (*Daily British Whig*)	No	Shinny	Canadian
	Total: 2			
	Total Pre-Montreal: 23			
Montreal (1st game)	1875 (*Gazette*, 3/3)	Yes	Hockey	Canadian
	1875 (*Gazette*, 4/3)	Yes	Hockey	Canadian
	1875 (*Daily Witness*, 4/3)	Yes	Hockey	Canadian
	1875 (*Evening Star*, 4/3)	Yes	Hockey	Canadian
	1875 (Ottawa *Times*, 5/3)	Yes	Hockey	Canadian
	1875 (*British Whig*, 5/3)	Yes	Hockey	Canadian
	Total: 6			

* Asterisk denotes references that do not give a name to the game; in those cases, we have used the name of the stick instead.

Quantity is not quality (or seniority), and thus it does not mean that claims with more references attached to them are "better." Still, one cannot help but wonder why the Halifax-Dartmouth claim continues to take a back seat to many other claims—one poll published in *The Hockey News* being the exception—when one considers the amount of evidence it has been able to present on behalf of its case. Even the prime minister of Canada, Stephen Harper, in his otherwise excellently documented *A Great Game: The Forgotten Leafs and the Rise of Professional Hockey*,[42] dismissed the Halifax-Dartmouth claim as a misnomer for the Windsor claim. It is surely nothing more than an amusing coincidence that, in 2013 (year that his book was published), all members of Parliament representing Halifax and Dartmouth happened to be members of opposition parties.

So, these are the eight known Canadian hockey-birthplace claims, and the 23 documents that support them. But to be able to study such claims, one has to know what hockey is.

Chapter 1 Notes

1. Garth Vaughan, *The Puck Starts Here* (Fredericton, N. B.: Goose Lane Editions, 1996).
2. Thomas Chandler Haliburton, *The Attaché; or, Sam Slick in England,* vol. 1 (London: Richard Bentley, 1844): 112–113.
3. "Early Sketches of Windsor," *Windsor Mail,* unknown date in 1876, clipping included in scrapbook, MG9, vol. 28, Nova Scotia Archives (Akins Collection): 5.
4. Russell A. McManus, "Wrong Pond," *Chronicle Herald* (Halifax, N. S.), 10 Jan. 2002.
5. Robert Grant, *East River Sketches, Historical and Biographical: With Reminiscences of Scottish Life* (New Glasgow, N. S.: S. M. MacKenzie, 1895): 41-42.
6. Garth Vaughan, "Game Chronology," *The Birthplace of Hockey,* Windsor Hockey Heritage Society, 5 Dec. 2005, Web, 30 Mar. 2014 <http://www.birthplaceofhockey.com/origin/game-chron/>.
7. *Colonial Patriot, and Miscellaneous Selector* (Pictou, N. S.), 4 Feb. 1829.
8. Augustus Henry Beesly, *Sir John Franklin* (London: Marcus Ward, 1881): 131.
9. John Franklin, *Narrative of a Second Expedition to the Shores of the Polar Sea, in the Years 1825, 1826, and 1827* (London: John Murray, 1828): 59.
10. John Franklin, Letter to Mary Anne Kay, 8 Nov. 1825, John Franklin papers, GB 0064 FRN/1/8, National Maritime Museum, London.
11. "Hockey's Birthplace?," *The National,* CBC News, 5 Jul. 2011, web, 22 Mar. 2014 <http://www.cbc.ca/player/Sports/Hockey/ID/2042935359/>.
12. Martin W. Jones, *Hockey's Home—Halifax-Dartmouth: The Origin of Canada's Game* (Halifax, N. S.: Nimbus, 2002).
13. Jones, viii–ix.

14. Tim Fashion, "Winter.—Now," *Acadian Magazine; or Literary Mirror* (Halifax, N. S.), Jan. 1827.
15. Harry Piers, "Artists in Nova Scotia," *Collections of the Nova Scotia Historical Society,* vol. XVIII (Halifax, N. S.: Nova Scotia Historical Society, 1914): 127.
16. *Halifax Morning Post,* 18 Jan. 1842.
17. Miss Grove, *Little Grace, or, Scenes in Nova Scotia* (Halifax, N. S.: C. MacKenzie, 1846): 106-107.
18. "Sabbath Desecration," *Acadian Recorder* (Halifax, N. S.), 22 Jan. 1853.
19. "The Young Men of Halifax," *British Colonist* (Halifax, N. S.), 4 Jan. 1859.
20. "Winter Sports in Nova Scotia," *Evening Gazette* (Boston), 5 Nov. 1859.
21. "Winter Sports in Nova Scotia," *British Colonist* (Halifax, N. S.), 15 Nov. 1859.
22. Quoted in Jones, 74.
23. The authors could not locate the original *Halifax Reporter* article. This text is quoted in Jones, 47–48.
24. Penrose Fitzgerald and Charles Cooper, *Memories of the Sea* (London: Edward Arnold, 1913): 261.
25. "Skating Scribblings," *Halifax Evening Reporter,* 19 Feb. 1867.
26. Henry Buckton Laurence, "Curling on the Lakes, near Halifax, Nova Scotia," *Sketches of Canadian Sports and Pastimes Dedicated by Kind Permission HRH Lieutenant Prince Arthur of the Rifle Brigade* (London: Thomas McLean, 1870), lithograph no 5.
27. *Acadian Recorder* (Halifax, N. S.), 3 Dec. 1869.
28. James Thomas Sutherland, "Origin of Hockey," *Hockey Year Book, 1924* (Toronto: George King, 1924).
29. Emanuel M. Orlick, "An Open Letter to the N. H. L. Governors On the Question of Hockey Hall of Fame," *The Gazette* (Montreal), 15 Sept. 1943.
30. Henry Arthur Freeling, Diary, Arthur Henry Freeling fonds, R4153-0-2-E, Library and Archives Canada.
31. *Kingston Chronicle and Gazette,* 15 Jan. 1840.
32. Horsey, Edwin, "Kingston Sixty Years Ago," *Daily British Whig* (Kingston, Ont.), 3 Mar. 1906.

33. Canadian Amateur Hockey Association, *Origin of Hockey in Canada* (Toronto: Canadian Amateur Hockey Association, 1942).

34. Richard George Augustus Levinge, *Echoes from the Backwoods; or Sketches of Transatlantic Life,* vol. 2 (London: Henry Colburn, 1846): 250.

35. *The Gazette* (Montreal), 3 Mar. 1875.

36. *The Gazette* (Montreal), 4 Mar. 1875.

37. *Daily Witness* (Montreal), 4 Mar. 1875.

38. *Evening Star* (Montreal), 4 Mar. 1875.

39. *The Times* (Ottawa), 5 Mar. 1875, and Daily British Whig (Kingston, Ont.), 5 Mar. 1875.

40. Paul Kitchen, *Win, Tie, or Wrangle: The Inside Story of the Old Ottawa Senators, 1883-1935* (Manotick, Ont.: Penumbra Press, 2008).

41. "Inductee Details," *Nova Scotia Sport Hall of Fame,* n.d., Web, 22 Mar. 2014, <http://www.novascotiasporthalloffame.com/Inductees/Search/InducteeDetails/tabid/571/Default.aspx?m=336>.

42. Stephen J. Harper, *A Great Game: The Forgotten Leafs and the Rise of Professional Hockey* (Toronto: Simon & Schuster Canada, 2013): 7.

What Is Hockey?

IT IS IMPOSSIBLE TO STUDY the subject of the birthplace of hockey seriously without first determining what constitutes hockey.

The Society for International Hockey Research comes to the rescue, as its Origins Committee, established in 2001 to look into "the claims that Nova Scotia is the birthplace of hockey"[1]—a mandate later refocused specifically on the Windsor claim[2]—spent considerable time and effort to come up with the most widely acceptable definition of hockey, which should be understood through the rest of this book as ice hockey, except when context indicates otherwise.

The SIHR committee's report was presented in May of 2002. As early as the summary that introduces the document, the committee announces its colours (in this chapter, the emphasis through underlining is ours and serves to highlight exactly which part of the quoted text represents the definition):

> The committee defined hockey as: <u>a game played on an ice rink in which two opposing teams of skaters, using curved sticks, try to drive a small disc, ball or block into or through the opposite goals.</u>[3]

Over the course of the report, the committee restates the definition four more times, twice with exactly (or almost) the same words, but twice more in a different form. While this may be viewed as potentially creating ambiguity, the effect is the opposite: restating the definition in a different way allows the committee to clarify the intent behind every element of it, as well as how to use the definition itself.

After the introduction, the report cuts to the chase, and under the heading "Methodology," it explains how it arrived at the definition it used to evaluate the claim:

> We felt it necessary to start with a definition of hockey. We wanted to apply the term as it is commonly understood by the public. As well, we wanted to avoid describing hockey in strictly contemporary, technical terms. By defining the game in such a rigid manner, we would have ruled out rudimentary forms from past times and would have been contemptuous of its spirit and genesis. We consulted numerous dictionaries and encyclopedias, looking for the common elements among the definitions. The wording we have agreed upon, borrowed or adapted from, in particular, the Houghton Mifflin and Funk and Wagnalls definitions, contains six defining characteristics: <u>ice rink, two contesting teams, players on skates, use of curved sticks, small propellant, objective of scoring on opposite goals.</u> Thus, **hockey** *<u>is a game played on an ice rink in which two opposing teams of skaters, using curved sticks, try to drive a small disc, ball or block into or through the opposite goals.</u>*[4]

Thus the committee established a list of all characteristics that were required for a game to be considered hockey, and then, through the addition of a verb, created the version found earlier in the summary—the definition that would end up being most often quoted.

The committee should be commended for acknowledging that hockey's "spirit and genesis" are inseparable from its current form, even though hockey has obviously evolved considerably, like any activity that is more than a hundred years old.

In a section of the report entitled "Evaluation of the Windsor Claim," the committee further examines and clarifies its intent in regard to the definition:

> We have stated what we believe to be the commonly accepted meaning of hockey: <u>a game played on an ice rink in which two opposing teams of skaters, using curved sticks, try to drive a small disc, block or ball into or through the opposite goals.</u> In adopting this definition, we have

consulted numerous dictionaries and encyclopedias to be sure we were capturing the essence of the game, as it is understood by most people. Our definition is inclusive to the extent that it accommodates early, rudimentary forms of the game as well as present features. It is exclusive to the extent that it rules out precursors of hockey that do not possess its essential or core qualities.[5]

Except for the inversion of "block" and "ball," this definition is identical to the "main" one; however, the committee drives the point home further regarding the origins of the game: by design, rudimentary forms will meet the definition, whereas precursors that "do not possess its essential or core qualities" will not make the cut. It is particularly telling that the game does not need to be *called* hockey. This leaves the door open to an activity known by a different name, and in particular does not dismiss offhand Windsor's hurly, Halifax's ricket or Kingston's shinty or shinney.

The paragraph continues:

> Thus, hockey may be played with a ball or a puck; it maybe [sic] played with six, or seven or any number of players aside; its rules, either written or unwritten, may be simple or complex; the playing surface may be large or small, and may be outdoors or indoors; the goals may be stones, poles or goal cages, and their width may vary. For a game to be recognized as hockey, all that is required is the presence of six defining characteristics: <u>ice surface, two contesting teams, players on skates, use of curved sticks, small propellant, objective of scoring on opposite goals.</u> The absence of any of these would exclude an activity from being accepted as hockey. Thus a game not played on ice is not hockey; a game in which players do not wear skates is not hockey, and so forth.[6]

This is a restatement of the second version of the definition, the one that lists the six essential qualities of hockey. A very small change can be detected: the "ice rink" has become an "ice surface." Considering that *rink* is not otherwise defined in the report, this slight variation allows the reader to assume that the rink is not to be interpreted in a restrictive sense. Boards are definitely not required, and a regular shape is likely just a bonus, too: the previous sentence makes it very clear that the definition will not be applied restrictively, accepting rinks that are "large or small," "outdoors or indoors."

Most importantly, the characteristics are clearly established as not only necessary, but also *sufficient*, through the use of the phrase "all that is required is the presence of six defining characteristics." This makes the committee's stance unambiguous: those are the requirements, and they are the only ones. The Windsor claim was evaluated based on them, and any other claim also would be.

Could the rules have been more specific? As we'll see in chapter 7, the mention of "passing" and "dribbling" (better known in the hockey world as "stickhandling") might have served to exclude some activities that most people would probably agree were not hockey, though it is not certain that such games ever even existed. Perhaps qualifying the sticks as "angled or curved" would have been more geometrically correct than just "curved." And a mention that the propellant is normally played on the ice could have quashed any conjecture that a game of modern hurling (in which the ball spends most of the time in the air), if played on ice with skates, could have qualified as hockey. But those are extremely minor points that would have made for a much longer definition, for the only purpose of excluding games that either never existed or were only a minuscule glitch in the timeline of stick-and-ball games. By and large, the definition that the committee gave to the world is an excellent one.

It is thus no surprise that the definition was picked up by many media at the time, and is still frequently used today. The *Winnipeg Free Press* of June 13, 2002, gave the Origins Committee report the better part of the front page of its "Canada/World" section.[7] In *Epidemiology of Injury in Olympic Sports,* published by the International Olympic Committee's Medical Commission in 2010, the chapter on ice hockey begins: "The Society for International Hockey Research defines ice hockey as 'a game played on an ice rink in which two opposing teams of skaters, using curved sticks, try to drive a small disc, ball or block into or through the opposite goals.'"[8] On February 24, 2001, the Canadian Broadcasting Corporation aired a report, as part of its coverage of Hockey Day in Canada, on the Windsor claim. The clip is archived on the CBC's website, and under the heading "Did You Know," the site mentions the six-point definition of hockey as contained in the Origins Committee report, as well as the committee's conclusion on the Windsor claim.[9]

Matching the Definition Is No Easy Task—Even Today

In the end, the exact definition did not matter much in the evaluation of the Windsor claim, as the primary evidence presented—as described in chapter 1—consisted of a mention of "hurly on the long pond on the ice," found in a work of fiction. We don't know whether the activity actually did take place in the nonfictional world, and even if it did, we still would not know what it consisted of.

But the committee did put its definition to good use, by taking the opportunity to designate newspaper coverage of the game played in Montreal on March 3, 1875, as "the earliest eyewitness account known to the committee of a specific game of hockey in a specific place at a specific time, and with a recorded score, between two identified teams."[10] Without a doubt, the committee made sure the game fit the six-point definition. This game shall be designated as the "first Montreal game" throughout the rest of this book, for easier reading.

The immense advantage that the first Montreal game holds over other birthplace claims is that it was clearly the first exposure of many people in Montreal to ice hockey. For this reason, the Montreal *Gazette* and *Daily Witness* published reports that contained many details that today help us to confirm that the game played was indeed hockey, although skates are not mentioned—but nobody doubts that they were used.

As indicated, this is an immense advantage over reports describing a game already well known to the readers. Rather than going back more than a century, let us take a look at more recent hockey game reports.

Stories about the deciding game of the 2013 Stanley Cup final between the Boston Bruins and Chicago Blackhawks by Dave Feschuk of the *Toronto Star*,[11] Eric Duhatschek of *The Globe and Mail*,[12] and Chris Kuc of the *Chicago Tribune*[13] add up to more than 3,000 words. Yet two of the six defining elements of hockey—skates and sticks—are not mentioned once in any of those three articles.

Better yet, the report on the NHL's website of the January 21, 2014, game between the Winnipeg Jets and Anaheim Ducks[14] does not mention ice, sticks or a puck (or ball or block, for that matter), and the only mention of skating is in the expression "pre-game skate," which does not imply that skating was part of the game itself. After all, pre-game pep talks do not also happen during the game. And Hall of Famer Glenn Hall engaged in a particularly well-documented pre-game activity that, thankfully, never happened during games.

The authors wish to draw attention to the fact that hockey references do not always list all six characteristics that define hockey to emphasize that accounts should not be dismissed simply because one or two of the six elements are missing. If one happens to come across the report of the very first game of hockey played in a city, there is a good chance that the article will provide good details as to how the game is played. But if the activity has been practised for decades—or more than a century—expecting to find every last detail of how the game is played is perhaps unfair to the reporter of the time, who was allowed to make reasonable assumptions as to the general knowledge of the readers.

Chapter 2 Notes

1.   Society for International Hockey Research, *Report of the Sub-Committee Looking into Claim that Windsor, Nova Scotia, is the Birthplace of Hockey* (Toronto: Society for International Hockey Research, 2002): 3.

2.   SIHR, 3.

3.   SIHR, 1.

4.   SIHR, 3.

5.   SIHR, 15.

6.   SIHR, 15–16.

7.   Conway Daly, "Cradle of hockey or cradle of myth?", *Winnipeg Free Press*, 13 Jun. 2002, B1–B2.

8.   Dennis J. Caine, Peter A. Harmer and Melissa A. Schiff, eds., *Epidemiology of Injury in Olympic Sports* (Chichester, U.K.: Wiley-Blackwell, 2010): 411.

9.   "The Birthplace of Hockey?", *CBC Digital Archives,* 16 Mar. 2012, web, 22 Mar. 2014, <http://www.cbc.ca/archives/categories/sports/hockey/the-spirit-of-hockey/the-birthplace-of-hockey.html>.

10. SIHR, 2.

11. Dave Feschuk, "Stanley Cup Final: Chicago Blackhawks had what it took to be winners," *Toronto Star,* 24 Jun. 2013, web, 22 Mar. 2014, <http://www.thestar.com/sports/hockey/2013/06/24/stanley_cup_final_chicago_blackhawks_had_what_it_took_to_be_winners_feschuk.html>.

12. Eric Duhatschek, "Blackhawks capture Stanley Cup with dramatic Game 6 victory," *The Globe and Mail,* 24 Jun. 2013, web, 22 Mar.

2014, <http://www.theglobeandmail.com/sports/hockey/blackhawks-provide-extraordinary-finish-to-an-unbelievable-nhl-season/article12792492/>.

13. Chris Kuc, "Blackhawks' 2nd Stanley Cup in 4 years comes in a flash," *Chicago Tribune,* 25 Jun. 2013, web, 22 Mar. 2014, <http://articles.chicagotribune.com/2013-06-25/sports/ct-spt-0625-blackhawks-bruins-chicago-20130625_1_dave-bolland-milan-lucic-jonathan-toews>.

14. Curtis Zupke, "Jets hand Ducks first regulation home loss," *NHL.com,* 22 Jan. 2014, web, 22 Mar. 2014, <http://www.nhl.com/gamecenter/en/recap?id=2013020--755>.

CHAPTER 3

The Perfect Matches

WE HAVE NOW REVIEWED existing birthplace claims, and established the framework for determining what is, and what is not, hockey. We will now focus on presenting our findings. To start, we cross the ocean to Great Britain—though most of our stops will be specifically in England. The Canadian claims have not been forgotten, however, and shall be returned to in chapter 14.

Virginia Water, Windsor, Berkshire, 1864

In England, it seems, if you want something to be in a newspaper, the best way is to somehow associate the Royal Family with it. This is as true now as in the 19th century. Before becoming king, Edward VII (1841-1910) was known as Albert Edward, Prince of Wales. One of the activities that he enjoyed very much was "hockey on the ice." On Friday, January 8, 1864, the prince had an afternoon of outdoor enjoyment accompanied by his seven-months-pregnant wife, Alexandra of Denmark, (1844-1925—she would go on to become Queen Alexandra). The couple had married just the year before and seemingly had a great time. The following is how the afternoon was reported in the press, in particular in *The Times* (London) the following day:

> Yesterday was a grand day on the ice at Virginia Water. His Royal Highness, the Prince of Wales left Frogmore Lodge at a quarter past 11 o'clock in the forenoon, in an open carriage and pair, with several gentlemen of

his suite, and arrived at Virginia Water shortly before 12 o'clock. Her Royal Highness the Princess of Wales followed in a close carriage, accompanied by her ladies in attendance.

Their Royal Highnesses immediately proceeded to the lake, where they were met on the ice by about 40 ladies and gentlemen, many of the gentlemen belonging to the London Skating Club.

Two sides were chosen for the game of hockey. Those on the Prince's side were distinguished by a white riband on the left arm. The game was kept up with great animation until 2 o'clock, when the Prince and his companions repaired to the Fishing Temple, where they partook of a sumptuous luncheon.

Afterwards they returned to the lake and resumed the game of hockey, which they kept up until a quarter to 5 o'clock, when the Prince left for Frogmore. His Royal Highness proved himself a first-rate skater and player, being as active with his hockey stick as he was on his skates, puzzling many of the most expert players.

Her Royal Highness the Princess of Wales, who is an excellent skater, seemed much interested in the game, and was occasionally driven about in a sledge. The Princess left Virginia Water at 4 o'clock. Besides the Royal visitors and suite, there were upwards of 500 people present, including a large number of ladies, who displayed much skill and grace in the performance of several difficult figures.

This exciting scene was much enlivened by the performances of the band of the Royal Horse Guards (Blue), who were comfortably seated round a large charcoal fire on the banks of the lake, near to the Fishing Temple.[1]

Thanks to the public's insatiable interest in all things royal, the article treats us to a wealth of details. We are informed that Their Royal Highnesses proceeded to the lake, where they were met by gentlemen belonging to the London Skating Club. It is no stretch of the imagination to conclude that skates were used, or that the lake was frozen, providing the required ice.

We also learn that "Two sides were chosen for the game of hockey." This not only tells us that there were "two opposing teams," but also that the activity was *called* hockey. While, as was pointed out earlier, this is not a prerequisite to suit the definition of hockey, it certainly reinforces the *possibility* that it is.

The following sentence provides yet more information as to the activity: "His Royal Highness proved himself a first rate skater and player, being as active with his hockey stick as he was on his skates, puzzling many of the most expert players." So, in case anyone was pondering a scenario in which the participants had started the afternoon skating, and then removed their skates to play hockey, well, ponder no more. They were skating and playing hockey at the same time. We also learn that they were playing with sticks, providing one more element of the definition of hockey, and we are told that there were experts, which means that the activity had been practised for some time. It is easy to draw a parallel with the Montreal announcement for the March 3, 1875, game: "some of the players are reputed to be exceedingly expert at the game."

So we have been able to mine four of the required six characteristics of hockey. A fifth will be made obvious by an illustration published, not with *The Times* article, but in London's *Penny Illustrated Paper* the following Saturday:[2]

The newspaper provided the following caption to the illustration: "Scene on the ice at Virginia Water on the day of the Princess of Wales's Accouchement: Her Royal Highness watching the Prince playing at Hockey."

For better viewing, let us provide an enlarged detail of the illustration:

We see the ice (even some skate marks on it), the skates, the ribbons on the arms distinguishing the teams, the sticks and the ball (above the right foot of the player in the foreground). The only thing not provided is the "objective of scoring on opposite goal." However, there is no secret that hockey was also played on the ground, then as now; ice hockey fans refer to this variant as "field hockey." And field hockey is sufficiently documented as of 1864 that we know that the object was to put the ball into the other team's goal.

So here we have a clearly documented instance of a game of hockey, where all the defining characteristics of the game are present, in addition to the game being actually called hockey, the teams wearing "colours" to identify themselves and having the future King of England participate. All this was more than 11 years before the March 3, 1875, game in Montreal.

As a footnote, it turns out that there was seemingly too much excitement in the day, and the princess ended up giving birth—to Prince Albert Victor "Eddy" (1864–1892)—in the evening, making it a memorable day in even more ways.

Brayton Hall, Aspatria, Cumbria, 1861–1865

We now turn our attention away from the suburbs of Britain's capital, and head up north, almost within earshot of Scotland, to consider three reports that originated in Aspatria within a span of four years, all of them published in the *Carlisle Journal*. Together, they provide a more complete picture than taken separately.

From Friday January 11, 1861:

Aspatria, January 10 —

After one of the severest frosts on record — the entire country having for some weeks put on an appearance attributed to the festive period of Christmas from time immemorial — a thaw commenced on Wednesday morning, or rather during Tuesday night, which lasted until this morning, when snow began again to whiten the ground, and continues falling at intervals, though the temperature is warmer than has been experienced lately. During the severe weather above referred to the streets were in a very slippery state, and numerous accidents have occurred from falls upon the ice-covered causeways, involving broken limbs, dislocated joints, and contusions of various parts of the body to many individuals who have had the misfortune to lose their balance when walking abroad for exercise.

Skating and hockey-playing upon the large fishpond at Brayton have been largely patronised, and many stout contests have been decided. The charms of music have even brought into requisition during the mimic warfare, and though sundry unintentional blows with the hockey-sticks have occasioned some trifling bloodshed, no serious accident has occurred to any of the numerous players.[3]

From Friday, January 8, 1864:

Our Aspatria correspondent writes: — The frost has rendered amusement upon the ice of the large fishpond at Brayton Hall a favourite relaxation for the people of the vicinity, and skating and 'hocky' playing are largely in the ascendant. Troups [sic] of people may daily be seen wending their way towards the pond, with their skates suspended from a formidable looking stick called a 'shinny'. At the pond a most lively scene presents itself. The worthy baronet kindly greets each comer as he recognises him, while himself and his sons—the legislator and the agriculturist—join heartily in the game.[4]

And from Friday, January 27, 1865:

THE FROST

The frost which set in at the beginning of this week has continued steadily. As usual when there is a great depression of the mercury in the thermometer, the shopkeepers who deal in skates at once displayed their stock in tempting array... Skating appears to have been general throughout the county...

Our Aspatria correspondent writes:—"During the past week the frost has been intensely severe, and the large fish pond at Brayton Hall has served as a daily place of recreation upon the ice for scores of people of all ages and ranks in society. About two o'clock sides are generally chosen, and the ball is thrown down for a game of 'hockey', which is vigorously contested until the shades of evening close upon the scene. It is quite an interesting sight to watch the groups of players; and numbers of elegantly-dressed ladies witness the game from the fine promenade on the western side of the pond. One or more of the most venturesome of these damsels may be seen taking lessons in skating, timorously leaning for support on the shoulder of some favoured swain, who is, of course, most happy in supporting the lady in case of an unlucky stumble resulting from inexperience of her novel position. Occasionally a ringing cheer proclaims that the ball has been driven home by one of the contending parties, or a burst of merriment is indulged at the expense of some unlucky wight whose heels may be seen in the position more properly belonging to his head; or what is still worse, who has suffered immersion by venturing upon the ice not calculated to sustain his weight. The venerable baronet (Sir Wilfrid Lawson) may almost daily be seen enjoying the sport, directing and encouraging the players, himself wielding the hockey with a dexterity sufficient to put to shame the clumsy attempts of many a novice, whose ill-directed strokes too often result in upsetting his own balance, to the great amusement of the spectators."[5]

It seems clear that, taken together, these articles contain all six elements defining hockey. The ice is clearly indicated on several occasions, with mention of particularly cold weather, while the skating is mentioned numerous times. There is one particular reference to the hockey players—in the sentence, "Troups of people may daily be seen wending their way towards the pond, with their skates suspended from a formidable looking stick called a 'shinny'." So the stick, in Aspatria, is called a "shinny" and can be used to suspend the skates. The teams and the ball are mentioned in a phrase that also mentions face-offs, which were conducted in the same style (thrown *down,* not *up*) as they are now: "About two o'clock sides are generally chosen, and the ball is thrown down for a game of 'hockey'." As for the objective of scoring goals, we see it here: "Occasionally a ringing cheer proclaims that the ball has been driven home by one of the contending parties." Assuming that the three articles, using the same term (or almost, as "hockey" is once spelled "hocky"), refer to the same activity, we have now pushed back the first instance of hockey played three more years, to 1861, now 14 years before the Montreal first game.

Bowood, Calne, Wiltshire, 1859

We return south, but about 80 kilometres west of the previously visited Windsor. On Thursday, December 22, 1859, the *Devizes and Wiltshire Gazette* reports:

> BOWOOD LAKE — On Monday and Tuesday this picturesque lake was one scene of animation, from the number of gentlemen who had assembled to enjoy a day's skating and a jolly good game at hockey, in which Lord Shelburne showed himself no novice in the handling of his golf.
>
> Sides were chosen, which were distinguished by pink and yellow ribbons worn on the arm, and in a very short time the *shinty,* which was painted red, began to dance over the ice right merrily, sometimes flying through the air and at others coming most unceremoniously against one's shins with a smart crack. The goals were denoted by pink flags at one end and yellow at the other. Both parties were victorious in their turns.
>
> We noticed on the ice Lord and Lady Somers, the Honourable Miss Flahault, the sons and infant daughter of Lord Shelburne; the latter of whom much enjoyed a little slide, and only smiled good humouredly at each little tumble. Through the usual kindness and liberality of Lord Shelburne the skaters were enabled to partake of refreshments, which, on such occasions, are always acceptable.[6]

Not a future king, but a lord. Hockey (on ice) appears to have been quite popular among the well-born of the time. Once again, we have ice and skates, we have teams ("Sides were chosen"), and once again, they are identified by colours ("...distinguished by pink and yellow ribbons worn on the arm"). We have the ball (here called a "shinty" and painted red), we have the sticks (here called "golf") and we have goals, "denoted by pink flags at one end and yellow at the other." We even have results, though not exact scores: we know that each team won one game; presumably, one team won on Monday and the other team won on Tuesday. And once again, the game is actually called "hockey" and is seemingly quite well organized, with the same teams having played several games, the wearing of colours to distinguish the two teams, the coloured flags to denote the goals and the ball ("shinty") painted red to make it more visible. As for the use of the terms *golf* and *shinty*, it is likely explained by the fact that Lord Shelburne's father was educated in Scotland, which is also where his wife was born and raised.

The Boy's Book of Sports and Games, Containing Rules and Directions for the Practice of the Principal Recreative Amusements of Youth, 1850

Here we have not a newspaper account of a game or games played, but a book for youth, describing how to play various games. The story of this book, its author known only as "Uncle Charles," is somewhat curious, as it is basically the same volume as one published two years earlier by Leavitt & Allan in New York, under the slightly different title *The Boys' Own Book of Sports, Birds and Animals* by "Uncle John." From the list of activities included, it is clear that the author is British, not American—a supposition strengthened by a book published later, also by "Uncle John," which was signed at Barnsbury Square, London in December 1858. Thus the appearance of this book in the United States before Great Britain is a mystery, but not one that makes much difference in our chronology. The British version, unlike the American one, includes colour illustrations by London engraver Henry Sears.

The article on hockey goes as follows:

HOCKEY, or SHINNEY

It will be necessary in this game, to provide yourselves with a vine stick having a hook at one end, and also a ball; or a good sized bung, is the best to play with.

The players must be equal in point of numbers, on each side. The bung is then placed in the centre of the playground, and the party winning the right of striking first, attempts to strike it to touch his opponent's goal, and he must be well backed by his party to enable him, if possible, to succeed.

This game affords excellent amusement and sport when the game is played by skaters, but they must be good ones, or it is dangerous.

This is called in Scotland, &c., shinney, from the players striking each other's shins, in trying to knock the bung from between their legs; but this I trust my young readers will not attempt, as it invariably produces much ill feeling, which should not exist between little boys.[7]

Clearly the description is intended to apply to both the field and ice versions of hockey, though the author may have had a preference for the latter, given his mention of the game providing *"excellent amusement and sport" when played by skaters.* Ice is not mentioned explicitly, but is implicit in the mention of skates. The first paragraph mentions the stick ("a vine stick having a hook at one end") and the ball, *or* bung ("a good-sized one"). This is the first suggestion that, on occasion, something similar to a puck might have been used instead of a ball when playing hockey.

The instruction that "The players must be equal in point of numbers, on each side" is a clear indication of the presence of teams, and the objective is to "touch his opponent's goal," which is not literally "into or through" the opposite goal, as per the accepted definition, but in effect amounts to the same thing. Who has never played an informal game of hockey with the goals set against the side of a building or a fence?

Croxby Pond, Lincolnshire, 1838

Lincolnshire is in the east of England, and Croxby Pond is in Lincolnshire Wolds, a range of hills designated by the British government in 1973 as an Area of Outstanding Natural Beauty. The pond was much bigger in the 19th century than it is now. The following was published in the *Lincolnshire Chronicle* of Friday, February 16, 1838:

On Saturday last, an amusing scene took place on a splendid sheet of ice which covered Croxby Pond. A large party from the neighbouring resi-dence of Geo. Alington, Esq., of Swinhop House, consisting of ladies and gentlemen, drove up in sledges to the pond; the ladies were drawn upon the ice in traineau, while the gentlemen performed various feats upon their skates: after going through several quadrilles, reels, &c., and playing a warmly contested game at hockey, the party partook of a cold collation, and again stepping into their sledges, glided swiftly away, leaving the ice-bound lake a 'dreary waste behind.' — Mr. Alington has travelled about 300 miles during the blast in his sledge.[8]

The same report, very slightly modified, also appeared on the same day in the *Stamford Mercury:*

A correspondent says, 'On Saturday the 3d inst. an amusing scene took place on the splendid sheet of ice which now covers Croxby Pond. A large party from the neighbouring residence of George Alington, Esq., consisting of ladies and gentlemen with a number of school-boys, drove up in sledges to the pond: the ladies were drawn upon the ice *en traineau,* while the gentlemen performed various feats upon their skates: after having gone through some quadrilles and reels, and played a warmly-contested game of hockey, the party partook of a *cold* collation, and again stepping into their sledges, glided swiftly away, leaving the ice-bound lake a dreary waste behind. — Mr. Alington has travelled about 300 miles during the blast in his sledge.'[9]

This account offers us fewer details, but it does mention ice and playing hockey on skates. Sticks, ball, teams and the objective of scoring goals are not mentioned, but if we accept that the word *hockey* already entailed all those elements, then we have another instance of ice hockey played in England, and one that takes place prior to the earliest of the Niagara Falls and Kingston references (1839 and 1843, respectively).

Why should we accept that, in 1838, "hockey," by definition, implied teams, sticks, a ball or puck and the objective of scoring goals? Because in 1838, *The New Sporting Magazine* said so.

The New Sporting Magazine, **1838**
This magazine was published monthly between 1831 and 1846. The March 1838 issue contained a letter written in February by someone identified only by the initials N. W.

THE

New Sporting Magazine.

VOL. XIV.]   MARCH, 1838.   [No. 83.

The letter gives a detailed description of the Fens during the winter season and the importance of skating for Fenmen (the words "skates," "skater," "skating," etc., appear 14 times).

The Fens are a naturally marshy region in eastern England. They reach into four counties—Lincolnshire, Cambridgeshire, Norfolk and a small area of Suffolk—and occupy nearly 3,900 square kilometres. Metal-bladed skates were probably introduced into the Fens by Dutch drainage workers in the 17th century; in earlier times, people had used sharpened animal bones to transport themselves across the ice.

For centuries, the frozen rivers and canals had—as in the Netherlands—been used for transportation, recreation, races, games and festivals. The author of the letter documents his personal recollections of those activities, dating back to the 1810s. Most of the places mentioned in the letter are located in modern Cambridgeshire.

The entire letter, available from the SIHR Hockey Origins Database, is nearly 2,000 words long and will thus not be reproduced in its entirety. We have chosen to quote only the beginning, the paragraph that describes hockey, and the signature.

Note that Peterborough is located at the western edge of the Fens.

THE ICE

THOMSON'S WINTER

On blithsome frolics bent, the youthful swains,
While every work of man is laid at rest,
Fond o'er the river crowd, in various sport
And revelry dissolved; ...
... and as they sweep
On sounding skates, a thousand different ways
In circling poise, swift as the winds along,
The then gay land is madden'd all to joy.[10]

HAVING read, among the 'Notes Off Hand' in your last number, a cursory notice of the *ice* in these parts, I am induced to suppose that the subject, in a more enlarged view, may not be unacceptable to many of your inland and highland readers, and I therefore proceed to a short narrative of scenes, most of which I have witnessed. . . .

The games chiefly practiced on the ice are *bandy* or *hocky,* as it is termed, fox-and-hounds, tick, and prison-bays. The latter speak for themselves—the first is played with sticks and a ball. A side is chosen, goals are fixed, and the ball bandied to and fro, like a foot-ball, until a goal is gained; twelve in general is *up,* and the goals three hundred yards apart . . .

Peterborough, February, 1838.
N. W.[11]

The spelling of *hockey* was seemingly not yet standardized at the time. In very few words, five of the six elements are present. The notion of team is perhaps less clearly indicated, but we are informed "A side is chosen," and the writer later mentions "the goals three hundred yards apart," making it difficult to imagine any setup other than two competing teams. In order to assume that such a thing as a game with more than two goals was being described, such a configuration would then have had to be specified.

Skates are not directly mentioned, but are omnipresent in the letter, with several paragraphs just prior to the one about "hocky" discussing skating races and the convenience of travelling long distances without effort—and it's safe, too: only three men had drowned in the last 20 years!

This letter from a Fenman is thus yet another instance of hockey in England, and it can be dated with good certainty as being from 1838, considering that the preceding winters had been quite warm with few days of skating reported. The winter of 1838, on the other hand, was particularly cold, and was termed "Murphy's Winter" after Patrick Murphy won fame and fortune from the sale of an almanac in which he correctly predicted the enduring frost.

From the letter, we can conclude that the Croxby Pond reference does indeed satisfy all of the hockey definition requirements, as we now know that hockey played on the ice with skates does satisfy the definition of hockey. For those wondering, Croxby Pond is less than 50 kilometres north of the northern edge of the Fens.

Shrewsbury, Shropshire, 1818–1825

Charles Darwin (1809-1882) was an English naturalist best known as the "father of evolutionary theory." He compiled and presented compelling evidence that all species of life have evolved over time from common ancestors.

Darwin was born in Shrewsbury in 1809 at the family home, located on a bluff overlooking the River Severn. The medieval town of Shrewsbury is the county town of Shropshire, in the West Midlands region of England. The portion of Shrewsbury known as "Old Town" is almost completely surrounded by a horseshoe-shaped bend in the Severn.

After attending the small local school, Darwin joined his older brother Erasmus in September 1818 to stay as a boarder at Dr. Samuel Butler's school, also known as the Shrewsbury School. At the time, the school was located at the town centre, and today the building houses the town library.

Charles remained at the Shrewsbury School for seven years till midsummer 1825, when he was 16 years old. In October of that year, he went on to Edinburgh University to prepare himself to enter the medical profession, but decided he was unfit to follow a medical career. So in January 1828, he went to Christ's College, Cambridge, with the idea of becoming a clergyman, but his passion for natural science led him, after having completed his degree in 1831, to his five-year voyage on the *Beagle*.

In a letter dated March 1, 1853, Darwin wrote to his son William Erasmus Darwin (1839-1914), and reminisced about the years when he attended Shrewsbury School:

> My dear old Willy,
>
> We were very glad to get your note this morning with so good an account of your examination, & of things in general. I trust the rest of the half-year — may go as quickly as this first week. What a curious thing infection is, yesterday Backy & Lizzie plainly had got the mumps, & this was about as long since you had them, as your attack was from the time the Hensleighs were here. They have had it very slightly, even slighter than you, Etty & Georgy. —
>
> I am glad you like the life of Napoleon; I thought it very interesting: I should be very glad to see you with more taste for reading; for by reading only can a man avoid being ignorant. A person, also, who reads on many subjects is interested in so many more things, & can talk so much more

pleasantly than another who is ignorant: and the pleasure of knowing things always goes on increasing the more one knows.

Georgy has learnt to slide & enjoys it very much, & goes down by himself to the village-pond: but this day's heavy snow will stop sliding & your skating.

Have you got a pretty good pond to skate on? I used to be very fond of playing at Hocky on the ice in skates. The weather is so bad, that I do not know when we shall be able to go & see the Crystal Palace building.

Goodbye my dear Boy | Your affectionate father | Charles Darwin Your note was well written.[12]

We've seen the "hocky" spelling before. It does not imply that this was the "original" spelling of hockey, as much older references already used the better-known—and current—"hockey."

So Darwin remembered playing "hocky on the ice in skates." In all likelihood, he learned to skate (and play hockey) as a young boy on the River Severn during the years when he attended Shrewsbury School. While a case could be made that Darwin was using the terminology used at the time he wrote the letter, which might have differed from that used when he was a child, he identified the game as "hocky," so what he played must have been very similar.

Even if we only consider the end year of Darwin's stay at Shrewsbury School (1825), we now have a reference older than the oldest Halifax-Dartmouth reference, the *Acadian Magazine* poem about "ricket with hurlies," and older than all of Franklin's references from Deline, as they were written in the later part of 1825—in the 1825/26 season, so to speak—while Darwin's stay at Shrewsbury ended after the 1824/25 hockey season.

But Darwin does not describe how hockey was played in his youth, so we shall provide two descriptions of hockey that predate his letter to his son, to make it clear that the game was already essentially what it still is today. Both references describe the game on the ground, but the four weather-independent aspects of the definition (teams, sticks, ball/puck and object of scoring goals) will be clearly established.

Chesham, Buckinghamshire, 1799

William Pierre Le Cocq (1785-1819) was the son of William Pierre Le Cocq Sr. and Rachel Reserson, who married in 1784. William was 13 years old when he left Guernsey for Mr. Simpson's school in Chesham, a town situated about 40 kilometres northwest of Central London. Le Cocq attended the school for at least two years, and the Priaulx Library has 45 letters from him to his parents covering this period.

The letter, dated Tuesday, December 17, 1799, and discovered by authors Gidén and Houda in August 2009, starts with a rather long introduction dedicated to the (sad) fate of a parcel containing pears that he received, with the letter accompanying them having to have the mashed pears scraped off of it, and the letter then being put to dry by the fire in the hopes it would eventually become legible. The young Le Cocq then abruptly changes subject:

> I must now describe to you the game of Hockey; we have each a stick turning up at the end. We get a bung. There are two sides one of them knocks one way and the other side the other way. If any one of the sides makes the bung reach that end of the churchyard it is victorious.[13]

Le Cocq then turns to a variety of other subjects, ending with the "news" that Dauphin Louis XVII of France was alive (he wasn't, at least according to official history) and that monarchy would return to France (it did, in 1814, going through various twists and turns until 1848).

The young Le Cocq had a talent for synthesis, defining quite clearly the game of hockey in few words, though of course there is no indication of whether it was played on the ground or on ice. As already mentioned, our intent in mentioning this letter is to make it clear that the main rules of hockey were already established at the time.

His subsequent letter to his parents, written in French, did not mention hockey or any stick-ball game, but did note that there was a lot of snow on the ground; so while Le Cocq and his schoolmates could conceivably have played hockey on ice, we do not have any information about this, neither do we know whether he ever skated while at school.

Juvenile Sports and Pastimes, to Which Are Prefixed, Memoirs of the Author: Including a New Mode of Infant Education, **1773**

Cumbersomely long book titles seem to have been the norm in the 18th century. This book, published by Thomas Carnan, at number 65 St. Paul's Churchyard in London, is not dated, but we were able to determine from newspaper reviews, that it was first offered on December 25, 1773. It not only describes in extensive detail how hockey was played, but the chapter about the game is titled "New Improvements on the Game of Hockey," which suggests that the game—and its name—had already been around for some time.

Yet, this reference, discovered by the authors in October 2011, is the oldest known contemporary use of the term "hockey," predating any other by about 20 years.

According to the book, its pseudonymous author, Richard Johnson (1734–1793), was sent at the age of seven to a boarding school within a day's travel by chaise (carriage) from London. He remained at this school for several years—probably until 1748—and during those years played the games described in the book. He recalls himself as a good reader, writer and draftsman, being given the nickname "Michel Angelo"—a name he constantly went by in the school—as a compliment by his drawing-master.

Here is the description he gives of hockey:

CHAP: XI.
NEW IMPROVEMENTS ON THE GAME OF HOCKEY.

THIS is a noble and manly exercise, but is proper only for the cooler months of the year, as it requires a great share of activity. It was undoubtedly first taken from the Irish game of Hurling, which it resembles in almost every respect.

The materials for this sport are only of three sorts; the goals, the hockey, and the hockey-sticks, all which are easily to be procured, and without much expence. Before I describe these matters to my little pupils, I must beg them to stop a moment, and view this picture; and I am inclined to believe they will wish it were possible for them to make one among these merry little fellows.

This sport can be pursued no where with pleasure, but in a wide spacious field, where the hockey may have its full scope. This game may be played by any even number of boys, divided into two parties. Each party must fix their goal at the greatest distance from one another the field will admit of, leaving however about ten feet space between each goal and the extremity of the field. The goals need consist only of a very long piece of briar, each end being stuck in the ground, and thereby forming a kind of erect arch. The goal at the upper end of the field is called the upper

goal, and the other the lower: the parties who play are likewise distinguished in the same manner.

Every one who plays must be provided with a hockey-stick. This is a matter of no small consequence, as I have known a boy give another almost any thing for one which has pleased his fancy; and I myself have parted with a minced pie upon the same occasion. I will now give you the description of a good hockey-stick. It is no matter what wood it is, so that it is tough, not liable to break, and has the desired form. It must be about a yard long, or rather in proportion to the size of the sportsman. The top of it, I mean that part of it which you hold in your hand, may be as thick as a common walking-stick; but the thicker it is at the bottom the better. The bottom, however, must not be strait, but crooked, and that in the form of a shepherd's crook is valuable beyond everything. The use of the crook part is to disengage the hockey from your antagonists, when it is so surrounded by them that you cannot get at it to give it a full stroke toward their goal.

The kockey must be made of the largest cork-bung you can get. Cut the edges round, and then it is prepared for use.

The goals being fixed, the hockey prepared, and the parties agreed on, you then proceed to your sport in the following manner. Both parties meet as nearly as possible, in the middle between the two goals, when the hockey is tossed up, and every one tries his best to beat the hockey through the goal of his antagonist; which being once accomplished, the game is over. I have known a game last for two or three hours, though followed up with the greatest ardour and alacrity, such have been the excellent sportsmen who composed the two parties.

There is a wide difference in *merely* playing this game, and playing it genteely. Some boys are of such an eager, warm disposition, that they care not whom they hurt, or whose skin they break, so that they get at the hockey; but this is the mark of a bad player. A right sportsman is always cool, and ready to take any advantage that offers, without having recourse to unfair proceedings. When he sees the kockey is so surrounded by both parties, that he cannot get a fair stroke at it, he makes one among them with his crook, and endeavours to get it between, so that, by a sudden jerk, he may disengage it from him; while others, who are as good players as himself on the other side, will endeavour to prevent it, by beating their hockey-sticks against his, and at the same time aiming to give it such strokes as may force it their away. All this may be done without much violence, or any hurt. I have played at this game for half a day together, without giving or receiving the least cause for complaint.

According to the rules of this game, you are never to touch the kockey with your hands, from the time it is tossed up till it is got through one of the goals; and, tho' you are allowed to push either of your antagonists aside, yet it is considered not only as foul play, but as very ungenteel also, to strive either to throw another down, or trip up his heels. Such proceedings always produce ill-will, quarreling, and sometimes fighting: but every young gentleman will wish to make his companion as happy as himself, since, without mutual harmony, the finest sport in the world will be rendered dull, insipid and disgustful.[14]

It is hard not to notice that the name of the cork/bung is written as "kockey" four times, only twice fewer than the presumably correct "hockey." As no explanation is given, it is quite possible that the typesetter was so unfamiliar with the term that he occasionally used the wrong letter. Johnson seems to have no doubt that the game came from the Irish hurling, "which it resembles in almost every respect." To be able to make such an affirmation, the author must have witnessed games of hurling, something he might have done in his own hometown, since it is known that Irish immigrants played hurling in London as far back as the 1730s.[15] Johnson also mentions "rules" and proceeds to mention a few: don't touch the "kockey" with your hands, don't throw the other players down or trip up their heels, though some body contact was permissible ("you are allowed to push either of your antagonists aside"), just like today's ice hockey.

Another point of interest is the comparison of the stick with a shepherd's crook, known in French as *hoquet* or *hocquet* at the time. The generally accepted etymology of *hockey* (though never proven with certainty) is that it came from that French term, due to the shape of the stick, and the article does confirm that hockey sticks were commonly compared to shepherds' crooks in the game's infancy. However, see chapter 12 for a further discussion on the origins of the word "hockey."

As the author recollects having played the various games of his book at his boarding school, it dates the activity as far back as somewhere between 1741 and 1748. Of course, the activity is only described as practised on the ground, not on ice, but this reference serves to establish the basic rules of hockey, so that any subsequent use of the term "hockey" can reasonably be assumed to correspond to the same activity.

Conclusion

From the passages reviewed in this section, it seems undeniable that ice hockey, as per the accepted definition, was widely played in England throughout the 19th century, in many different regions, and under the designation "hockey," though other terms were used as well, like the "shinney" encountered in *The Boy's Book of Sports and Games* or the "bandy" mentioned in *The New Sporting Magazine.*

The references to hockey on ice included in this chapter were selected specifically because each could undoubtedly be demonstrated to satisfy the Society for International Hockey Research's definition of hockey. In no way do they constitute the entirety of all hockey references from England prior to 1875. On the contrary, there is a wealth of such material, and we shall present more. Our observation is that the reporting of hockey and ice hockey in England got significant boosts from the following events:

1. Most of the earliest mentions of hockey on ice were related to accidents, quite often the ice breaking and a poor player drowning or being narrowly rescued.
2. With Prince Albert's interest in the game, which he passed on to his son the future Edward VII, every instance of his participating

in the activity was reported with paparazzi-like zeal. His grandson Prince Albert Victor, Duke of Clarence and Avondale (1864–1892), also had ice hockey in his blood.

3. The interest around the Agapemone "sect" made for tabloid-like reporting involving religion, sex, crime and... hockey, though in this case it was strictly field hockey.

4. The Tishborne trial (1845–1848) was a fixture of newspapers of the era, and we will examine it in chapter 8, when we return to the subject of the various names used to designate hockey-like games.

But before we cast our net wider, we will continue to explore even further the favour in which ice hockey was held in 19th-century England.

Chapter 3 Notes

1. *The Times* (London), 9 Jan. 1864.
2. *Penny Illustrated Paper* (London), 16 Jan. 1864.
3. *Carlisle Journal*, 11 Jan. 1861.
4. *Carlisle Journal*, 8 Jan. 1864.
5. *Carlisle Journal*, 27 Jan. 1865.
6. *Devizes and Wiltshire Gazette*, 22 Dec. 1859.
7. "Uncle Charles," *The Boy's Book of Sports and Games, Containing Rules and Directions for the Practice of the Principal Recreative Amusements of Youth* (London: Henry Allman, 1850): 2-3.
8. *Lincolnshire Chronicle*, 16 Feb. 1838.
9. *Stamford Mercury*, 16 Feb. 1838.
10. James Thomson, *Winter: A Poem (London: John Millan, 1726)*.
11. N. W., "The Ice," *The New Sporting Magazine*, March 1838: 153-156.
12. Frederick Burkhardt and Sydney Smith (eds.), *The Correspondence of Charles Darwin: 1851*-1855, vol. 5 (Cambridge, U.K.: Cambridge University Press, 1989): 121-122.
13. William Pierre Le Cocq, Letter to Parents, 17 Dec. 1799, Priaulx Library, Island of Guernsey.
14. Michel Angelo (Richard Johnson), *Juvenile Sports and Pastimes, to Which Are Prefixed, Memoirs of the Author: Including a New Mode of Infant Education* (London: Thomas Carnan, 1773): 91-96.

15. *Daily Advertiser* (London), 16 Aug. 1733: "Yesterday a match at Hurling was plaid for 50 guineas a side in Hyde-Park by gentlemen of Ireland." Also, "Yesterday in the Evening a Match at a Game call'd Hurling, was play'd for 50 Guineas a Side in Hyde-Park, by Gentlemen of Ireland, the County of Kildare against the County of Meath," *Whitehall Evening-Post* (London), 16 Aug. 1733.

Also Organized

T HE SOCIETY FOR INTERNATIONAL Hockey Research's 2002 report
on the Windsor claim contained not only a conclusion on this claim, but
also an affirmation regarding Montreal. In a section titled simply "Montreal,
March 3, 1875," the report stated:

> On March 3, 1875, the Montreal *Gazette* reported that "a game of
> Hockey" was to be played that evening at the Victoria Skating Rink. It
> said, "some of the players are reported to be exceedingly expert at the game."
> The next day, the paper reported the event, noting that "hockey, though
> much in vogue on the ice in New England and other parts of the United
> States, is not known much here." The reporter covering the event identified
> the members of the two teams, described the play, and gave the final score.
>
> The match appears to be unique. It is the earliest eyewitness account
> known, at least to this SIHR committee, of a specific game of hockey in
> a specific place at a specific time, and with a recorded score, between two
> identified teams.[1]

This game is now widely accepted as the first game of organized hockey,
and the SIHR report played a significant part in its acceptance. However,
the report does not define "organized hockey," and the word "organized"
itself does not even appear in the report (except once, in the bibliography—it
is part of the title of one of the references). In the absence of such a definition,
we look at what caught the attention of the SIHR Origins Committee:

- a specific game of hockey;
- in a specific place;
- at a specific time;
- with a recorded score;
- between two identified teams.

Is there any chance that a hockey game fulfilling all of the above criteria took place before this game in 1875?

Elsham, Lincolnshire, 1871

On Friday, January 13, 1871, the *Stamford Mercury,* a newspaper in Lincolnshire, reported:

> At Elsham Hall ponds on Friday last a party of gentlemen got up a skating match between eight of Brigg and eight of Elsham, the inspiriting game being hockey on the ice. Colonel Astley, a thorough lover of sport, kindly invited a party from Brigg to a contest with the village folk. The play went on for an hour and a half, and the result was a drawn game. After the struggle was over the combatants were entertained in the finishing course with good refreshment.[2]

This was not the only newspaper to report on the game. The next day, *Bell's Life in London and Sporting Chronicle* had the following:

> Colonel Astley invited eight gentlemen from Brigg to play a hockey match against an equal number of Elsham, on the Hall Ponds, on Friday in last week, and after the contest had lasted an hour and a half it ended in a drawn game.[3]

Elsham Hall Park and Gardens is a mere 20 kilometres northwest of Croxby Pond, mentioned in the previous chapter. The complex includes a house dating to the 1760s, a 19th-century coach house and stables, and a large medieval carp lake. Brigg is a small market town on the River Ancholme, about 6 kilometres south of Elsham.

The colonel identified in these accounts is Sir John Dugdale Astley (1828–1894), dubbed "the sporting baronet." Born in Rome, in a house on the Pincian Hill, he was sent to Eton College in September of 1842, a period when hockey flourished at the school. In March 1848, Astley was gazetted ensign of the Scots Fusiliers Guards, and for the next few years his diary is full of descriptions of such diversions as racing, cricket, boxing, punting and running—he was a first-rate sprinter at 150 yards.

In 1858, he married Eleanor Blanche Mary (ca. 1839-1897), only child and heiress of Thomas George Corbett (1797-1868) of Elsham Hall, Brigg. Astley's financial security having seemingly been assured, he devoted himself to sports, including horse racing and boxing. He was a popular figure on the turf, known familiarly as "the Mate" and for winning and losing large sums of money.

Just before his death in 1894, he published *Fifty Years of My Life in the World of Sport at Home and Abroad.* He writes the following about December of 1846:[4]

> My first term at Oxford was remarkable for the very heavy floods. The Thames overflowed all the meadows for miles, and while the water was still out there was a severe frost, which produced some first class ice. We had some real good hockey—one of the best games, in my humble opinion, that man can play.[5]

Upon examination of the two game reports, we find that we have:

- hockey played on ice with skates (so the six characteristics are present);
- a specific game of hockey;
- in a specific place (the lake in the park of Elsham Hall);
- at a specific time (the time is not reported, but neither is it ever in 2014 for games that took place a week earlier; however, it is extremely hard to imagine that 16 players from two different towns would have agreed to play a game of hockey without deciding on the time in advance);
- with a recorded outcome (a draw—the exact score is not known);
- between two identified teams, Elsham and Brigg.

We also know that there is a specified number of players—eight per side, which is actually closer to today's hockey than the number of players in the first Montreal game.

Perhaps dissatisfied with having to settle for a tie (they did not think of staging a shootout), the teams met again a month later. This time, the game was reported in the *Hull Packet and East Riding Times,* a Yorkshire newspaper, on Friday, February 10, 1871:[6]

> **ELSHAM.**
> SPORT.—An interesting match at hockey was played on the lake in the park on Saturday last, between eight of Elsham Club and the same number of the Brigg Club, which resulted in the victory of the former by eight goals (Brigg *nil*) in one hour and a quarter. Brigg gave in a quarter of an hour before time was up. The ice was in splendid condition. The goals were obtained in the following order :—First goal, 10 minutes ; second, 15 ; third, 6 ; fourth, 7 ; fifth, 5 ; sixth, 8 ; seventh, 6 ; eighth, 4.

As with the earlier Elsham–Brigg game, we have here a specific game of hockey, in a specific place, at a presumed specific time—though not reported—between two identified teams. Once again, we have the number of players, which has remained at eight per team. This time, we also have the recorded score: 8–0 for Elsham. In addition, we have the exact times of the goals (not available for the first Montreal game) and the exact duration, as well as the *originally intended* duration of the game (as the Brigg club "gave in" with 15 minutes to play). This information is also not available for the Montreal game; in that case, we know that the game ended (due to a brawl with skaters who wanted to take to the ice while the players intended "to have another game"), but it is not clear whether a set duration had been agreed to in advance, or if the players simply wished to go on a little longer still.

So it would appear that all criteria specified in the SIHR report are satisfied, twice in a row—save for the exact score of the first game, which is not exactly known, though we know it ended in a draw.

Did anything else of interest happen in 1871?

Bluntisham-cum-Earith, Huntingdonshire (Cambridgeshire), 1871

Right from the hockey heart of the Fens (the parish of Bluntisham-cum-Earith, encompassing the villages of Bluntisham and Earith) came this announcement, published in London's *Morning Post* on Wednesday, January 4, 1871:

Champion Skating Matches in the Fens

There are now several very eager aspirants for the title of champion skater of the Fens, and there will be some most exciting contests on the river Ouse at Littleport and Huntingdon. A slight thaw set in yesterday, but last night it was freezing hard, and there appears to be no likelihood of the frost breaking up. There has been another great match at Earith, at which Dann, of Mepal, beat the once celebrated Turkey Smart, the ex-champion of the Fens. Several thousand spectators were present…

A cricket match and some hockey matches are pending.[7]

So the game was announced in advance, though with few details. The game report, however, provided a wealth of information, as seen in *The Penny Illustrated Paper* (London) of Saturday, January 7:

Hockey-Match on the Ice

On Wednesday week [January 4] a great hockey-match was played on the ice at Earith, between Bluntisham and Earith, against Over and Swavesey. The ball was thrown up a little before three o'clock, and there were twenty picked men on each side, under the captaincy of Mr. C. Robinson, for Over and Swavesey, and Mr. T. P. Tebbutt for Bluntisham and Earith. There was a little too much snow on the ice, otherwise there was a famous field. From the first the play of the Bluntisham and Earith men was such that it was evident the others stood but a poor chance of coming off victorious. At the conclusion of the game the Bluntisham and Earith men had scored two goals, and the Over and Swavesey none.[8]

This game was necessarily played on Bury Fen located between Bluntisham and Earith, as this was where Earith played all of its home games. The following excerpt from *A Handbook of Bandy; or, Hockey on the Ice* by Arnold Tebbutt offers an exceptionally detailed description of how hockey or bandy rinks were created.

Adjoining the village [of Earith] on the west is a low-lying tract of meadow land, some hundred acres in extent, lying alongside the river, but protected from its floods by banks in which are small sluices. These meadows are divided into "Little Fen" and "Bury Fen", both for shortness usually called "Bury Fen". It has been the practice of the occupiers of these fens during times of winter flood to open these sluice gates, and let the muddy river water flow in upon the fen some foot or two deep. This "white" water, as it is called, then deposits its fertile sediment upon the land, and having done so may be drawn off at pleasure as soon as the river has fallen. But as the water may be left upon the land for many days, if not weeks, without any serious damage being done to the grass, a little management has enabled the villagers to have a fine skating and bandy ground at little or no expense. The tract is large enough when all covered to furnish half-a-dozen or more full-sized bandy grounds.[9]

The team from the twin villages of Bluntisham and Earith was often referred to as "The Bury Fen team," which had been playing bandy since the mid-1700s. It is located in the historical county of Huntingdonshire, today a part of Cambridgeshire.

The two villages of Swavesey and Over are located about 5.5 kilometres south of Bluntisham-cum-Earith.

The game, which took place just two days prior to the first one mentioned in this chapter, also appears to have been organized hockey. The account describes:

- hockey played on ice with skates;
- a specific game of hockey;
- in a specific place (Earith);
- at a specific time ("a little before three o'clock");
- with a recorded outcome (2–0 for Bluntisham and Earith);
- between two identified teams (Bluntisham and Earith, and Over and Swavesey).

This time, as a bonus, we have:

- the type of faceoff (performed by throwing the ball up, not down);
- the number of players on each side (20—a high number for hockey, but as described in the quote from Tebbutt earlier, the ice surface was extremely large);
- the names of the captains: Mr. C. (Charles) Robinson

(1832–1918) for Over and Swavesey, and Mr. Charles Prentice
Tebbutt (1824–1910), incorrectly identified by the initials
T. P., for Bluntisham and Earith.

Could this have been the first organized game of ice hockey? Perhaps not!

Swavesey, Cambridgeshire, 1857

Swavesey is a village in the Fens, about 15 kilometres northwest of Cambridge.
The village of Over is located about a kilometre north of Swavesey. Mare
Fen (also known as Mere Fen) was used for skating races and bandy matches
during most of the 1800s, and is still used for skating to this day. It is located
just north of Swavesey and west of Over.

The following report was published Saturday, February 7, 1857, in the
*Cambridge Independent Press, Huntingdon, Isle of Ely, Bedford, Peterborough,
and Lynn Gazette* (despite the long-winded title, this was a single newspaper
and not six).

THE CAMBRIDGE INDEPENDENT PRESS, HUNTINGDON, ISLE OF ELY, BEDFORD, PETERBOROUGH, AND LYNN GAZETTE, FEBRUARY 7, 1857

SWAVESEY — SKATING — There has been plenty of skating at this place
during the past week, in which a youth named Dodson, aged 18, greatly
distinguished himself. On Tuesday [February 3] several Willingham
heroes of the ice, came to contest the honours of championship with
him but to no purpose; Dodson still maintaining his position. On Wednesday there was a mixed drawn match between the Over and Swavesey
skaters, at which Dodson was again victorious. On Thursday there was
a bandy match on the ice, between Over and Swavesey, and a race for
£4, the Swaveseyites being successful in both. Swavesey has been visited
this week by many skaters from St. Ives, Cambridge, and adjacent villages.
Great credit is due to Mr. [Hanslip] Long for allowing about 40 acres
of land to remain covered with water, that the skaters should not be dis-
appointed in having a fine piece of ice to exhibit upon. Host Dodson,
of the White Horse, has been overwhelmed with visitors and rendered
them all the accommodation in his power, and to their utter satisfaction.
The following were the competitors, and those with an asterisk were successful [in the Races]:

SWAVESEY	OVER
C. Dodson *	S. Bicheno
F. Carter *	D. Silk
J. Fear	G. Silk *
G. Dodson	C. Bicheno *
J. Richman *	B. Silk
C. Richman	C. Gifford *
C. Allen *	B. Catrell
T. Mansfield *	W. Mustell
J. Metcalfe	W. Ingle *
G. Thorp	F. Hall *
A. Metcalfe *	F. Edwards[10]

In chapter 8, we will return to the question of whether 19th-century bandy can be considered hockey. Like the previous examples in this chapter, this game also satisfied the majority of conditions: on ice with skates, specific game, in a specific place (Mr. Hanslip Long's land in Swavesey), specific time (not explicit, but implied), recorded outcome (the Swavesey team won, though the exact score is not known) and two identified teams (Over and Swavesey).

Once again, we also have an additional element—in this case, the names of all players.

Were these four games organized hockey? In the absence of a strict definition, the answer has to be at least a qualified yes: none of the games was improvised; they were all planned somewhat in advance and involved clearly identified teams, typically two opposing villages, with a fixed number of players, though that number was high (20 per team) for one of the games.

But there was more to the first Montreal game than just those elements. The next chapter will examine this.

Chapter 4 Notes

1. Society for International Hockey Research, *Report of the Sub-Committee Looking into Claim That Windsor, Nova Scotia, is the Birthplace of Hockey* (Toronto: Society for International Hockey Research, 2002): 14–15.

2. *Stamford Mercury,* 13 Jan. 1871.

3. *Bell's Life in London, and Sporting Chronicle,* 14 Jan. 1871.
4. The frost set in in early December 1846. In Scotland, the skating season began on December 1 (*Glasgow Herald,* 7 Dec. 1846), in Northern England a few days later (*Westmorland Gazette* [Kendal, Cumbria], 5 Dec. 1846), and in London on December 14 (*Morning Chronicle* [London], 15 Dec. 1846).
5. John Dugdale Astley, *Fifty Years of My Life in the World of Sport at Home and Abroad,* vol. I (London: Hurst and Blackett, 1894): 30.
6. *Hull Packet and East Riding Times,* 10 Feb. 1871.
7. *Morning Post* (London), 4 Jan. 1871.
8. *Penny Illustrated Paper* (London), 7 Jan. 1871.
9. Arnold Tebbutt, *A Handbook of Bandy; or, Hockey on the Ice* (London: Horace Cox, 1896): 3–4.
10. *Cambridge Independent Press, Huntingdon, Isle of Ely, Bedford, Peterborough, and Lynn Gazette,* 7 Feb. 1857.

CHAPTER 5

Having It All

Before we continue our study of games of hockey played in England prior to 1875, let us turn our attention to the subject of whether skates were used when hockey was played on the ice.

"But were they wearing skates?" The question is commonly raised whenever reports have surfaced of hockey—or some other "stick and ball game"—being played on ice. An article on the Deline claim, written by Randy Boswell of Postmedia News and published in 2011, offers a perfect example:

> When Franklin and the members of an overland expedition wintered at Fort Franklin in 1825, the Royal Navy commander wrote in a letter to Britain that his men were playing games of "hockey on the ice" to keep their spirits up. And in a separate reference in his diaries, Franklin noted that "skating" was among the winter "amusements" enjoyed by his men.
>
> Whether Franklin's men were playing their rudimentary form of hockey at the same time that they [were] wearing skates remains unknown.[1]

We know they were playing a game called hockey, we know they were playing it on the ice, and we know that they had skates. But we're still wondering whether they actually wore the skates *while playing hockey*.

Without specifically examining the case of the Franklin expedition, let us take a look at skating in England in the 18th and 19th centuries.

Cold Broth and Calamity, *a watercolour created by the London printmaker and caricaturist Thomas Rowlandson (1757-1827) in 1792,*[6] *demonstrates perfectly how all classes of the population had taken to skating—despite the obvious risks.*

We know that, in the 1700s, skates became available for all classes of the population. On February 18, 1720, the London newspaper *The Post-Boy* reported, "On Sunday last, as several Persons were scating [sic] upon the Ponds in Hyde-Park, [the ice broke...]"[2]

On December 18, 1742, *The Newcastle Courant* contained the following, from London: "On Tuesday several Persons skaiting [sic] on the Canal in the [St. James's] Park, were heartily duck'd by the breaking of the Ice."[3]

In that same year, or near it, the Edinburgh Skating Club, the very first skating club in the world was created.[4]

Two more decades later, skating—or "scating," or "skaiting"—did not seem to be going out of fashion. Sadly, neither did the related accidents. From *The Whitehall Evening Post; Or, London Intelligencer* on January 12, 1760:

Last Sunday among the great Number of Skaiters on the Canal in St. James's Park, one Man broke his Back by a Fall, and another had his Leg broke.[5]

In 1772, the first book ever written on figure skating, *A Treatise on Skating* by Captain Robert Jones,[7] was published. Jones also manufactured his own model of skates that could be more firmly attached by screws through the heels.[8]

Ads for skates can be found at least as far back as 1729, when London's *Daily Post* offered "Dutch SLIDEING [sic] SKATES — OF all Sorts and Sizes..."[9] Less than 15 years later, English models had become available.

> GEORGE BARRETT...TAKES this Opportunity to acquaint all Gentlemen and Ladies that are Lovers of the Diversion of Skaiting, that they may, by applying to me, be serv'd with all sorts of Dutch and English Skaits, completely fix'd up with Leathers or Strings, after the strongest and most approv'd manner...[10]

The English schools adopted the concept of healthy exercise for boys. For example, in 1911, Ralph Nevill wrote about "the manly character induced by games and sport."[11] As a consequence, as these youngsters grew up, it became acceptable and even well-viewed for gentlemen to skate. Good figure skaters were mentioned in newspapers, as in London's *Morning Post* in 1823:

> THE SERPENTINE RIVER...The best skaiters performed their evolutions on the South Side...Those who excited the most interest were Mr. ATKINSON, Messrs. LONGLAND, MURRAY, and MASTERS. These adroit performers exhibited the "mazy round," in a set of quadrilles, with the most captivating correctness;...Here a new set of figures were introduced, called a Polish dance, something resembling a waltz. In this movement some Gentlemen connected with the Russian Embassy were conspicuous.[12]

An obituary of Shute Barrington (1734–1826), the Eton- and Oxford-educated Bishop of Durham, commented, "As a young man, he excelled in graceful exercises; he was one of the best skaiters of his day;..."[13]

In the early 1800s, it even became fashionable for private estates to have their own skating ponds, so that the owners would not have to mingle with the lower classes at the common lake — though some of the more "generous" noblemen did invite the general population to enjoy their quality ice. Being able to offer guests perfect conditions for skating brought status and prestige.

Witness the (unrewarded) generosity of Mr. Berkeley:

> Although, at the time of our last publication, the frost had every appearance of leaving us, it has again set in with increased rigour, and the skaters have resumed their diversions upon the Spetchley and neighbouring pools. Mr. Berkeley, whose kindness will be long remembered, has, we hear, been greatly annoyed this week, in consequence of several mischievous fellows having cut down a number of his young trees in the plantations adjoining the pool, for their amusement upon the ice, notwithstanding sticks had been previously provided them on the margin of the pond. Mr. Berkeley's kindness has been further requited by having his gates thrown off their hinges, and his fences destroyed. We are glad to hear that the real lovers of skating in this city feel indignant at this disgraceful conduct, and that it is their intention to form a club, not only for the protection of the property of those gentlemen who, as in the case of Mr. Berkeley, have shown them so much kindness, but to use very endeavour to punish any person found acting in the wanton and disgraceful way above mentioned.[14]

We will return to Spetchley and Mr. Berkeley's estate later in this chapter.

At this point, most gentlemen still practised the "genteel" figure skating and did not yet participate in the more virile sports, like hockey. At the same time, however, the younger generation was learning hockey in schools and bringing it to the military academies and to their own private estates as they grew up.

When Albert, Prince Consort, husband of Queen Victoria, took up ice hockey in the 1840s, it established the activity as the "in" thing to do. His son the Prince of Wales (the future Edward VII) took up the game, as did the royalty of other countries. There are several reports between 1863 and 1869 that Czar Alexander III (1845-1894) of Russia played ice hockey at the Winter Palace Ground in St. Petersburg.[15] In France, Napoleon III (1808-1873), also known as Louis-Napoléon Bonaparte, played on "Le Lac de Madrid" in the Bois de Boulogne in Paris in January 1864[16]. His son, Napoleon IV (1856-1879), also played, while in exile, at Trentham Hall, Staffordshire England, in late December 1878.[17] The Swedish crown prince, later to become King Gustaf V (1858-1950), played at Idrottsparken in Stockholm in January 1897.[18]

Londoners are playing hockey on ice—and on skates—in this woodcut drawing, "The Thames Frozen Over at Richmond," from the Illustrated London News *of Saturday March 3, 1855.*[19] *In the detail on the opposite page, we can see that every single player is wearing skates—and that the object has straight edges, making it probably not a ball, but rather a bung, as was very commonly used then.*

It follows that any game of hockey played on ice at a private estate was always on skates. The nobles would not have risked ridicule or accident by clumsily running around in boots on the slippery ice. The objective of engaging in a hockey game was to demonstrate one's skill and agility, something that could only be done on skates.

The Search for Organized Hockey Continues

In the previous chapter, we cited a number of cases that not only fit the Society for International Hockey Research's definition of (ice) hockey, but that also satisfied all or most of the specific qualities that the SIHR Origins Committee report attributed to the March 3, 1875, game played in Montreal, which is generally considered the first organized game of hockey ever played. Some of the reports also contained additional elements not available for that first Montreal game.

However, the Montreal *Gazette* that appeared on the day that the game was held, and the newspaper reports published the next day, contained more elements than SIHR report highlighted. Examining them in detail, we find that they also contained all of the following points:

- a clear description of the object used to play (resembling a puck, but without a proper name at the time, and thus described as a "flat block of wood" — interestingly, the rules published in Montreal in 1877 designated that object as... "the ball");
- the exact number of players on each side and their names;
- the names of the team captains;
- a mention of the audience;
- the approximate distance between the goal posts (eight feet), though the wording is subject to interpretation, as the article might have been describing "hockey in general," and not necessarily that specific game; and
- the time at which the game ended.

Thus the articles provided a great many details about the game — though as mentioned previously, this was in part due to the fact that it was, for many readers, if not the majority, their first exposure to this game.

We certainly do not pretend that a report of a game played in England prior to 1875 contained every single one of these details, but we do believe that some reports' level of detail in their description of the game was as high as for that Montreal game.

Moor Park, Hertfordshire, 1871

On Saturday, February 4, 1871, *The Morning Post* (London) reported on this game:[20]

HOCKEY AT MOOR PARK. —A well-contested match at hockey was played upon the ice at Moor Park on Thursday between seven gentlemen from Oxfordshire and seven of Moor Park. The Oxon seven consisted of Messrs. Charles and C. G. Marsham, Ottaway, Tubb, Hadow, Harrison and Dewar. Their opponents were Messrs. Grosvenor, R. A. Fitzgerald, N. Grosvenor, R. Barker, A. H. Grosvenor, Kay, and R. C. Grosvenor.

At first it seemed as if neither side would be able to penetrate the adverse goal, so evenly did they appear matched. However, after several severe struggles and no lack of prostrations on both sides, Moor Park got the first goal. Not very long after the same colours were again successful, and a 10 minutes' rest was taken.

On resuming the game fortune changed sides and Oxon obtained the ascendant, making two goals in a very short time. The fickle goddess, however, from that moment turned her back upon the Oxonians, and the three remaining games that were played, being seven in all, fell to the lot of Moor Park.

The winning strokes were obtained for Oxford by Messrs. C. G. Marsham and Tubb; for Moor Park, by Messrs. N. Grosvenor, A. H. Grosvenor (3), and R. C. Grosvenor.[20]

If the opening phrase of the report sounds familiar ("A well-contested match at hockey..."), it could be because of a similar sentence in *The Gazette*'s report of the 1875 Montreal game: "The match was an interesting and well-contested affair..."

Moor Park is a private residential estate in Hertfordshire with several hundred acres of parkland, located approximately 25 kilometres northwest of central London. It takes its name from a country house that was originally built in 1678–79 for James Scott, the first Duke of Monmouth, and was reconstructed in the Palladian style circa 1720 by Giacomo Leoni. The manor of Moor (La More) is, however, much older and was first mentioned about 1180.

In 1828 the estate was bought by Robert, the 2nd Earl of Grosvenor (1767-1845), who later became the 1st Marquis of Westminster. Upon his death in 1845, the estate passed to his third son, Robert Grosvenor (1801–1893), made 1st Baron Ebury in 1857. The Grosvenors were to remain at Moor Park until the death of Robert Wellesley Grosvenor, the 2nd Baron Ebury, in 1918. His heir sold the mansion and the grounds by auction, and the place was converted to golf courses. It is today occupied by the Moor Park Golf Club.

At this point, the reader probably does not need to be convinced that this game featured hockey. The skates are not mentioned, but as demonstrated at the beginning of this chapter, there can be no doubt that they were used, especially in light of the participation of Algernon Henry Grosvenor (1846–1907), an excellent sportsman (he had a long cricket career in particular) who became the president of the London Skating Club in the 1890s, writing a prefatory note to George A. Meagher's 1895 book *Figure and Fancy Skating*.[21] He became a keen ice hockey player and even went on to appear as a goalkeeper (at age 49) in the first indoor game ever played in England—on February 1, 1896, at the National Skating Palace, also known as Hengler's Grand Cirque, on the site now occupied by the London Palladium. In that game, a team representing England had defeated a team representing Canada by a score of 3-0.[22]

As for the Moor Park game, it is a specific game in a specific place, certainly at a specific (though not reported) time, with a recorded score (5-2 for Moor Park) and identified teams: Oxfordshire and Moor Park.

We also note that the number of players per team: seven, the same number that was used in eastern Canada between 1880 and 1912, and in western Canada until 1922, whereas the first Montreal game (1875) had nine.

Furthermore, the report specifies:

- the names of all players;
- the identity of the scorers;

- the mention of a "rest" (intermission), specifying its duration (10 minutes); and
- a goal-by-goal description of the game, giving in particular the score at the intermission (2-0 for Moor Park).

It seems difficult to imagine that this game could not be considered organized hockey. Was it the first?

Spetchley Park, Spetchley, Worcestershire, 1870

A little more than a month before the Moor Park game, a game involving 10 players a side had been contested in another part of England. Reports of the game were published in two different newspapers, with nearly identical wording. First, from the *Worcestershire Chronicle* of Wednesday, December 28, 1870:

MATCH ON THE ICE. — On Tuesday a very spirited and well-contested hockey match on the ice was played between ten gentlemen of Worcester and an equal number of Spetchley and neighbourhood, which ended in favour of Spetchley. The match was played at Spetchley Park, and the garden pool in front of the mansion had, by the express wish of R. Berkeley, Esq., been reserved for the occasion.

The following are the names of the gentlemen who took part in the match: Worcester—Messrs. J. Baxter, A. Everill, F. Everill, T.J. Elliot, W. Grafton, Harry Lane, W. Parsons, J. Rea, J. Tyler, F. Yeates. Spetchley—T. Aston, Esq., F. R. Berkeley, Esq., H. Chamberlain, Esq., F. Chamberlain, Esq., Messrs. J. Dale, W. Dale, Don Francisco, Palmer, Tayler, Jack Allen, T. Wheeler.

For Worcester Messrs. Tyler, Yeates, and A. Everill obtained goals; and for Spetchley Messrs. Tayler, Wheeler, W. Dale, and Don Francisco.[23]

The same report, with only very minor differences, appeared the following Saturday in *Bell's Life in London, and Sporting Chronicle*—under the heading SKATING. The name of F. Chamberlain is omitted, and a few other players have their names spelled differently.[24]

Spetchley Park, in the hamlet of Spetchley, about five kilometres east of Worcester, has belonged to the Berkeley family since 1605. The present home, designed by London architect John Tasker, is a magnificent Georgian mansion constructed at the beginning of the 19th century, but the estate's history goes back to Tudor times, when it was a more of a simple moated Tudor house, and home to the Lyttleton family.

The Berkeley family is unique in English history in that it has, to this day, an unbroken male line of descent from a noble Saxon who lived before the Norman conquest of England in 1066. The family also retains possession of much of the land it held from the 11th and 12th centuries, centred on Berkeley Castle in Gloucestershire.

Prior to this game, several reports about stick-and-ball games and hockey on the ice at Spetchley exist from the 1800s. A skating club was formed about 1840, and as late as on June 30, 1888, the *Worcestershire Chronicle* noted that "Spetchley is still famous for its unrivalled avenue of elms, its well-wooded park and fine lake, which last is, by the liberality of the Berkeley family, freely and largely used by the citizens of Worcester for skating."[25]

While the article mentions that there were 10 players per side, the first report shows 11 members of the Spetchley team. So the mention of F. Chamberlain in the first report might have been in error. The usual information is present: hockey on ice with skates, specific date, implied specific time (since it is mentioned that "the garden pool had been reserved for the occasion"), score (4–3 for Spetchley) and two teams (Worcester and "Spetchley and neighbourhood"). As for the Moor Park game, all players are listed; in this case, their titles, where applicable, are indicated as well. The scorers are also identified—all goals were scored by different players.

So was it organized hockey yet?

It would appear that these games—not part of a regular schedule, but necessarily decided in advance; featuring clearly identified teams, whose players are all named; being reported not only with the final score but the identity of the goal scorers—had as many of the elements of organized hockey, though not exactly all of the same ones, as the first Montreal game in 1875. Certainly, the absence of the size of the goals used in the

Moor Park and Spetchley Park reports does not make these games any less organized.

But what is so special about that Montreal game in 1875 goes beyond what has been explored so far. Beyond how well the game was documented, beyond how structured its organization was. For the first time, hockey players were *not* answering this call: "All right gentlemen, let's go out and play!"

Chapter 5 Notes

1. Randy Boswell, "Birthplace of hockey still great debate," *Edmonton Journal,* 18 Sep. 2011, web, 22 Mar. 2014 <http://www2.canada.com /edmontonjournal/news/story.html?id=e41ebf06-55cf-4032-b5bc-2a160a92009c&p=1>.
2. *Post Boy* (London), 18 Feb. 1720.
3. *Newcastle Courant,* 18 Dec. 1742.
4. Edinburgh Skating Club, Minute-Books, GB233/MS.24641-24649, National Library of Scotland, Edinburgh.
5. *Whitehall Evening Post; Or, London Intelligencer,* 12 Jan. 1760.
6. Thomas Rowlandson, *Cold Broth and Calamity, study for a satirical print, London, 1792,* 1931,114.87, British Museum, London.
7. Robert Jones, *A Treatise on Skating; Founded on Certain Principles Deduced from Many Years Experience: by which that Noble Exercise Is Now Reduced to an Art* (London: John Ridley, 1772).
8. Denis L. Bird, "Skating, A Brief History of Ice and the National Skating Association of Great Britain," *NISA History: National Ice Skating Association of Great Britain and Northern Ireland,* 12 Jan. 2010, web, 22 March 2014, <http://www.iceskating.org.uk/about/history>. Website describes *A Treatise on Skating* as "the world's first book on the sport."
9. *Daily Post* (London), 7 Feb. 1729.
10. *Daily Advertiser* (London), 4 Dec. 1742.
11. Ralph Nevill, *Floreat Etona, Anecdotes and Memoires of Eton College* (London: Macmillan, 1911): 125.
12. *Morning Post* (London), 13 Jan. 1823.
13. *New Times* (London), 28 Mar. 1826.
14. *Berrow's Worcester Journal,* 15 Feb. 1838.

15. *The Standard* (London), 9 Mar. 1869, and *Leeds Mercury,* 5 Nov. 1894.
16. *Otago Daily Times* (Dunedin, New Zealand), 21 Mar. 1864.
17. Ronald Charles Sutherland-Leveson-Gower, *My Reminiscences* (London: Kegan, Paul, Trench, 1883): 255.
18. *Tidning för Idrott* (Stockholm, Sweden), 25 Feb. 1897.
19. "The Thames frozen over at Richmond," *The Illustrated London News,* 3 Mar. 1855: 197. The following text below accompanied the illustration: "Among the memorabilia of the recent frost was the freezing of the entire width of the river Thames at Richmond, which had not occurred for seventeen years.... Some of the Richmond skaters took advantage of this rare state of the river, but the greater number, including a few ladies, preferred the smoother ice of the large ponds in Richmond-park."
20. *The Morning Post* (London), 4 Feb. 1871.
21. George Alfred Meagher, *Figure and Fancy Skating* (London: Bliss, Sands, and Foster, 1895): 8–10.
22. *The Echo* (London), 3 Feb. 1896.
23. *Worcestershire Chronicle* (Worcester), 28 Dec. 1870.
24. *Bell's Life in London, and Sporting Chronicle,* 31 Dec. 1870.
25. *Worcestershire Chronicle* (Worcester), 30 Jun. 1888.

CHAPTER 6

The Game That Came In from the Cold

T HE TITLE SAYS it all. In *Putting a Roof on Winter: Hockey's Rise from Sport to Spectacle,* author Michael McKinley makes it very clear that transporting the game indoors, which happened for the first time at that Montreal game on March 3, 1875, was the defining moment when ice hockey became a sport. McKinley writes: "James Creighton didn't invent hockey on that winter's night under the roof of that Montreal rink, but rather, he had found its temple. In W. P. Kinsella's *Shoeless Joe,* which provided the basis for the movie *Field of Dreams,* a mysterious voice says, "If you build it, he will come." Hockey's corollary could well be "If you move it inside, it will become."[1]

McKinley goes on to explain that the roof puts hockey in a protected environment, safe from the elements of snow and wind. Of course, hockey was not safe from the cold, since the ice, even inside, was still natural in the early days, so the temperature indoors was very close to that outside.

There is no doubt that bringing hockey indoors was a brilliant idea. It did prevent occurrences of games where players had to fight the snow, such as in NHL's 2014 Winter Classic game between the Pittsburgh Penguins and the Chicago Blackhawks—a memorable game, but no fan would want all games to be played under such conditions.

So the question is not whether bringing hockey indoors was a good idea, but whether it is a prerequisite for the game to be considered hockey, or organized hockey, or "hockey as we know it." The very existence of the NHL's Winter Classic and Heritage Classic games certainly appears to cast a serious doubt over whether such a requirement really exists, but the subject is worth exploring further.

It would be difficult to draw any conclusion by looking at hockey in isolation. If we expand our scope, we immediately see that a large number of sports have succeeded, and even thrived, outdoors. Two of North America's major sports, football and baseball, are still to this day usually played outside, though of course there are now a few covered fields. Golf and skiing, which can be badly affected by elements, have become immensely successful outdoors, both as sport and spectacle, to use McKinley's words.

Speed skating (long track) is a particularly good example to study, because its conversion is quite recent. The Olympic competition was first held indoors in 1988 in Calgary, and the next Winter Olympics, in Albertville, France, in 1992, was the last time it was held outdoors. All 11 ISU Speed Skating World Cup events held in the 2013/14 season took place indoors.[2] Yet the change appears to have so little importance or relevance that it is not even mentioned in the sport's entry in Wojciech Liponski's *World Sports Encyclopedia*.[3] Surely the skaters would have conceded that snow and wind (and sometimes unbearable cold) had to have affected them in outdoor competitions of old.

Figure skating also moved indoors — the last outdoor Olympic competition was in 1956. Yet James R. Hines, Jr. identifies the elimination of school (or compulsory) figures as the most radical change the sport experienced over the years,[4] not the move indoors. Surely figure skaters (and the 78-rpm records from which their music was played) were even more affected by weather conditions than hockey players.

So is ice hockey unique in some way that makes the indoor form the only truly valid one? We already know that the NHL's Heritage Classics, Winter Classics and Stadium Series games, which have occurred a total of 13 times[5] as of the end of the 2013/14 season (though one, at Vancouver's BC Place stadium on March 2, 2014, ended up being played with the roof closed due to snow and rain), were huge successes, and the games counted in the standings — they were not exhibition games. The fact that the NHL has been programming more and more of these games[6] in fact appears to confirm that outdoor hockey does qualify as "true," and organized, hockey.

Now obviously, these games, which only started in 2003, are played in an extremely structured environment, with boards identical to the ones used in NHL arenas and artificial ice. So the point could be made that, while there is no roof, and while the players are at the mercy of the elements (except, again, in Vancouver), in most other aspects, the games themselves barely differ from indoor ones.

These NHL games, however, are far from the only organized ones—for elite-level adults—that have been played outside. In fact, only four of the first twenty-eight IIHF World Championships (including the Olympic tournaments) had all their games played indoors: the tournaments of 1934, in Milan, Italy; 1937 and 1950, in London, England; and 1951, in Paris, France. The tournament moved indoors permanently only in 1962.

The opening game of the 1948 Winter Olympic hockey tournament in St. Moritz, Switzerland, played outdoors at the St. Moritz Olympic Ice Rink.

Of course, these rinks, while built outdoors, had the benefit of boards all around the ice, a fixture of hockey that naturally came from the sport having, at one point, been moved inside. So maybe the key development isn't that the game moved indoors, but that it was played with boards.

However, the following photographs say otherwise:

Spengler Cup game played December 30, 1938, between LTC Praha of Prague, Czechoslovakia, and IK Göta of Stockholm, Sweden. The Spengler Cup, competed for in the Swiss resort city of Davos since the winter of 1923/24, is the oldest continuously held invitational ice hockey tournament for club teams in Europe.

Game played on January 21, 1914, between Germany and Bohemia as part of the Ligue Internationale de Hockey sur Glace (LIHG) championship. Germany won the game 4–2, while England won the tournament.

The observant reader will have noticed that all these examples feature European hockey, which, for some, is not—or at least, was not at the time—"real" hockey. Maybe "real" North American hockey can only be played indoors, or at least in ultra-modern 21st-century open stadiums?

Hardly.

While most of the exhibition games played between 1875 and 1882 in Montreal were played indoors (and nearly all of those at the Victoria Skating Rink),[7] the very first time in the history of ice hockey that a tournament was played, with a champion designated, was at the Montreal Winter Carnival hockey tournament of 1883, with the first two games played on the St. Lawrence River! (Warning to readers: Do not attempt this in the 21st century.) An artist's rendition[8] of one of the games, below, is quite clear:

This engraving, simply titled "Hockey," is one of nine by Henry Sandham that illustrated the article "A Canadian Carnival" by William George Beers in the December 1883 issue of Wide Awake.[9]

And it was not just a one-time affair. The following year (1884), all but one of the tournament's games were played on the (outdoor) McGill University rink,[10] as can be seen here:

A photograph of the 1884 Montreal Winter Carnival hockey tournament, taken by Alexander Henderson of Montreal.

In 1886, an outbreak of smallpox[12] caused the cancellation of the Montreal Winter Carnival, but a "replacement" hockey tournament was held in Burlington, Vermont, which was the very first international hockey competition. The games were played on the reportedly windy Lake Champlain[13] (Even in the 21st century, Lake Champlain still freezes sufficiently in most winters to allow it to be the site of an annual tournament, the Lake Champlain Pond Hockey Classic, which takes place on Malletts Bay.)

So while there is no question that moving the game indoors was indeed a defining moment for hockey, it does not mean that games played outdoors could not be considered "organized" or "real" hockey.

There are still further arguments that are made to explain that the Montreal first game, and all those that followed from it, had something that the previous games, wherever they were held, did not have. We will continue examining those in the next chapter.

Chapter 6 Notes

1. Michael McKinley, *Putting on a Roof on Winter: Hockey's Rise from Sport to Spectacle* (Vancouver: Greystone, 2000): 11.
2. International Skating Union, *ISU Results*, n.d., web, 22 Mar. 2014, <http://live.isuresults.eu/>.
3. Wojciech Liponski, *World Sports Encyclopedia*, (St. Paul, Minn.: MBI, 2003) 508-509.
4. James R. Hines Jr., *Figure Skating: A History*, (Champaign, Ill.: University of Illinois Press, 2006).
5. The outdoor (or intended to be outdoor) NHL regular-season games so far:

    22 Nov. 2003, Heritage Classic, Montreal Canadiens 4, Edmonton Oilers 3
    1 Jan. 2008, Winter Classic, Pittsburgh Penguins 2, Buffalo Sabres 1 (shootout)
    1 Jan. 2009, Winter Classic, Detroit Red Wings 6, Chicago Blackhawks 4
    1 Jan. 2010, Winter Classic, Boston Bruins 2, Philadelphia Flyers 1 (overtime)
    1 Jan. 2011, Winter Classic, Washington Capitals 3, Pittsburgh Penguins 1
    20 Feb. 2011, Heritage Classic, Calgary Flames 4, Montreal Canadiens 0
    2 Jan. 2012, Winter Classic, New York Rangers 3, Philadelphia Flyers 2
    1 Jan. 2014, Winter Classic, Toronto Maple Leafs 3, Detroit Red Wings 2 (shootout)
    25 Jan. 2014, Stadium Series, Anaheim Ducks 3, Los Angeles Kings 0
    26 Jan. 2014, Stadium Series, New York Rangers 7, New Jersey Devils 3
    29 Jan. 2014, Stadium Series, New York Rangers 2, New York Islanders 1
    1 Mar. 2014, Stadium Series, Chicago Blackhawks 5, Pittsburgh Penguins 1
    2 Mar. 2014, Heritage Classic, Ottawa Senators 4, Vancouver Canucks 2

6. More than four years elapsed between the first and second such games. Since then, there has been at least one every season (except for lockout-shortened 2012/13). In 2013/14, there were six.
7. Games played between 1875 and 1882 in Montreal, elsewhere than the Victoria Skating Rink:

    28 Feb. 1879, McGill University Rink (outdoors), McGill 6, Britannia 0 (source: Montreal *Evening Post*, 1 Mar. 1879).
    20 Jan. 1882, Crystal Palace Skating Rink, McGill vs. Quebec Hockey Club–game ended in a draw (source: *The Gazette* [Montreal], 1 Jan. 1882).

8. Henry Sandham, "Hockey," *Wide Awake*, December 1883: 43.
9. *Daily Witness* (Montreal), 1 Feb. 1883.

10. Alexander Henderson, "Playing Hockey on the Skating Rink, McGill University, 1884," C-081683, Alexander Henderson fonds, Library and Archives Canada, Ottawa.
11. *The Gazette* (Montreal), 12 Feb. 1884.
12. *Boston Evening Transcript,* 17 Feb. 1886.
13. *Burlington Weekly Free Press,* 5 Mar. 1886: 2.

CHAPTER 7

Hockey Rules!

THERE ARE GAMES, AND THEN there are sports. People rarely pay hundreds of dollars to see others play games, but they may part with their money to see top-level athletes taking part in a sport.

What's the difference? Perhaps we should seek out an authority figure to tell us — say, the head of a national government. A member of this exclusive club wrote the following: "What distinguishes any modern sport from its 'folk pastime' status is the formal codification of rules by James Creighton, the fixing of dimensions, the fixing of numbers of participants, and time frames. And that was clearly done in Montreal in 1875. It's also possible that it might have been done in other places as well, but it's clear that the sport we know today evolved from that 1875 event."[1]

This was written by Canada's hockey historian and prime minister, Stephen Harper, in the foreword to *How Hockey Explains Canada: The Sport That Defines a Country,* a book co-written by national hockey hero Paul Henderson with Jim Prime. The prime minister does not provide his sources, but the difference, as defined, between a "modern sport" and a "folk pastime" is generally accepted. For example, the source could have been Quebec sports historian Donald Guay, who gave a six-point definition of sport, with the fifth point being (our translation): "Sport, a rule of conduct: Sport being a competition motivated by stakes, it is essential that the opponents be subject to the same rules, in order to minimize the variables that could favour one of the opponents, because only the sports value of the participants should determine the winner."[2]

It is well known that, two years after the first Montreal game, *The Gazette* published a set of seven rules for hockey.[3] It is also generally accepted that the games played before the rules were printed had implicit, maybe even explicit rules known to the participants. After all, it makes little sense to bring 18 grown men to engage in a game—advertised in the newspaper, no less—without telling them what they're expected to do, what is allowed and what isn't. In fact, many believe that "some" rules had been used, in Montreal, as far back as 1872 or 1873, when the eventual participants in the Montreal first game were practising for the "big day," as recounted by Henry Joseph in interviews published in *The Gazette* in 1936[4] and 1943.[5]

It would be difficult to disagree that the rules published in 1877 were largely inspired by then-existing English field hockey rules. Specifically, they were based on the rules of the Hockey Association, which had been formed (on April 10) and had published those rules in 1875. The Association was created to group together the seven clubs of Teddington, Richmond, Surbiton, Sutton, East Surrey (Croydon), Upper Tooting and the Strollers. The Blackheath Club, which participated in the discussions, declined to join, because the hockey it played did not resemble the form played by the other clubs, being more akin to rugby (whereas the other seven clubs could be said to have been inspired more by football/soccer).

Lending credence to the theory that the Montreal hockey players were using rules prior to 1877 is the fact that the Hockey Association's rules had started being used the year before, as this *Gazette* game report, published February 7, 1876, attests: "The game was conducted under the 'Hockey Association' rules, Messrs W. Hutton, President of the Rink, and Philip Cross acting as umpires."[6]

Seemingly unfamiliar with the English Hockey Association, Emanuel M. Orlick would, on September 18, 1943, formulate the following hypotheses: "This tells us two important things, namely that a 'Hockey Association' was functioning in Montreal as early as 1876 and that some time prior to February 5, 1876, a set of rules for the game of ice hockey had already been codified.[7]

To his credit, Orlick was half right (the second half), though in a different way than he might have thought.

Is it reasonable to assume that rules could have crossed the Atlantic in just one year? Almost certainly. A few years later, in 1883, the news of the adoption of the NSA (National Skating Association) rules was commented on in the *Toronto Daily Mail* just a few weeks after the announcement in London.[8]

Below is a rule-by-rule comparison of the 1875 Hockey Association rules and the 1877 *Gazette* rules. As can be seen, the sequence of the rules was rearranged, and five of them were dropped, while one new rule was added — a rule about how disputes are resolved that says nothing about how hockey was played. Words, or letters, from the English rules that were left out of the Montreal rules are underscored on the left, while underscored words on the right designate words that were added in Montreal:

Hockey Association (England), 1875[9]	The Gazette, 1877[10]
3. The game shall be commenced and re-newed by a bully in the centre of the ground. Goals shall be changed at half-time only.	1. The game shall be commenced and re-newed by a Bully in the centre of the ground. Goals shall be changed after each game.
6. When a player hits the ball, any one of the same side who at such moment of hitting is nearer to the opponents' goal-line is out of play, and may not touch the ball himself, nor in any way whatever prevent any other player from doing so, until the ball has been played, unless there are at least three of his opponents nearer their own goal-line; but no player is out of play when the ball is hit from the goal-line.	2. When a player hits the ball, any one of the same side who at such a moment of hitting is nearer to the opponents' goal line is out of play, and may not touch the ball himself, or in any way whatever prevent any other player from doing so, until the ball has been played. A player must always be on his own side of the ball.
7. The ball may be stopped but not carried or knocked on by any part of the body. No player shall raise his stick above his shoulder. The ball shall be played from right to left, and no left or back-handed play, charging, tripping, collaring, kicking or shinning shall be allowed.	3. The ball may be stopped, but not carried or knocked on by any part of the body. No player shall raise his stick above his shoulder. Charging from behind, tripping, collaring, kicking or shinning shall not be allowed.
4. When the ball is hit behind the goal-line by the attacking side, it shall be brought out straight 15 yards and started again by a bully; but if hit behind by any one of the	4. When the ball is hit behind the goal line by the attacking side, it shall be brought out straight 15 yards, and started again by a Bully; but, if hit behind by any one of the side

side whose goal-line it is, a player of the opposite side shall <u>hit</u> it out from within one yard of the nearest corner <u>flag post, and</u> no player shall be <u>allowed</u> within 20 yards of the <u>ball until hit out.</u>

whose goal line it is, a player of the opposite side shall it out from within one yard of the nearest corner, no player <u>of the attacking side at that time</u> shall be within 20 yards of the <u>goal line, and the defenders, with the exception of the goal-keeper, must be behind their goal line.</u>

5. When the ball goes is <u>in touch,</u> a player of the opposite side to that which hit it out shall roll it <u>in</u> from the point on the boundary line <u>where it left the ground in a direction</u> at right angles with the boundary line <u>at least 10 yards,</u> and it shall not be in play until it has touched the <u>ground,</u> and the player rolling it in shall not play it until it has been played by another player, every player being then behind the ball.

5. When the ball goes <u>off at the side,</u> a player of the opposite side to that which hit it out shall roll it <u>out</u> from the point on the boundary line <u>at which it went off</u> at right angles with the boundary line, and it shall not be in play until it has touched the <u>ice,</u> and the player rolling it in shall not play it until it has been played by another player, every player being then behind the ball.

<u>11.</u> On the infringement of any of the above rules, the ball shall be brought back and a bully shall take place.

(New)

<u>6.</u> On the infringement of any of the above rules, the ball shall be brought back and a Bully shall take place.

7. All disputes shall be settled by the Umpires, or in the event of their disagreement, by the Referee.

1. The maximum length of the ground shall be 150 yards, and the minimum length shall be 100 yards; the maximum breadth of the ground shall be 80 yards, and the minimum breadth shall be 50 yards. The length and breadth shall be marked off with flags, and the goals shall be upright posts six yards apart, with a tape across them seven feet from the ground.

(No rule specified the dimensions of the playing field.)

2. The sticks used shall be curved wooden ones approved by the committee of the Asso-

(No rule described the stick.)

ciation. The ball shall be an ordinary sized
cricket-ball.

8. To obtain a goal a player must hit the ball
between the posts and under the tape.

(No rule defined how goals were scored.)

9. No goal shall be allowed if the ball be hit
from a distance of more than 15 yards from
the nearest goal-posts.

(No rule was made for conditions disallowing
a goal.)

10. In all cases of a bully, every player shall be
behind the ball.

(No rule defined how face-offs–bullies–
needed to be played.)

12. The ordinary number of players shall be
eleven a side.

(No rule specified the number of players.)

A full chapter could be devoted to the differences between the field hockey
rules and the ice hockey ones. Iain Fyffe, in *On His Own Side of the Puck:
The Early History of Hockey Rules,*[11] has done an excellent job of providing
such an analysis. Let us simply point out what has most attracted our attention:

- Excluding Montreal rule 7—which, as mentioned, does not contribute in any way to describing how the game is played—269 of
  the 323 words in the first six Montreal rules are copied directly from
  the Hockey Association rules, which means that only 16.7 per cent
  of the wording of the rules is specific to Montreal.
- The seemingly essential rule (HA rule 8) defining how goals are
  scored is surprisingly absent from the Montreal rules.
- While, in one instance (Montreal rule 5), the word *ground* is replaced
  by *ice,* in another (Montreal rule 1), it isn't.
- Montreal rules 4 and 5 appear to introduce typographic errors not
  found in the Hockey Association rules, including the absence of the
  word *hit* from the Montreal version, and the suggestion that the
  ball should be rolled *out* after going off to the side, rather than being
  rolled *in.*

- For some reason, the Montreal rules spell *Bully* (the term for a face-off) with a capital *B*.
- The addition of the words "from behind" in Montreal rule 3 *may* have been intended to allow some form of bodychecking.
- In apparent contradiction with Harper's description, the Montreal rules do not specify dimensions (English rule 1 was dropped), number of participants (English rule 12 was dropped) or time frames (not mentioned in English rules, either).
- One thing we know is that, three years after the rules were published, during the winter of 1880, the number of players inconspicuously went from nine to seven[12] and the "authorities" never looked back, the game keeping seven players for several decades, before permanently settling on six. This aspect, as well as the time frames, would be included in the next set of rules, enacted in 1886.
- Skates are not mentioned.

These rules published in 1877—and used since the previous year—would remain on the books until January of 1886, when four Montreal clubs would agree to a season-long tournament and draw up a new set of 14 rules[13] that would be only slightly altered upon the creation of the first formal ice hockey league, the Amateur Hockey Association of Canada (AHAC), established in Montreal in December of 1886.[14]

Note that, prior to the Hockey Association in 1875, Eton College had published, in 1868, its own extremely detailed rules, 30 of them, for field hockey.[15]

Part of what makes the 1875 Montreal game so special is the fact that it was soon followed by the publication of rules—the ones shown above—which are undeniably a major milestone in the progression of a game to the status of sport.

Were there ever rules for ice hockey in England? And what is the difference between a description of hockey and a list of rules? Simply the fact that the rules are numbered? Or should the rules be formally identified as such—i.e., "Here are the rules of hockey"?

Let us provide an overview of the progression of the definition of hockey rules in the England of the 19th century and even before. At least at first, unsurprisingly, the rules were intended for the game played on the ground.

Francis Willughby's Book of Games, c. 1665

Francis Willughby (1635-1672) was an English ornithologist and ichthyologist born in Middleton Hall, Warwickshire, as the only son of Sir Francis Willoughby (1590-1665) and Cassandra Ridgway (c. 1600-1675). In 1662, Willughby and naturalist John Ray (1627-1705) travelled to the west coast of England and into northern Wales to study the breeding seabirds. Between 1663 and 1666, they toured Europe together, travelling through the Netherlands, Germany, Switzerland and Italy. Upon returning to England, they made plans to publish the results of their studies. Willughby, however, died from pleurisy at Middleton Hall during the preparation of this work. Ray posthumously published Willughby's *Ornithologia libri tres* in 1676, with an English edition two years later, a work considered to be the beginning of scientific ornithology in Europe.

It is believed that Willughby's interest for the subject of games, or "plaies," began during the journey in May and June of 1662. Around 1665, he must have decided to put together his collected notes following the same principles of systematic observation, description and classification he developed in his work on natural history. He did not live to finish this work, but the text survived in a folio volume with a number of loose sheets and notes attached. It was clearly a work in progress, heavily amended in some parts and bearing marks referring to other sources or to topics requiring further investigation. The manuscript was printed and published for the first time in 2003 as *Francis Willughby's Book of Games: A Seventeenth-Century Treatise on Sports, Games, and Pastimes.*

Below is the entry on "bandie ball" (the editor's notes are from the 2003 publication):

Bandie Ball

The Bandie Ball staves they strike the ball with are crooked at one end like Baseting* sticks. They hold them by one end at **A** and strike the ball with the crooked end **B C**. All the plaiers beeing aequally divided they stand at two gaoles, as in Football, the ball lying just in the middle. At a signe given, they both run from the gaoles to get the first blow, & they that can strike the ball thorough their adversaries gaole first win. The best place to hit the ball is just at the bending **B**.**

[* Editor's note: Baseting—altered from Basetting, follows cancellation

Basti—meaning unknown: perhaps a curved stick used in stuffing fabric items to be based?]

[** Editor's note: Versions of this game are well attested from the Middle Ages onward, and it continues to be played under the name Hockey or Field Hockey. The name Bandy, Bandy-Ball, or Ball and Bandy, appears between the 17th century and the 19th. The game also existed on the Continent; it was known in French as "la crosse."][16]

The description, of a game played on the ground, is very summary and could hardly be called a set of rules, especially considering that it was not published at the time, so they were certainly never used as rules. Yet, while the ice and skates are non-starters in 1665, the other four aspects of the definition of hockey are fully established. Of particular interest are the details provided regarding the stick and how to use it, details further augmented by a hand drawing:

Chapter 8 will examine how closely related bandy and hockey were, until the late 19th century in England.

Willughby's work having not been published in his lifetime, the book that contained the first form of (field) hockey rules would be, in 1773, *Juvenile Sports and Pastimes* by Richard Johnson, already examined in chapter 3.

The Book of Games (Tabart & Co.), 1805

The firm of Benjamin Tabart & Co. was one of the most innovative British publishers of children's books in the early 19th century; the firm published 174 books between 1801 and 1818. *The Book of Games,* whose first edition was released in 1805, is attributed to Richard Phillips (1767–1840), son of a Leicestershire farmer and energetic hack writer who often used pseudonyms for his works. In his youth, he was sent to prison for selling Thomas Paine's *Rights of Man.* In 1807, in recognition of his publishing empire and his work to improve conditions in jails, Phillips became a sheriff of London and Middlesex. He was knighted when he presented an address from the corporation to George III.

Rather than taking the traditional (and perhaps already well-worn) approach of describing how the games the book described were played, the author instead chose to tell a fictitious story, along the course of which twenty-four different games were "encountered" and described. Hockey came very early in the story (page 7), and is described as follows, with the characters being 10-year-old Thomas White and his father, Mr. White:

> As they could not immediately procure fresh horses at one of the places they stepped at, Mr White, with a view of diverting his son, proposed taking a little walk, to which Thomas readily consented. After they had walked for some time in a path which skirted a wood, they came to an open place, where some well looking boys were at play. Each of them had a sort of hooked stick, with which they were beating a ball. Thomas stood for some time looking at them, and then asked his father what game they were playing at?
>
> MR WHITE. — It is called Hockey. Those boys seem to play well; but I cannot say it is an amusement of which I am very fond.
>
> THOMAS. — Why not, sir? I it seems a very pretty game.
>
> MR WHITE. — I cannot help thinking it a rather dangerous one; though I believe it is, in reality, not more so than many others; it was a favourite amusement among us, when I was a boy at school, but it was put a stop to by a very melancholy accident.
>
> THOMAS. — Pray, sir, what was that?
>
> MR WHITE. — You have heard me speak of James Robson, a boy of whom I was particularly fond.
>
> THOMAS. — O yes, often; he is Captain Robson now, is he not? The gentleman who dined at our house one day last Christmas, and who has only one eye?
>
> MR WHITE. — The same; he lost his eye playing at Hockey.
>
> THOMAS. — Dear, did he? Did you knock it out, for I have heard you say you always played together?

MR WHITE. —No, fortunately. I did not. A boy who had not been long at the school, and whom Robson was teaching the game, in striking at the ball, missed his aim, and gave him so severe a blow, as to occasion the loss of his eye.

THOMAS. —O how unhappy the poor boy must have been who did it!

MR WHITE. —Indeed I believe he was, for he was a good boy, and, very fond of Robson.

THOMAS. —Pray, sir, was it long before it got well?

MR WHITE. —Yes, a great while, and he had nearly lost the sight of the other eye, in consequence of the violent inflammation which the pain occasioned. This accident banished Hockey altogether from the school, and I have never liked the thoughts of the game from that time to this.

THOMAS. —Pray, sir, will you tell me some of the rules of it, for I do not very well understand the game, from only seeing it played.

MR WHITE. —Willingly: those I remember; but I believe I have not seen it played these thirty years. In the first place, then, do not you see a piece of stick with both ends stuck in the ground, just there?

THOMAS. —What, that bit of briar, which is bent into the form of an arch?

MR WHITE. —Yes, that is called the goal, and there is another which answers to it, at some distance, the other side the boys.

THOMAS. —Yes, I see it; are they always made of briars?

MR WHITE. —Mostly; for it is easier to find a long piece of that wood which will bend, than any other. You know briar is extremely pliable. Well, when the goals are erected, the players divide into two parties; to each of whom belongs the care of one of them. The game consists in endeavouring to drive the ball (which is either made of wood or cork; and old bung cut round at the edges answers the purpose very well, and called the hockey) through the gaol of your antagonist.

Both parties meet in the middle space between the gaols, and the ball is then tossed up. The players next endeavour to strike the hockey, and drive it through their adversaries' goal. In this the art of the game consists; for it requires a good deal of skill to send it through so small a space at such a distance. I have known a game last for more than two hours, if the parties have been well matched.

Hockey, *an engraving by an unknown artist, printed in*
The Book of Games, *published in 1805. Notice the flat
bung, similar to a "puck," referred to as "the hockey."*

The players on each side must defend their own goal, while they endeavour to send their ball through that of their opponents. These boys all seem to play with much dexterity. See with what address that little boy in the dark coat parries the stroke of his antagonist.

THOMAS. —Ah! look, it is over, is it not? The tall boy has driven the hockey through the sticks; the goal, I think, you call it.

MR WHITE. —Yes, it is usually so called; and the sticks are known by the name of hockey sticks.

THOMAS. —I think hockey seems a pretty game. I wonder whether I could play at it.

MR WHITE. —Not without a good deal of practice, I dare say; but it is not a game which is now in very general use. The eagerness with which boys are too apt to play at it, has been the occasion of many accidents, and it is I believe forbidden in many schools.

THOMAS. —I wonder whether it is permitted at Dr. Benson's; do you think it is, sir?

MR WHITE. —Indeed I do not know; I rather think it is not, for I re-member he once said he did not very much like the game. But come, Tom, I dare say they have got horses by this time, let us return to the inn.

During the remainder of the journey, Mr White kindly gave his son much excellent advice, for his future conduct. Deeply engaged in attending to his father's interesting conversation, Thomas was much surprised to find, when the chaise stopped, that they had reached Kingston, which was the name of the village where the Doctor resided.

Dr. Benson came out to welcome them, and received his young pupil with a degree of kindness which greatly encouraged and relieved him. There was in the mild benignity of this excellent man, something which never failed inspiring all who knew him with love, as well as respect and esteem. Thomas experienced the truth of this, and before the tea-things were removed found himself tolerably at ease.[18]

Little Thomas specifically asked his father for the "rules," so if his father was an honest man, we have to accept that those were the rules of hockey at the time. They are very much in line with those described in *Juvenile Sports and Pastimes*—which may, in fact, have largely inspired the author

of the *Book of Games,* who also termed the object of play—not the stick—
"the hockey."

"On Eton Games," 1832

Eton College, to this day a boys-only full boarding school, is situated in
Windsor, just 30 kilometres west of central London. In 1832, *The Eton
College Magazine,* edited by student Sir John Wickens (1815-1873), published an article entitled "On Eton Games." The passage below was written
by an unidentified student, though Alfred Guy L'Estrange, in his autobiography *Vert de Vert's Eton Days, and other Sketches and Memories,*[18] credits
the passage to "G. W. (Lord) Lyttleton," though the correct spelling would
be Lyttelton.

George William Lyttelton, 4th Baron Lyttelton (1817-1876), was born
in London as the eldest son of William Henry Lyttelton, 3rd Baron Lyttelton,
and Lady Sarah Spencer. He was a good sportsman and played for a number
of cricket teams, including Cambridge University, Marylebone Cricket
Club and Birmingham.

Here is the part of the article dedicated to hockey and "foot-ball":

> We ought, perhaps, to proceed to hockey and foot-ball, which are in
> winter what cricket and rowing are in summer...
>
> In the two games, Eton may assume to herself, if not superiority, at
> least the merit of originality, and great distinction from other establish-
> ments. We say 'if not superiority' not because we think her in the least
> degree inferior therein, but because she has never had the opportunity
> of measuring her strength with that of any other 'Eleven' at either game...
>
> It is only among ourselves, then, that we enjoy these two amusements;
> and, as we said before, we stand alone in both of them: in hockey, because
> Eton is almost the only place in England in which this ancient game is
> kept up; in foot-ball, because it is practised among us, as we said before
> of fives, in a manner totally different from that of any other school or
> club. We will proceed to give some account of both.
>
> Hockey we believe to be a very old and indigenous game, never heard
> of beyond the channel, and almost forgotten even in England; consisting,
> as of course our readers well know, in two parties endeavouring to send
> a small ball of great hardness, through the *goals* of their adversaries; and
> played with strong sticks resembling a shepherd's crook.

It is a game, in which, as in poetry, *mediocrity* is not tolerable; indeed, a bad game at hockey is one of the most stupid sights poor mortal can see; but, on the other hand, when it is played, as at Eton, with a considerable degree of dexterity, we think it one of the most elegant and gentlemanlike exercises there is, being susceptible of very graceful attitudes, and requiring great speed of foot, and skill in not missing the blow aimed at the ball; neither is it a very dangerous game, though by no means unattended with peril; for a severe blow on the shins with so weighty a weapon as a hockey-stick, is attended with very great pain.

But upon the whole, we think that fewer are seen hobbling back from the distant hockey fields, than from the less remote scene of foot-ball playing; and that many enter without fear into a 'bully' at hockey, who would dread the more dense 'rouge' at foot-ball.

Before we dismiss this game, we must except from the general sentence which we pronounced against other youthful establishments, of ignorance of it, the Royal Military College at Sandhurst, where it is played, but in a manner decidedly inferior to Eton; indeed we have lately heard that far the best performer there at present is one who has but recently left Eton, and though a very distinguished player, was by no means in the first rank of hockeyists.[19]

It is tempting to draw the attention to the "very old and indigenous game" part of the description, but the segment that immediately follows it, mentioning "almost forgotten even in England," is an indication that the author might not have done that much research into the history of the game. However, the description of how it is played is spot on, and as a bonus, we see the stick described as "resembling a shepherd's crook," which is of course the most commonly accepted etymology—though not necessarily the correct one—of the word *hockey,* from the French *hocquet* or *hoquet,* meaning a shepherd's crook.[20]

Every Boy's Magazine, 1862

Every Boy's Magazine began its publication in January 1862 and was issued under a few slightly different names until 1888, when it merged[21] with *Boy's Own Paper.* The magazine was edited by Edmund Routledge (1843–1899), the second son of the well-known English publisher George Routledge, whose publishing house Edmund joined in 1859.

Rev. John George Wood (1827–1889) was born in London, the son of a surgeon, and became a well-known writer and lecturer on natural history. His first book, *The Illustrated Natural History,* published in 1851, was followed by over 50 others. Wood also produced several works on gymnastics, sports, etc., and was for a period the editor of the *Boy's Own Magazine.* Under the pseudonym George Forrest, he was also the author of the first edition of *Every Boy's Book* (1855) and *The Playground; or, The Boy's Book of Games* (1858). Wood would also contribute to the second edition of *Every Boy's Book* (1869), which was edited by Edmund Routledge and published in 1869, his third work dealing with hockey.

The third issue of *Every Boy's Magazine* had an (illustrated) article about hockey, announced on the cover:
Here is the full article:

IN all the general principles, hockey bears a great resemblance to football, the game consisting in driving a ball through a goal.

The ball, however, is of much smaller dimensions, even where a ball, and not a bung, is used; and it is impelled, not by the foot, but by certain sticks, or clubs, called hockeys, or hookeys, because the end with which the ball is struck is more or less hooked.

The shape and dimensions of the hockey-stick are entirely arbitrary, being left to the peculiar taste of the owners. Some like their hockeys to be sharply hooked, while others prefer them merely bent over at the end. Some players like a very thick, heavy stick, which can be put down in front of the ball in order to neutralize the blows of the opposite side, while others can play best with a slight and springy weapon, that can be used with one hand, and is employed to tap the ball away just as an opponent is about to strike, and to coax it, as it were, towards the goal through the mass of adverse sticks.

The four sticks shown in the engraving are very good samples of the forms best adapted for use.

FIG. 1 —is much in favour with some players, and is therefore given; but for my own part I never could play to my own satisfaction with it, the large and deep curve deceiving the eye and causing the player to let the ball pass through the hook, besides running the risk of entanglement in the opponent's stick.

FIG. 2 —is usually a favourite, but the angle of the head with the handle is arranged according to the fancy of the player. Some like the head to be made of horn, backed with lead like a golf-stick; but this formation is hardly necessary, costing a rather large sum, and not conveying correspondent advantages.

FIG. 3 —is a queer and eccentric form, which is not suitable to every player on account of its weight and generally large proportions. I have, however, seen it employed with extraordinary effect by a player who was accustomed to drive his opponents into a state of considerable excitement by his faculty of stopping the ball with this overgrown weapon, and then planting it so firmly that all the opposing sticks could not get at the ball in spite of their battering. In this way he would save many a game that had well-nigh been given up as hopeless, and by thus checking the ball on its way to the goal, would give time for his own side to come up and turn the tables. The great hooked end of this club was bound with very strong iron wire.

The same player was equally successful with a stick the exact reverse of the preceding, and represented as FIG. 4. This was a very slight ashen stick, with a small, but rather heavy head, so that when shaken it would bend and spring like whalebone. This little stick was used for darting among the struggles and clatter of contending weapons, and giving the ball just a wee pat now and then at critical moments, so as to edge it a little nearer the goal, and at the same time to knock it away just as the blow of the opponent descended.

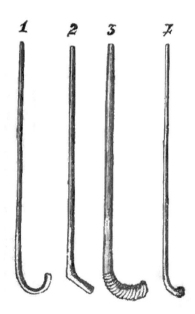

The ball used for this game is sometimes an ordinary cask bung. As this would speedily be knocked to pieces, it is generally quilted with string, as shown in the illustration, for the better preserving its integrity. Sooner or later, however, it goes to pieces, for the string is sure to be cut or worn through, and the cork soon gives way.

Balls, too, are apt to get their jackets knocked off, and, if struck hard, will sometimes fly in the face of a player, who cannot avoid it at so short a distance, and do no small damage.

A hollow india-rubber ball is very good; but the best that I have yet seen, was a common globular india-rubber bottle, such as can be procured at any stationers, with the neck cut off, and partly filled up by leaving a strip of the neck and securing it by the proper varnish.

It made a capital ball. Nothing could hurt it and it could hurt no one. I have had it driven into my face at two yards' distance, and felt little the worse for it five minutes afterwards. It would not roll very far by itself, but required to be edged carefully by the sticks; it never could get cut against flints, or spoiled by thorns or splinters; it was big enough to be easily seen if knocked into a ditch or over a hedge, and if struck into water it would not sink but come to the surface at once, bobbing about as if to draw attention to its presence. It remained in constant action for two years to my knowledge, had been employed for several seasons before I made its acquaintance, and for aught I know may be in use now. If fact, if it were only kept out of the way of a fire or an ostrich, I know nothing that would hurt the ball except burning or swallowing. Even in the latter case I fancy that the ostrich would be sufferer rather than the ball.

Having now described the instruments, we will proceed to the method of playing the game.

As has already been mentioned, this game is in principle similar to football. Two goals are set up, at a convenient distance from and exactly opposite to each other, as in football. The same goals indeed will answer as for that game, only the cross pole should be lashed to the uprights at a much lower elevation, say three feet six inches or four feet from the ground, and the uprights should be within six feet of each other. Very good and simple goals can be made by taking long osiers, willow branches or brambles, pointing the two ends, bending them over and sticking the pointed extremities into the earth, so as to make an arch.

A peg is driven exactly half-way between the goals, goal-lines are drawn as at football, and the ground is then laid out.

The players, hasving previously chosen their sides, arrange themselves between the goals, facing each other, and always having their left sides towards the enemy's goal and their right towards their own.

The ball is then thrown in the air, so as to fall on or near the wooden peg, and each party try with their sticks to drive it through the goal of the enemy.

The rules of this fine game are few and simple:

1. The game is won by the ball passing through the enemy's goal.

2. The ball must be struck through the goal with the stick, not thrown or kicked.

3. Each player shall strike from right to left, and any player infringing this rule is liable to the penalty of a blow on the shins from any of the opposite side.

4. Each player shall remain on his own side, and if he crosses to that of the opponents is liable to the same penalty.

5. No player shall raise the head of his stick higher than his shoulder, on pain of the same penalty.

6. The ball may be stopped with the stick, or with any part of the person, provided that the intervening player is on his own side.

7. If the ball be kicked or thrown through the goal, or if struck beyond the goal-lines, it is to be fetched by the junior player of the side who struck the last blow, and gently thrown towards the centre peg.

8. Any player willfully striking another, except when inflicting the penalty contained in rules 3, 4, and 5, is immediately to be excluded from the game.

By means of these rules, the game of hockey is shorn of the danger consequent on the loose and unrestrained play that is sometimes seen, the sticks brandished in all directions, and the two sides so intermixed that it is hardly possible to discriminate between them.

Many a person has been seriously damaged by such undisciplined play, and teeth have been struck out, or even eyes lost in the contest. By strict adherence, however, to the above rules, there is no fear of incurring any injuries, and this really fine game is rendered as safe as it is exciting.

As a general rule, a good player seldom if ever strikes the ball with any violence, but keeps it well in hand, trundling it along rather than knocking it forcibly, and endeavouring, if he finds it likely to pass out of his control, to strike it gently towards another of his own side, who may keep it in its course towards the enemy's goal.

A bad player, on the contrary, rushes about without any definite purpose, shouts continually at the top of his voice, brandishes his stick to the danger of other persons' eyes and the detriment of his own hands which are sure to be painfully blistered in half an hour, and exhausts his strength and breath so early in the game, that he fails just at the critical moment, and sees the ball driven past him without being able to check it.

As a parting word of advice, let me recommend to our readers to play this game as quietly as they can contrive to do, and as a golden rule, always to keep the head of the hockey-stick close to the ground.

Above all, keep your temper intact, and don't lose it even if one of your own side should make some stupid mistake, and lose you a winning game. Take especial care to keep strictly to the rules, and if your opponent should break them and render himself liable to the penalty, be merciful to his shins, and inflict the punishment as a warning to deter from future transgression, and not as a spiteful opportunity for giving a blow which cannot be returned.[22]

Here we have a clear list of exactly eight rules — possibly the first ever "real" field hockey rules — along with a detailed analysis of hockey sticks, with the conclusion that the one (fig. 2) that most closely resembles current-day ice hockey sticks is considered, in 1862, "a favourite." Compare this "angled" stick with the "curved" stick of fig. 1, found to be disappointing, as it lets the ball pass through the hook. The ball is also described: a globular india-rubber bottle with the neck cut off is deemed "the best," but a flat cask bung quilted with string, resembling a hockey puck, is the one illustrated.

The punishment for infractions seems harsh and quite surprising, at least for our 21st-century sensitivities, but physical punishment did have its believers at the time.

Rule 4 may be interpreted as meaning that the field is separated in two halves, and that the players of each team must remain in their own half, implying that any goal could only be scored by hitting the ball at least half the distance of the entire field. Note that, even played in that way—which would have made it particularly boring—the game would still conform to the six-point definition of hockey, which is why, in chapter 2, the authors suggested that the mention of passing and dribbling in the definition of hockey might have served to eliminate some forms of the game that are clearly not hockey for most observers. However, there seems to be no doubt here that this is not the way rule 4 was meant to be understood; in all likelihood, the intent was to specify that the traditional offside rule applied (similar to football/soccer).

What do these field hockey rules have to do with ice hockey? For one thing, they remove any possible doubt that ice hockey evolved from field hockey, something not that commonly accepted in the hockey birthplace debate these days.

Yet what we are really after are rules for ice hockey. Could the first set have been published just a year after the ones from *Every Boy's Magazine*?

The Boy's Handy Book of Sports, Pastimes, Games and Amusements, 1863

This book, one among many in the crowded field of "boy's books" describing physical activities that girls should never even dream of practising, was published in April of 1863, judging from the advertisement found in London newspapers at the time. The author of the chapter about hockey is unknown. Here is the chapter:

> HOCKEY may be called a very simplified form of golf. It is called Shinty in Scotland, and Hurley in Ireland.
>
> Two captains are chosen, and by these the players are alternately selected until they are all divided into two sides each, under a captain.
>
> Each player is armed with a strong hooked stick, called a hockey-stick; and one of the captains takes in his hand a small hard ball, like a golf ball. Only one ball is used in the game. The captain throws this straight

BALL-PLAY.

Illustration from The Boy's Handy Book *from the chapter on hockey.*

---

up into the air, and, as it falls, the players of the opposite side strike at it, and endeavour to send it to the goal, or home of their enemies; for, as in foot-ball, each side has a goal, and that party wins who can lodge the ball in the fortress of the foe.

In striking at the ball, each of the opposing troops must keep to its own side. The ball may not be touched, except by the hockey-stick. A player may receive the blow aimed by an antagonist at the ball upon his stick, and then endeavour to drive the ball away before the adversary has recovered from his surprise. Sometimes, instead of tossing the ball in the air, the captain who gains the toss is allowed a fair stroke at the ball from his own goal towards his adversaries'.

In Scotland bats called 'clackans' are sometimes used instead of hockey-sticks.

Hockey is a capital winter game, and is sometimes played on the ice, and even by skaters.

But care should be taken in all these venturous undertakings; for the zeal of boys frequently outruns their discretion, and falls upon the ice are uncommonly hard, especially when a few random blows from hockey-sticks increase the amenities of the fallen champion's position. A broken limb or a fractured collar-bone is too high a price to pay for a few hours' amusement, and we should advise our young friends accordingly to be content to pursue the sport of Hockey on *terra firma*, where it will be found a safe as well as a diverting pastime.[23]

While not numbered, or identified as "rules," parts of the above certainly do read like rules. And the possibility of playing it on the ice, "even by skaters," is evoked, though the last paragraph tries its hardest to dissuade the practice of that form, recommending instead to confine the game to solid ground.

So can a set of rules, mentioning that hockey can be played on the ice with skates but advising against it, be considered a set of rules for ice hockey? Well, the NHL advises against fighting, and even imposes "major" penalties on those who nevertheless engage in it, yet the league considers fighting part of hockey, as Gary Bettman told Peter Mansbridge of CBC News in 2013: "It has been, it is, but it's been declining in its frequency. There's less fighting in the game than we had years ago. I mean, we penalize it. It's part of the fabric."[24]

So the short answer is yes: if a group of players wanted to play on the ice with sticks, they could certainly have used the rules described above and ignored the warning, in much the way that smokers buy packages of cigarettes with labelling that "strongly" advises them not to smoke.

As for what the rules say, without being particularly detailed, they reinforce the definitions provided by several other sources and, with ice and skates now allowed though not recommended, indisputably adhere to the Society for International Hockey Research's six-point definition of ice hockey.

Yet this is not entirely satisfactory. Surely there could have been a set of rules that provided for the game to be played on ice with skates, and actually embraced the practice?

The Boy's Own Book, 1828–1868

The Boy's Own Book was first published in 1828 and was reprinted numerous times in London and in North America up to the late 1800s.

The 25 London editions that followed the first one, published between 1828 and 1846, were all identical (though slightly augmented relative to that first one), with the page count unchanged at 462. Then, in 1849, the publisher released a "New Edition, greatly enlarged and improved," with 611 pages. This version was reissued, with identical content, until 1864. In 1868, the publisher offered "A New Edition, thoroughly revised and considerably enlarged," with 696 pages. Nine more editions would be released until 1889, mostly identical to previous ones, though the 1885 one was described as "partly rewritten," but the article on hockey was unchanged. On the other side of the Atlantic, in the U.S., at least 17 editions of *The Boy's Own Book* were published between 1829 and 1884; however, hockey wasn't mentioned before 1881, though a somewhat outlying edition from 1854 (released by a different publisher) did contain an article about Cornish hurling.

Beginning on page 110 is a list of the 36 London editions that the authors have been able to identify. An immense debt of gratitude is owed to SIHR member Mike Barford, whose help in compiling the list was invaluable. Mr. Barford is the current president of the Richmond Hockey Club, founded in 1874, which the attentive reader will recognize as one of the clubs that participated in the writing of the first Hockey Association rules of 1875.

Not too much should be read into some of the very small changes in page counts, which could simply be explained by library staff counting pages in a slightly different way. Except where mentioned, the hockey articles always appeared exactly on the same page and were always perfectly identical.

The first (1828) edition did not have an article about hockey.[27] Neither did the second one (also 1828), but that one did have an article about "Goff, or Bandy-Ball."[28] The activity described was not the game of bandy, but rather golf (under an alternate spelling used at the time) or a related game, in which each player has his own ball, and "The game consists in driving the ball into certain holes made in the ground; he who achieves which the soonest, or in the fewest number of strokes, obtains the victory."

It is only in 1849, when the book underwent a major rewrite, that hockey was added. The author of the article is not known.

> Here we have a fine, exhilarating, and truly English game, for it is popular in every county in England, and should be played with sticks of good old English oak or crab, —none other will give confidence and success to the player. It is an amusement for all seasons, —in the summer on the turf, in the winter on the ice.
>
> Sides are to be chosen by the two best players, selected alternately. Every player must be provided with a good strong tough stick, hooked or turned up at the end in an oblique angle, so that when held by one or both hands in a slanting position, the end lies flat on the ground. A cork bung is usually the object of contention.

Year	Edition	Publisher
1828 (June)	1st	Vizetelly, Branston & Co., Fleet Street[26]
1828 (October)	2nd	Same
1829	3rd	Same
1829	4th	Same
1830	5th	Same
1830	6th	Same
1831	7th	Same
1834	8th	Same
1834	9th	Same
1835	10th	Same
1836	11th	Same
1838	13th	Same
1839	15th	Whitehead and Co.
1839	16th	Same
1840	17th	Same
1840	18th	Longman, Orme and Co.
1842	20th	Longman, Brown and Co.
1844	21st	Same
1845	23rd	Same
1846	26th	Same
1849	No longer numbered	David Bogue, 86 Fleet Street
1852	–	David Bogue
1855	–	Same
1859	–	W. Kent and Co., Fleet Street
1861	–	Lockwood and Co., Stationer's Hall Court

Title	Pages	Notes
Boy's Own Book; A complete Encyclopedia of all the Diversions, Athletic, Scientific and Recreative, of Boyhood and Youth	448	No article about hockey
Same	460	Slightly augmented, now contains an article about "Goff, or Bandy-Ball," which is in fact golf
Same	Same	Identical to previous edition
Same	Same	Unchanged. This edition is available online.
Same	Same	Unchanged
Same	Same	Unchanged
Same	Same	Unchanged
Same	Same	Unchanged
Same	Same	Unchanged
Same	Same	Unchanged
Same	Same	Unchanged
Same	Same	Unchanged
Same	Same	Unchanged
Same	Same	Unchanged
Same	Same	Unchanged
Same	Same	Unchanged
Same	Same	Unchanged
Same	Same	Unchanged
Same	Same	Unchanged
Same	Same	Last edition before major rewrite
Same, catalogue adds "New edition, greatly enlarged and improved"	611	First edition of new version, now includes hockey (p. 41). Available online.
Same	Same	Unchanged
Same	Same	Unchanged
Same	624	Page count slightly increased, but hockey article unchanged
Same	632 (623+9 ads)	Page count changed only due to inclusion of advertising

Year	Edition	Publisher
1864	–	Same
1868	–	Lockwood and Co., 7 Stationer's Hall Court
1870	–	Same
1872	–	Same
1877	–	Crosby, Lockwood and Co., 7 Stationer's Hall Court
1880	–	Crosby, Lockwood and Co., 7 Stationer's Hall Court, Ludgate Hill
1881	–	Crosby, Lockwood and Co.
1882	–	Same
1885	–	Same
1886	–	Same
1889	–	Crosby, Lockwood and Son

The best ground is a large field or meadow, — the opposite hedges or boundaries, the two goals. The sides are arranged in two lines opposite each other, the players standing several yards apart.

The first strike is decided by chances. At about two-thirds distance from the striker's goal, the bung is laid down. When all are ready, the striker calls 'Play!' and with his utmost force sends the bung forward, which is 'taken up' by the rest, and the game has then begun, each player endeavouring to send it back or forward toward his respective goal.

Should the striker miss his first hit, his opponent immediately takes advantage of it, and strikes it in the contrary direction, which being but a short distance, frequently decides the game; otherwise, with many players, it may be kept up for a long time, the striker and his opponents following on to assist their party. When the bung is driven to or over either of the respective goals, the game is decided, and fresh sides may be chosen.

Title	Pages	Notes
Same	624	Identical to 1859. Last edition of this version.
The Boy's Own Book: A Complete Encyclopædia of Sports and Pastimes; Athletic, Scientific, and Recreative	696	Has the mention "A New Edition, thoroughly revised and considerably enlarged." Hockey article (p. 146) is augmented significantly.
Same	716	Additional pages mostly due to advertising
Same	Same	Unchanged
Same	724 (incl. 2 ad.)	Unchanged except for ads
Same	726	Unchanged except for ads
Same	726 (incl. 2 ad.)	Unchanged except for ads
Same	726	Unchanged except for ads
Same	726	"New Edition, thoroughly revised and partly rewritten." Hockey article unchanged.
Same	726 (incl. 2 ad.)	Unchanged except for ads
Same	726	Hockey article still identical to 1868 version

This is decidedly one of the most popular sports of English youth. In the north of England it is called 'Shinney,' we believe, from the custom of the players striking the shins if the bung or ball get between the legs; but this practice we earnestly protest against, as tending to create angry feelings.

With a party of good skaters, this game affords fine sport, but of course can only be played on a sheet of ice of great extent.[29]

The entry establishes in no uncertain terms that hockey can and should be played on the ice as much as on the ground: "It is an amusement for all seasons,—in the summer on the turf, in the winter on the ice." There might even be a suggestion, in the last paragraph ("this game affords fine sport"), that the version played on ice by good skaters was even better than the ground game. As in numerous other examples already seen, the article states that the game can be played on ice, without specifying the use of skates;

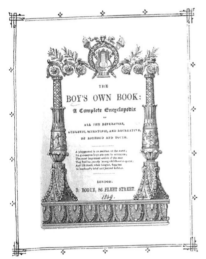

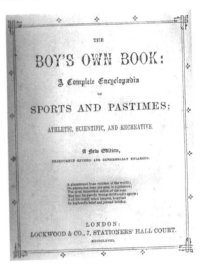

Cover pages of The Boy's Own Book, *for the first and second editions (both from 1828), and the "greatly enlarged and improved" (1849) and "thoroughly revised and considerably enlarged" (1868) editions. The year is handwritten in the 1849 edition, but an ad in* The Patriot *of December 17, 1849,[26] (opposite) attests that the year is correct.*

THE FAVORITE PRESENT FOR BOYS.
Just published, embellished with several Hundred Engravings
on Wood, new binding, price 3s. 6d.,
THE BOY'S OWN BOOK : a complete
Encyclopædia of all the Diversions, Athletic, Scientific,
and Recreative, of Boyhood and Youth. New Edition, greatly
enlarged, with the addition of many Engravings, beautifully
ornamented with gold borders.
David Bogue, Fleet-street.

---

however, it is unequivocally implied by the "good skaters" mention, as if any other way of playing on the ice was not even worth mentioning.

The description suggests that, as soon as a goal is scored (the game is decided), the teams may be shuffled before the next "game" starts. We also learn that the game is called "shinney" (and we find out why), in the north of England, adding some credence to the posit that hockey and shinney were interchangeable names for the same activity at the time.

Are these rules? They are not numbered, and they are not presented as "rules." But there is an unmistakable level of detail that very much resembles what one would expect from a formal set of rules. But the best was yet to come.

The Boy's Own Book, 1868 Edition

The "Encyclopedia" has become an "Encyclopædia." The title page of the "thoroughly revised and considerably enlarged" edition gives the publication year of 1868, but according to advertisements in the British newspapers, the book was released in the middle of December 1867, just prior to Christmas. As most of the contents had been rewritten and several new articles added, the subtitle from earlier editions was changed from "all the diversions" to "Sports and Pastimes."

The article about hockey, on page 146, starts with a nearly identical text to the 1849 and subsequent editions, but has been extended:

> HERE we have a fine, exhilarating game, popular in every part of England, and played with sticks of good old English oak or crab. Hockey is an amusement for all seasons—in the summer on the turf, in the winter on the ice.
>
> Sides are chosen by the two best players, selected alternately. Every player is provided with a good strong, tough stick, hooked or turned up at the end in an oblique angle, so that when held by one or both hands

HOCKEY.

HOCKEY.

Here we have a fine, exhilarating game, popular in every part of England, and played with sticks of good old English oak or crab. Hockey is an amusement for all seasons—in the summer on the turf, in the winter on the ice. Sides are chosen by the two best players, selected alternately. Every player is provided with a good strong, tough stick, hooked or turned up at the end in an oblique angle, so that when held by one or both hands in a slanting position, the end lies flat on the ground. A large cork bung is the object of contention. The best ground is a large field or meadow,—the opposite hedges or boundaries, the two goals. The sides are arranged in two lines opposite each other, the players standing several yards apart. The first strike is decided by chance. At about two-thirds distance from the striker's goal, the bung is laid down. When all are ready, the striker calls "Play!" and with his utmost force sends forward the bung, which is "taken up" by the rest with their hockey sticks. The game has then begun, each player endeavouring to send the bung back or forward toward his respective goal. Should the striker miss his first hit, his opponent immediately takes advantage of it, and strikes it in the contrary direction, which being but a short distance, frequently decides the game; otherwise, with many players, it may be kept up for a long time, the striker and his opponents following on to assist their party. When the bung is driven to or over either of the respective goals, the game is decided, and fresh sides may be chosen. In the north of England the game is called "Shinney," from the custom of the players striking the shins if the bung or ball get between the legs; but we protest against this practice as tending to create angry feeling. With a party of good skaters, this game affords fine sport, but of course can only be played on a sheet of ice of great extent. The following are the rules :—

1. The ball must be struck with the stick, and not kicked with the foot or touched by the hand.

2. The ball must be struck fairly through the goal, before the side can claim the game.

3. The goals must be marked by lines at either end; and in the centre a line must be drawn across to determine the side which has possession of the ball.

4. If the ball bound against the person of a player, he must allow it to fall to the ground before he strikes at it.

5. Any player striking another with stick or hand, kicking, or otherwise unfairly playing the ball, is out of the game.

6. A captain on each side is to be chosen to regulate the game; and it is the duty of any player, when directed by the captain, to fetch the ball when struck to a distance.

These six rules will be sufficient. As to the ball or bung, an ordinary bung of good size cut round the edges and bound with strong string, will last much longer than the mere cork. Some players use an India-rubber bottle cut close to the neck. This answers much better, and is much stronger than the balls ordinarily sold at the toy-shops.

in a slanting position, the end lies flat on the ground. A large cork bung is the object of contention.

The best ground is a large field or meadow, — the opposite hedges or boundaries, the two goals. The sides are arranged in two lines opposite each other, the players standing several yards apart.

The first strike is decided by chance. At about two-thirds distance from the striker's goal, the bung is laid down. When all are ready, the striker calls 'Play!' and with his utmost force sends forward the bung, which is 'taken up' by the rest with their hockey sticks.

The game has then begun, each player endeavouring to send the bung back or forward toward his respective goal. Should the striker miss his first hit, his opponent immediately takes advantage of it, and strikes it in the contrary direction, which being but a short distance, frequently decides the game; otherwise, with many players, it may be kept up for a long time, the striker and his opponents following on to assist their party. When the bung is driven to or over either of the respective goals, the game is decided, and fresh sides may be chosen.

In the north of England the game is called 'Shinney,' from the custom of the players striking the shins if the bung or ball get between the legs; but we protest against this practice as tending to create angry feeling.

With a party of good skaters, this game affords fine sport, but of course can only be played on a sheet of ice of great extent.

The following are the rules:—

1. The ball must be struck with the stick, and not kicked with the foot or touched by the hand.
2. The ball must be struck fairly through the goal, before the side can claim the game.
3. The goals must be marked by lines at either end; and in the centre a line must be drawn across to determine the side which has possession of the ball.
4. If the ball bound against the person of a player, he must allow it to fall to the ground before he strikes at it.
5. Any player striking another with stick or hand, kicking, or otherwise unfairly playing the ball, is out of the game.
6. A captain on each side is to be chosen to regulate the game; and it is the duty of any player, when directed by the captain, to fetch the ball when struck to a distance.

These six rules will be sufficient. As to the ball or bung, an ordinary bung of good size cut round the edges and bound with strong string, will last much longer than the mere cork. Some players use an India-rubber bottle cut close to the neck. This answers much better, and is much stronger than the balls ordinarily sold at the toy-shops.[30]

So, just as ice hockey has a six-point definition, in 1868 it is governed by six rules. Those rules are numbered, and the words "The following are the rules:" make it somewhat difficult to not acknowledge them as such.

To be sure, they are not specific to ice hockey. They are formally presented as applying to both the "on the turf" and "on the ice" versions of the game. But there is nothing wrong with that. The 1875 Montreal rules were only slightly different from field hockey rules, and even contained the word "ground," just like rule 4 above. One would be hard pressed to find anything in these six rules above that could be said to be inapplicable to hockey played on the ice. Rule 3 requires lines to be drawn, but it is quite easy to etch lines with the blade of a skate. As a bonus, these rules actually do indicate how goals are scored, unlike the first Montreal rules.

The last paragraph also gives yet another bonus: the suggestion that the ball be replaced by an "India rubber bottle cut close to the neck," which is actually *better* than typical balls, meaning that English hockey players used a rubber puck (though it was not called that yet) long before their Canadian counterparts, though the exact shape of India rubber bottles is unknown and may have resembled balls more than the modern puck. India rubber, also called natural rubber, is made from the latex obtained from *Hevea brasiliensis,* otherwise known as the rubber tree. The vulcanization process discovered/invented by Charles Goodyear in 1839 caused a boom in the manufacture of India rubber objects in the 1840s.[31] The first mention of the use of an India rubber bottle in place of a ball for play was in *The Playground; or, The Boy's Book of Games* by John George Wood (under the pen name George Forrest) in 1858.[32]

More Rules!
The National Skating Association (NSA) was founded on March 1, 1879. One of its objects was "To provide rules and regulations for the game of hockey on the ice."[33]

In January of 1882, the *Handbook of Fen Skating,* by Neville Goodman and Albert Goodman, was published. Its fifth chapter, credited to Albert, was called "The Game of Hockey" and contained a 2,600-word description of ice hockey, with illustrations of two types of sticks and of how the players should align on the field, followed by a 266-word comparison of the racing skate and the distinct hockey skate, with extremely detailed drawings of all parts used in the manufacture of such, including the "S. R." (Standard Racing) or "S. H." (Standard Hockey) hallmark that needed to be affixed to each, as appropriate. The difference between the two types of skate was that, with the hockey skates, "the blades are stronger made, and are more rounded at the bottom, they will therefore be preferred by most hockey players, by heavy people, and also by ladies and others who prefer ease in turning to speed, not wishing to go fast or to perform long journeys."

Quoting from a published circular of the NSA, Albert Goodman specified that the Standard Running skates were the only ones accepted by the Association—as decided at a general meeting on October 14, 1881—and that the skates should be marked with the Association's registered marks.

On the other side of the Atlantic, according to Martin Jones, the specific Starr hockey skate (manufactured in Halifax) was patented c. 1893-1895. Very late in the process of producing the *Handbook of Fen Skating*, a set of rules was drawn up by the Bluntisham and Earith Skating Hockey Club, a club whose name indicated that they only played "skating hockey" and not "field hockey." The rules were added to the handbook as Appendix A:

I.   The maximum distance between the goals shall be 220 yards, and the goals shall be upright poles with tape or lath across the height of 7 feet. The maximum width of the goals to be 22 feet, but if sufficient ice is not available to get a length of 220 yards with a proportionate width, then the goals shall be in the proportion of 1 foot wide to every 10 yards apart.

II.   The hockey used shall not be more than 6 feet long, or more than 3 inches wide or thick in any part.

III.   The ball to be used shall be a solid india rubber ball with a diameter of not more than 2 3/4 in. and not less than 2 1/4 in.

IV.   In commencing, the Umpire or one of the Captains shall throw

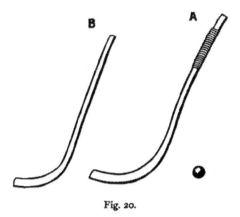

Fig. 20.

Hockey sticks, as illustrated in the Handbook of Fen Skating.

---

the ball straight up half half-way between the goals. At half time and whenever a goal is obtained the players shall change ends and recommence in the same way. [The time during a match was to last should be fixed beforehand by the captains]

V.   When a bye is hit, the goal-keeper shall hit the ball off within 6 yards of the goal posts, when no opponent shall be within a distance of 12 yards in front of the goal lines, this being the only restriction as to where the players shall stand, except that no player shall persistently stand within a distance of 12 yards of an opponent's goal, thereby impeding the movements of the goal-keeper.

VI.   If the ball is hit off the ice or beyond that line which is considered the boundary, it may be picked up by the first comer who must take it to the place from where it left the boundary and he shall have a free hit from that point.

VII.   If the ball rises into the air it may be stopped by the body or hand of the player, but if caught it must be dropped instantly at the feet of the person who caught it, except in the case of the goal-keeper, who shall have the liberty of throwing the ball away from him.

VIII. The hockey may be used to catch, lift or bear down the hockey of

Fig. 21.

Player positioning, as recommended in the Handbook of Fen Skating.

a player, but no player under any circumstances whatever to be allowed to raise his hockey higher than his shoulder, and any charging, holding with the hands or hockey, any tripping or rough play of any sort to be peremptorily put down by the Umpire or Captains.

IX.   The full number on each side to be 15, but in case of short goals etc., Captains to arrange the number as convenient.

X.   To obtain a goal the ball must pass between the goal-posts and under the tape.

XI.   If any player throws or drops his hockey, an opponent may pick it up and throw it away.

XII.   No player to be allowed the use of more than one hockey at the same time.

XIII.   All players disobeying these rules after being once warned or called to order by the Umpire or Captains may be prevented from taking further part in the game.

      FREDERICK JEWSON

      ARNOLD TEBBUTT

      HON. SECS.[34]

These 13 rules have it all: size of the goals (with flexibility), dimensions of the playing surface (with flexibility), number of players per side (with flexibility), dimensions of the stick, dimensions of the ball, how goals are scored. The duration of the game is not set, but the rules stipulate that it must be "fixed beforehand by the captains."

Note in particular that the width of the goals is to be adjusted according to the length of the field, being one foot wide for each 10 yards of length (recommended at 22 feet and 220 yards respectively). If the length of the field is adjusted to the current NHL standard (200 feet, or 66 2/3 yards), we obtain a goal six feet, eight inches wide, quite close to the NHL standard of 6 feet.

Also note that, while the recommended number of players per team may seem high (15 on each side), the field was considerably larger than today's NHL ice rinks. In fact, even with 15 players a side, each player in a full field (according to the rules, and assuming a field "width to length ratio" similar to that of today's NHL rinks) would have had four times as much space—a little over 6,000 square feet—as current NHL players, who have to make do with just slightly more than 1,400 square feet each.

These rules would be the earliest known ice hockey rules to have been published by a structured sports organization, pre-dating the Canadian AHAC rules by more than four years.

The NSA Rules, 1883
It would take several meetings, but the NSA would finalize its own set of rules and publish them on November 21, 1883.[35] The development of the rules had been eagerly followed by the press—witness this December 19, 1882, article from the *Exeter and Plymouth Gazette*, titled WEEKLY NOTES ON SPORTS AND PASTIMES—BY A COUNTRY SPORTSMAN: "Yesterday a meeting was held at St. Ives for the purpose of settling the rules of hockey on the ice. We have cricket on the ice and football on the ice. Hockey, I venture to predict, will, wherever introduced, surpass either cricket or football in popularity. Matches are pending between Metropolitan and Fen hockey players."[36]

Talk about enthusiasm! In the end, the NSA drew up two sets of rules, one for the traditional method of play practised in the Fens, and another for "the Metropolitan district." The long-awaited publication of the rules had echoes as far as Toronto, in the December 10, 1883, edition of the *Daily Mail:* "Prince Alexander, of the Netherlands, has presented a valuable piece of plate to the National Skating Association of Great Britain for an

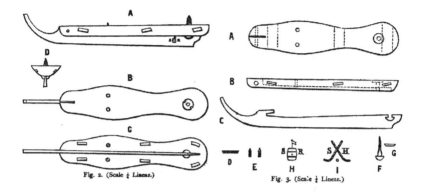

Fig. 2. (Scale ¼ Linear.)   Fig. 3. (Scale ¼ Linear.)

Skates approved by the National Skating Association.

international race open to all amateurs. The association has adopted a set of rules for hockey on the ice, one of the grandest of all games."[37]

Here are the rules for the Fens:

> DEFINITIONS: The 'Field' is the defined area within which the game is played. The 'Goal' is the defined space between the goal posts. The goal of either party of players is that which they defend.
> Rule 1.—Where space allows, the field shall be a right-angled parallelogram 200 yards long by 150 yards wide.
> 2.—The goals shall be opposite and parallel in the centre of the shorter sides or 'goal lines', 15 feet wide, between two uprights, with a tape or lath across at the height of 6 feet 6 inches.
> 3.—The number of players on each side shall be 15, including the captain.
> (The above rules, 1, 2, and 3, may be modified by agreement, as circumstances may require.)
> 4.—The ball used in play shall be solid, of India rubber, and not less than 2 inches, or more than 2½ inches in diameter.
> 5.—The bandy or hockey sticks shall be of wood, not more than 4 feet long, and not more than 2½ inches wide in any part.

6.—The first choice of goals in every match shall be determined by lot.

7.—A goal is won by either side when the ball is passed through their opponents' goal under the tape.

8.—The time during which a match is to last shall be fixed beforehand by the captains, and the sides shall change goals whenever a goal is made, or at half-time when a goal has not been previously made.

9.—The players shall wear the colours of their side on the arm, and on their bandy or hockey sticks.

10.—The game shall be commenced in all cases by the umpire throwing the ball perpendicularly into the air from the centre of the field, and as it descends it is in play.

11.— *(a)* The ball must not be carried or thrown, and if caught must be at once dropped upon the ice. *(b)* No player may catch hold of, or intentionally charge or impede an opponent. *(c)* No player may throw his bandy or hockey stick, or use it to trip an opponent, or intimidate him, or strike his stick from his hand, nor may he raise his own stick above his shoulder to strike the ball when any player is within reach.

Any player who violates any of the sections of the above rule may, on appeal to the umpire, be disqualified from playing again until a goal is won.

12.—When the ball is struck beyond the side lines the player who sends it beyond the boundary, or a player on his side, must carry it back to the place where it crossed the boundary and at once strike it at right angles into the field.

13.—When the ball is passed across the goal line on either side of the goal by one of the attacking players the ball shall cease to be in play, and the keeper of that goal shall have a free hit from any point on the goal line within six yards of the goal. But if the ball is passed across the goal line by one of the defending players an attacking player shall have the right to a free hit either from the corner of the field or from any point on the goal line not nearer to the goal than forty yards. The free hit shall be from the side of the goal on which the ball passed.

14.—Whenever a free hit is allowed, no opponent shall stand within twenty yards of the striker.

15. —No player shall place himself within twenty yards of his opponents' goal except in following up the ball.

16. —A match is won by the players whose side wins the greater number of goals.

17.—In all cases of dispute an appeal shall be made to the umpire, whose decision shall be final.

And in the Metropolitan district:

1.—To be played within a parallelogram, 200 yards long by 75 yards wide, or proportionately reduced. Distance between golf [sic] standards to be 10 feet. This area may be marked out by driving into the ice, sharp pointed, bright iron, or steel wire rods, carrying small square red and blue flags of bunting to indicate goal and touch line of the respective sides. The goal standards to be considerably higher, and the half distance and knock off flags in touch lines, to be more prominent than the other boundary flags.

2.—Players to carry the colour of their sides, either red or blue ribbon, tied down on their hockey sticks; and to skate on club skates, *i.e.,* the skate irons to have rounded not pointed ends.

3.—The hockey sticks to be straight (Bamboo canes are recommended), not exceeding 1½ inches in diameter, and to be carried and worked in the right hand only, and on the right hand side only of the body.

4.—The hockey stick may be used to catch, lift, or bear down that of an opponent; but any charging, holding with the hands or hockey sticks, any tripping, or rough play of any sort, is to be peremptorily put down by the umpire and captains.

5.—A solid, or hollow inflated India rubber ball, 2 inches or 2½ inches in diameter, is to be used.

6.—Eleven to play on each side.

7.—Duration of game, an hour; or longer, if so arranged before the match commences, sides to be changed at half time only.

8.—The game shall be begun by the respective captains facing each other on their mutual sides of half distance line, crossing sticks and tapping the ice three times, and then starting the ball towards one or other of the goals.

9.—During the progress of the game the ball is to be worked along the surface of the ice by the hockey sticks only; no player under any circumstances shall strike, throw, carry, kick or handle the ball.

10.—Any player who shall take up a position, or advance to a position nearer to his adversaries' goal line than that occupied by the player who is working the ball, shall be 'off side', and out of play, until he has put himself, or been put 'on side' again, by occupying a point anywhere between the ball in play and the goal line of his own side. Any player who is 'off side', shall immediately retire to a position which puts him 'on side' again.

11.—If the ball rise into the air, it may be stopped by the body or hand of the player; but if caught it must be dropped instantly at the feet of the player who caught it.

12.—If the ball cross touch line it shall be gently and fairly thrown in at right angles to the touch line and from the point at which it left touch line. No player meanwhile, other than the thrower in, is to approach within six yards of this point.

13.—If the ball cross goal line, but not between the goal standards, it shall be carried out by one of the side whose goal line it has crossed, to any point at least 25 yards in front of their goal line, and from touch line, and be started towards the opposite goal. Until the ball is started on the ice, the other side are to remain beyond half distance line.

14.—To obtain a goal the ball must pass between the goal standards; but it is 'no goal' if the ball be struck, thrown, carried, kicked, or handled through, between the goal standards; and if such has been the case, and so decided by the umpire, the ball shall be re-started as provided in Rule 13.

15.—After a goal has been won the winners shall start the ball from the 25 yards line, as provided in Rule 13. Five minutes interval if asked for by either side shall be allowed.

16.—The greatest number of goals won during the term of play to decide the match.

17.—Any player who has been once warned by the umpire or by the captain of his side, for disregarding any of the above Rules, may be ordered, for any second or further breach of these Rules, to retire from the game.[38]

These are the first known rules drawn up by a national association, pre-dating the Montreal AHAC rules by more than three years.

History tells us that the teams from the Fens followed "their" rules much more closely than the Londoners followed "theirs," the latter continuing in particular to use a flat brewer's bung, covered with leather, instead of an India rubber ball. As mentioned at the beginning of this chapter, the reader is encouraged to read *On His Own Side of the Puck: The Early History of Hockey Rules* by Iain Fyffe for an in-depth analysis of the early English and Canadian rules of hockey.

Chapter 7 Notes

1. Paul Henderson and Jim Prime, *How Hockey Explains Canada: The Sport That Defines a Country* (Chicago: Triumph Books, 2011): viii. Harper's original text appears to be missing some words, as Creighton did not codify the rules for all sports—he is the one who did it for hockey.

2. Donald Guay, *L'histoire du hockey au Québec* (Chicoutimi, Que.: Les Éditions JCL, 1990):18-19. The other five "dimensions" of sport, as Guay calls them, involve:

   1. A physical activity.
   2. A competition.
   3. Something at stake so the participants are motivated to try to win.
   4. Playfulness: the participants want to win to show they are better at the sport, not because they are enemies.
   5. Sportsmanship.

3. *The Gazette* (Montreal), 27 Feb. 1877.
4. *The Gazette* (Montreal), 22 Dec. 1936.
5. *The Gazette* (Montreal), 27 Nov. 1943.
6. *The Gazette* (Montreal), 7 Feb. 1876.
7. *The Gazette* (Montreal), 18 Sep. 1943.
8. *Toronto Daily Mail,* 10 Dec. 1883.
9. J. Nicholson Smith and Philip A. Robson, *Hockey Historical and Practical* (London: A.D. Innes, 1899): 12-13.
10. *The Gazette* (Montreal), 27 Feb. 1877.
11. Iain Fyffe, *On His Own Side of the Puck: The Early History of Hockey Rules* (San Francisco: Blurb Inc., 2014): 23-30.
12. *The Gazette* (Montreal), 20 Jan. 1880, and the *Daily Witness* (Montreal), 21 Jan. 1880.
13. *The Gazette* (Montreal), 8 Jan. 1886.
14. *The Gazette* (Montreal), 23 Dec. 1886.
15. "Rules of Hockey," *The Eton College Chronicle,* no. 96, (20 Feb. 1868): 1. They are as follows:

    i. The Ground is 200 yards long, and 50 yards broad, marked out by sticks.

    ii. At the distance of 20 yards from the line of the goal sticks, two sticks are placed along the side line, one on each side of the ground. These are called "Lamming Sticks."

    III.   Goal sticks are placed at each end, 20 feet apart, and 7 feet high.

    IV.   The sticks used may be according to the fancy of each player, as long as it is recognized as fair by the Keepers. No player may have more than one stick in his hand at a time.

    V.   A large sized tennis-ball is used.

    VI.   The two sides do consist of 11 players each: these being two "Guards" and one "Goal-keeper" to each side. The rest forming the "Bully".

    VII.   A "Bully" is formed by each side being drawn up in a long line in the direction of the length of the ground, having their right hands towards their own goals: the ball being placed between the sticks of the middle player on each side.

    VIII.   No player is allowed to raise his stick above the knee, except when inside the "Lamming Sticks", when he may hit as hard as he likes, due regard to safety being had.

    IX.   The stick must be held on the right side of the player, and the ball struck with it in that position, in order that all collision of bodies and roughing be avoided.

    X.   If any player violating this rule impedes his adversary he can with impunity be struck on the shin.

    XI.   The ball may be stopped, but not kicked with the foot.

    XII.   The ball may be stopped in the air with the hand, but not held.

    XIII.   Any player violating the two above rules to leave the ball alone until it has been touched by an adversary.

    XIV.   It is the duty of the two "Guards" to stand outside the Bully, and endeavour to keep the ball in the middle of the ground, and to prevent any adversary from passing them with it; also to prevent "sneaking."

    XV.   No player may "corner" or "sneak."

    XVI.   On any player violating the above rule, any one of the opposing party may claim a Bully at the spot where the offence was committed.

    XVII.   Play lasts an hour, and is commenced by a Bully in the middle.

    XVIII.   Goals are changed at the half-hour.

    XIX.   If the ball goes out of bounds, a Bully is found opposite to where it went out.

xx. A goal is obtained when the ball passes between the Goal Sticks, provided by the Striker be inside "Lamming Sticks."

xxi. If the ball pass between the Goal Sticks, struck from beyond the "Lamming Sticks," it counts only a "Behind."

xxii. If the ball passes on either side of the Goal, when struck from within "Lamming Sticks," a "Behind" is counted.

xxiii. If the ball goes behind, when struck from beyond Lamming Sticks, there is a Hit-off.

xxiv. When a Behind is obtained, a Bully is formed in front of goals at 10 yards distance from them.

xxv. The Striker-off is at liberty to throw the ball up for a half volley if he pleases, or to strike it in the air or on the ground.

xxvi. No player of the adverse side may come within 20 yards of the Striker-off.

xxvii. After a Goal, play is resumed by a Bully in the middle.

xxviii. The Game is decided by the number of Goals each side has obtained.

xxix. The Game cannot be ended until the Ball has crossed the side line.

xxx. In the absence of Umpires, the Captain of each side acts as Umpire for his own side, and his decision is final.

16. David Cram, Jeffrey L. Forgeng and Dorothy Johnston, *Francis Willughby's Book of Games: A Seventeenth-Century Treatise on Sports, Games, and Pastimes* (Aldershot, U.K.: Ashgate Publishing, 2003): 179.

17. Richard Phillips, *The Book of Games, or, a History of the Juvenile Sports, Practised at the Kingston Academy; Illustrated with Twenty-four Copper Plates* (London: Tabart & Co., 1805): 7–16.

18. Alfred Guy Kingan L'Estrange, *Vert de Vert's Eton Days, and other Sketches and Memories* (London: Elliot Stock, 1887): 56–57.

19. George William Lyttelton, "On Eton Games", *The Eton College Magazine,* no. 8 (19 Nov. 1832) 282–283.

20. For example, David Levinson and Karen Christensen, eds., *Encyclopedia of World Sport: From Ancient Times to the Present* (Oxford, U.K.: Oxford University Press, 1996): 168: "...hockey (from the French *"hoquet,"* the shepherd's crook) ..."

21. *The Spectator* (London), 3 Nov. 1888: 42.

22. George Forrest (John George Wood), "Hockey," *Every Boy's Magazine*, no. 3 (April 1862).

23. "Hockey," *The Boy's Handy Book of Sports, Pastimes, Games and Amusements* (London: Ward and Lock, 1863): 221–222.

24. "The National: Bettman describes his love for hockey–NHL Commissioner says he's a fan of the game," CBC Sports, 30 Sep. 2013, web, 2 Apr. 2014 <http://www.cbc.ca/sports/hockey/nhl/the-national-bettman-describes-his-love-for-hockey-1.1874134>. Here is the quote with more context:

   BETTMAN: It's played in a confined space. Every now and then, there needs to be an outlet to keep the temperature from worse things happening, and I think, by and large, the players understand their responsibilities, the coaches understand their responsibilities, and the officials do a good job of regulating the game.

   MANSBRIDGE: So fighting is something, then, that you see as part of the game. A necessary part, at times.

   BETTMAN: It has been, it is, but it's been declining in its frequency. There's less fighting in the game than we had years ago. I mean, we penalize it. It's part of the fabric and it evolves, and the game constantly evolves, and when you're making changes, because we respect the history, the tradition and the vibrancy of the game, you just don't throw a light switch and effectuate a major change. We try to let the game evolve within certain parameters. There's a balancing act . . .

25. "The Vizetelly London firm of printers, engravers and publishers was active at 135 Fleet Street under various names from c. 1827–1890. Founded by James Henry Vizetelly with various associates, the firm was reorganized at his death in 1838, by the eldest son, James, with his younger brother Henry as associate." "Inventory of the Vizetelly and Company (1850–1855) letters and documents, 1785, 1838–1854," Online Archive of California, web, retrieved 22 Mar. 2014, <http://www.oac.cdlib.org/findaid/ark:/13030/kt8x0nc282/>.

26. *The Patriot* (London), 17 Dec. 1849.

27. *The Boy's Own Book; A complete Encyclopedia of all the Diversions, Athletic, Scientific and Recreative, of Boyhood and Youth* (London: Vizetelly, Branston and Co., June 1828).

28. "Goff, or Bandy-Ball," *The Boy's Own Book; A complete Encyclopedia of all the Diversions, Athletic, Scientific and Recreative, of Boyhood and Youth* (London: Vizetelly, Branston and Co., October 1828): 18.

29. "Hockey," *The Boy's Own Book: A Complete Encyclopedia of all the Diversions, Athletic, Scientific, and Recreative, of Boyhood and Youth* (London: David Bogue, 1849): 41.

30. "Hockey," *The Boy's Own Book: A Complete Encyclopaedia of Sports and Pastimes; Athletic, Scientific, and Recreative. A New Edition, thoroughly revised and considerably enlarged* (London: Lockwood & Co., 1868): 146.

31. John Loadman, "Timeline: 1819–1875," Bouncing Balls: Everything You Ever Wanted to Know About Rubber, web, retrieved 26 Mar. 2014, <http://www.bouncing-balls.com/index2.htm>.

32. George Forrest (John George Wood), *The Playground; or, The Boy's Book of Games,* (London: George Routledge, 1858): 204–206.

33. John Moyer Heathcote, Charles Goodman Tebbutt and Thomas Maxwell Witham, *Skating* (London: Longmans, Green & Co., 1892): 256.

34. Neville and Albert Goodman, *Handbook of Fen Skating* (London: Sampson Low, Marston, Searle, and Rivington, 1882).

35. As reported, in particular, in *Bell's Life in London, and Sporting Chronicle* and the *Ipswich Journal,* 24 Nov. 1883.

36. *Exeter and Plymouth Gazette,* 19 Dec. 1882.

37. *Toronto Daily Mail,* 10 Dec. 1883.

38. National Skating Association of Great Britain, "Hockey on the Ice: Rules," *Rules of the National Skating Association of Great Britain* (Cambridge, U. K.: Digby and Son, 1883): 15–18.

CHAPTER 8

What's in a Name?

Canadians are, to say the least, not very familiar with the game of bandy. How many Canadians lamented the 22-1 loss of the Canadian men's team to Russia in the quarter-finals of the 2014 world championship of bandy? The Canadian women's team has been faring better, but still no world championship medal as of 2014—although there have been three fourth-place finishes so far.

Yet bandy is quite similar to hockey. It is played on ice, with skates, sticks, a ball, two teams, and an objective of putting the ball in the opposing team's goal. So it is hockey, then? Well, in 2014, it certainly is not: there is no bodychecking in bandy; the game is played with a ball, not a puck; the rink and goals in bandy are much bigger than in hockey (though there exists a smaller "rink" version); the number of players is different; the goalkeeper does not use a stick; and so on. So bandy and hockey have evolved quite differently, but was there always a difference between bandy and hockey?

In *How Hockey Happened,* hockey historian J. W. (Bill) Fitsell dedicated a chapter to bandy, and mentions that it "has been cited as an obvious ancestor of ice hockey."[1] But the chapter does not offer a comparison of the two games as played in the 19th century or earlier.

It is the authors' strong belief that, prior to the 1891 creation of England's Bandy Association, there was no difference between hockey and bandy in England—at least, no more difference than there was between regional variations of hockey itself. In fact, whether the games played were called hockey or bandy was mostly a regional consideration, and we shall provide some of the evidence supporting this claim.

Glossary of North Country Words, in Use, 1829

John Trotter Brockett (1788–1842) was an antiquarian and attorney born in Witton Gilbert, County Durham, in northeastern England. In his early youth, his parents moved to Gateshead. He became an attorney, and practised for many years in Newcastle, where he was respected as an able and eloquent advocate in the mayor's and sheriff's courts.

Brockett was a member of the Society of Antiquaries, a secretary of the Newcastle Literary and Philosophical Society, and one of the council of the Society of Antiquaries of Newcastle-on-Tyne.

Northern England, also known as the North, is a cultural region within England. The southern extent of the region is roughly the River Trent, while the northern boundary is the border between England and Scotland. The North might be considered to comprise the six ancient counties of Cumberland, Northumberland, Westmorland, Durham, Lancashire and Yorkshire. Some words occurring in "far" northern accents reflect the Viking influence; estimates have suggested that as many as 7 per cent of West Cumbrian dialect words are original Norse or derived from Norse.

In 1825, Brockett published the first edition of his *Glossary of North Country Words, in Use.* A second edition, to a large extent rewritten, was published in 1829; a third was in preparation at the time of the author's death, and was published, under the editorship of W. E. Brockett, in 1846.

Below are some entries from the second edition:

CLUBBY, a youthful game, something like DODDART; which see.

DODDART, a bent stick used in the game called *doddart;* which is played in a large level field, by two parties of nearly balanced powers, either as to number or dexterity, headed by two captains who are entitled to choose their followers by alternate votes. A piece of globular wood, called an *orr* or *coit,* is thrown down in the middle of the field, and the object of each side is to drive it to one of two opposite hedges assigned respectively before the game begins, as the *alley, hail, goal,* or boundary.

HOCKEY, another name for the game of DODDART—*hooky,* from the bent stick used. So the synonyme [sic] bandy, *bendy.* The verb *bandy* appears borrowed from the game, and directly allusive to it. "I will not *bandy* with thee word for word" — *3d. Part, Henry VI.*

SHINNEY, a stick crooked or round at the end, with which to strike a small wooden ball or coit, in the game called SHINNEY, or SHINNEY-HAW, and sometimes SHINHAM — played in the Northern counties.
    The same as DODDART; which see.[2]

So hockey is "another name" for doddart, whose description does appear to match the definition of field hockey, and bandy or bendy is synonymous with hockey. Then we know that bandy, like hockey, started off on the ground before being adapted to be played on the ice. We also discover that the faceoff, in doddart, was done modern ice hockey style.

The Fens, Cambridgeshire, 1838
In chapter 3, we were introduced to the long letter from "N. W." that was published in the March 1838 edition of *The New Sporting Magazine.* Let us reproduce here the paragraph describing hockey — or, rather, "hocky":

> The games chiefly practiced on the ice are *bandy* or *hocky,* as it is termed, fox-and-hounds, tick, and prison-bays. The latter speak for themselves — the first is played with sticks and a ball. A side is chosen, goals are fixed, and the ball bandied to and fro, like a foot-ball, until a goal is gained; twelve in general is *up,* and the goals three hundred yards apart.[3]

There is no doubt that the author is describing one game, not two, when he writes "bandy or hocky," as he adds "as it is termed," not "as they are termed" and, further, "the first is played with sticks and a ball," not "the first two are played . . ."

Holiday Sports and Pastimes for Boys, 1848
Henry D. Richardson (d. 1851) was born in Scotland and as a young man lived in Edinburgh. While in that city, he was president, or captain, of the Holyrood Gymnastic Club and was known as the swimming champion of Newhaven. An entry in *The Scotsman* from August 1836 reports of him winning the standing jump at five feet, one-half of one inch.[4]

Soon afterward, Richardson moved to Dublin, Ireland, and started publishing works on natural history, breeding, rearing and the general management of various domestic animals. Being a keen sportsman, Richardson also wrote *Holiday Sports and Pastimes for Boys,* published in 1848. This book, with a strong Edinburgh flavour, describes a great number of indoor and outdoor sports, including many performed at Scottish Highland Games. Richardson writes in the preface, signed in Dublin on November 10, 1847:

> I can also assure them [my youthful readers], that I have not for many years experienced more real pleasure than while employed in inditing these pages for their amusement and direction; for the task has recalled, in the most vivid manner, sweet recollections of bygone days of youth, of those happy times when as yet there was no past, when the present day was full of joy, and when the future seemed as clear and unclouded as the blue sky of sunny Italy...[5]

While written in Dublin and drawing on memories from Edinburgh, the book was sold throughout the United Kingdom,[6] and thus should not be perceived as intending to present a regional view. Below is the book's entry for a game that appears to have many names:

> HURLEY, BANDY, HOCKY, SHINTY—are synonymous for one very capital game. The best place for playing it is a large but smooth field, not overburdened with grass.
>
> The game is as follows:—two long and upright poles are stuck into the ground in a conspicuous part of the field, and about two hundred yards from them, and as nearly opposite to them as possible, two other sticks are planted; each pair of posts are about six feet apart. Sides having been chosen as in rounders, one party of players select one pair of posts as their own, the opposite side takes the others. The implements of the game are very simple, consisting of a ball, or, in its absence, the bung of a cask, and in each player's hand a stick, with a curved extremity.
>
> All being ready, one of the party takes the ball, lays it on the ground in front of the post, or *"call",* as it is technically termed, of his party, and strikes it to as great a distance in the direction of the opposite *"call"* as he is able. The game has now commenced—the object of each party

being to drive the ball or bung between the posts or stakes constituting their opponents' *"call"*; if the ball be driven *past* the call, instead of between, the party so striking it gain nothing, but on the contrary the game ceases, and a new one commences the proprietors of the call so passed having now the right of first stroke, precisely as if they had been victorious. This error of passing the call, confers, in short, a sort of tacit, negative victory on the party to whom it belongs, resembling "stale mate" at chess.
It is necessary to observe that each party should, in this game, keep to its own side. Those who strike downwards, and those who strike upwards, have no right, under any circumstances, to cross over; if they do so, the offending party is liable to a crack on the shins with the bandy, accompanied by the cry, — oh! how our hearts yearn back to the days of happy youth at the recollection of 'Shin your sides'.[7]

We have seen many ways of describing the game in various books, and this is perhaps one of the less effective, but it does correspond to the same game as the others, with the confusing "keep to its own side" referring to having to hold the stick right-handed to avoid collisions. One thing that is not confusing, however, is that the various names given to the game—hurley, bandy, hocky, shinty—are all "synonymous for one…game."

Skating, 1892
This is the most extensive work about ice sports published during the 1800s. A first edition of this book was published in 1892, a second in 1894 and a third in 1902. It contained chapters about figure and speedskating, curling, toboganning, ice-sailing and bandy.
    Charles Goodman Tebbutt (1860–1944), who wrote the chapter about bandy, was highly responsible for both the indoor and outdoor dissemination of the game in middle and north Europe. He was born in the village of Bluntisham in the Fen district and became an eminent bandy player and speed skater. His four brothers, as well as his ancestors, were all active bandy players on the team playing on the Bury Fen. Tebbutt was an active writer and published several works about bandy and speed skating.
    Here is the beginning of the chapter on bandy:

THE game of bandy, otherwise known as hockey and shinney, or shinty, is doubtless one of the earliest pastimes of the kind ever known. In its most primitive form it is simply played down the middle of a village street by boys who, armed with bent sticks, make themselves warm on a winter's evening by knocking a 'cat' about, all against all. At other times sides are chosen and it becomes a more regular game, the hedges or houses forming the side boundaries, and a couple of stones, some hundred yards apart, marking each goal.

From this rough-and-ready frolic, however, the present games of hockey and bandy are derived.

The word 'hockey' is now given to a well-established game under definite rules, played with boundaries and goals as foot-ball is on grass, while 'bandy' has long been identified with a game played like hockey, but on ice; and it is with this game we are now concerned.[8]

Later in the chapter, Tebbutt recalls a game played in Brockett Hall Park, Hertfordshire, between the teams of Hatfield and Hoddesdon:

Bandy, or, as it is often called, 'hockey on the ice', is too good a game to have been always confined to one district of England. During a prolonged frost wherever a large piece of water gave scope games had been played. Thus, in 1864, a Hatfield eight played a Hoddesdon eight at Brockett Hall Park.[9]

So for Tebbutt, there is no difference between bandy and "hockey on the ice"; they are interchangeable terms. Many parts of England, as we've already seen in numerous examples, do not even bother with the "on the ice" part of the name, when the context is clear.

Still further along in the chapter, Tebbutt recounts a game played in the winter of 1890/91 between the Bury Fen Club, which had travelled all the way to London to meet a "combination team" called, for the occasion, the "Virginia Water Team."

During the winter of 1890-91 several matches were played near London, the principal being Virginia Water v. Mr. G. E. B. Kennedy's eleven, which was closely contested, victory falling to Virginia Water, two goals to one. After this a combination team was chosen to meet the Bury Fen Club, under the captaincy of H. Blackett, and called 'The Virginia Water Team'. For the first time the club left their native fens for the metropolis,

The Bury Fen and Virginia Water club badges.

and met on Virginia Water the representative London team.... Some of the Londoners had been used to the leather-covered bung and light ash sticks, so the first half was played with these, during which the Londoners obtained one goal. At half-time the bandy and ball were played with, and the 'off-side rule', to which the Fenmen were unused, was agreed upon. The Londoners increased their goals by eight, whilst the Bury Fen club only made three. It was a very fast game throughout, the home side including some of the best hockey players of England, showing great speed, combination, and hitting power.

The teams consisted of,... In consequence of the great interest this match created, and the necessity of having uniform rules now that bandy was becoming general, a meeting of bandy players was held to consider rules and form a Bandy Association.[10]

Here, Tebbutt mentions that the two teams are used to different equipment and rules, those of course being described as the "as played in the Fens" and "as played in Metropolitan District" rules detailed in the last chapter, which were established in 1883, and at the time (both) formally designated as "hockey on the ice rules."

Ice-Sports, 1901
This book contains a section, written by Sydney Charles King-Farlow (1864–1957), containing what was likely the first set of rules for indoor bandy/ice

hockey devised in England, though the exact date of their creation is not known with certainty. The first indoor game in London was played in February 1896, and must have been played with "some" rules, but since these rules have not yet been located in a publication earlier than this book, all we can say for certain is that they were written between 1895 and 1901. King-Farlow was a member of the Virginia Water Hockey Club.

Bandy, is otherwise known as Hockey on the Ice, or Shinty.

Ice-rinks have been popular in North America and Canada in particular, for a long time past; and in the latter country much ice hockey is played— usually four or five a side—under cover.

The game is very similar to that played in our ice-rinks, except that the bandies used by the Canadians are longer, and curved at the end in such a way that their backs are able to 'loft' the puck into the air, well clear of the ice, without difficulty.

THE BANDY ASSOCIATION — RULES OF ICE-RINK HOCKEY

Rules of Bandy or Ice Hockey, November 25th, 1895, applied to ice-rink bandy.

The main points worth noting are:

1. The "ground" is, of course, limited to the size of the rink, the width between the goal posts being regulated accordingly.

2. The number of players is usually five a-side, sometimes six.

3. The bandy, as in rule 3 of Bandy Rules. [Rule 3 of Bandy rules states the following: "The bandy, shall be of wood, not exceed 2 ins. in width in any part, not more than 4 ft. long as measured along the handle and round the curve, and shall have no metal fittings or sharp edges."]

4. A "puck," or flat piece of indiarubber (borrowed from Canada), is used instead of a ball.

The reason for this is obvious: in a small ice-rink a ball would travel too fast.

5. There are no "corner" hits.

6. The "puck" remains in play except when it strikes a small space specially marked off on either side of the goal posts. It

is then, and then only, said to be "behind", and is hit out by
the goalkeeper from goal. — See plan below.

7. There are no side lines. The "puck" remains in play until
it has actually passed over the barrier with which ice rinks are
surrounded. The barrier is usually about 3 ft. 6 ins. high.

8. There is no off-side rule.

Save as mentioned above, the rules of November 25th, 1895, apply
to ice-rink bandy.

This plan represents an ordinary ice-rink with a team of five in position.

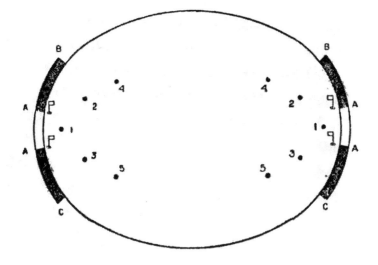

A A are the goals; 1 is the goalkeeper; 2 and 3 the backs; 4 and 5 the
left and right forwards respectively; B A and C A are "behind" lines.

If six a-side play, the extra man usually acts as half-back, supporting
both the backs and the forwards, and making himself generally useful.[11]

It is now 1895, and Canada's "takeover" of hockey has started, with the
rules making their way across the Atlantic in the direction opposite to what
was happening less than 20 years earlier, and yet the author still writes
"Bandy, or ice hockey" as the title of his section, then offers the alternative
names "hockey on the ice" and also "shinty."

Interestingly, a schism, caused by some London teams upset at not being invited to the "New Niagara Hockey Tournament," led those teams to form their own circuit, the Rink Hockey Association, which formulated its own rules, published in *The Field* on April 17, 1897.[12] Those rules were also very detailed.[13] However, this association does not appear to have met with much success, as it left hardly any documentary trace in the subsequent hockey season.

A Handbook of Bandy; or, Hockey on the Ice, 1896

This is the very first book solely devoted to ice hockey (or bandy). Only a few copies of this book seem to have survived. Although only Arnold Tebbutt (1858-1940) is mentioned as author on the cover, two of his brothers, Charles Goodman (1860-1944) and Neville (1852-1929), contributed to the book. All five Tebbutt brothers were prominent players in the now-familiar Bury Fen Club—credited with a tradition of playing bandy since the mid-1700s.

The book covers activities of hockey until the end of the winter of 1894/95, but also includes the revised rules of the National Bandy Association from November 25, 1895. The indoor rinks opened in London during the mid-1890s completely changed the conditions for the game—and the first indoor game in England was actually played on February 1, 1896, only two weeks after the publication of the book.

In the book, the term "bandy" is used more often than "hockey," but both appear numerous times, in particular in the often used expression "the bandy, or hockey stick," the former term having always designated the stick as well, even in other sports. We will reproduce here just the beginning of the first chapter:

CHAPTER I
HISTORY OF THE GAME
BY NEVILLE TEBBUTT

THE game of Bandy, or, as it is often called, 'Hockey on the Ice', is not of modern origin, although until within the last fifteen or twenty years it had, perhaps, never been systematically played elsewhere than in the eastern counties, and few persons outside that district had never seen it, or, indeed, heard of its existence.[14]

Arnold Tebbutt and Charles Goodman Tebbutt, two of the authors
of A Handbook Of Bandy; Or, Hockey On The Ice.

Neville continues with a geographical analysis of where the game was played
(in England), analysis that we now know was far from accurate, in view of
the numerous references now known to exist of hockey played on ice with
skates throughout much of England's territory. In 1896, information did
not travel very fast, and thus Tebbutt was likely mostly aware of hockey
played in his own region (the Fens) and London and its surroundings.

The title of the book should convince anyone that indeed, at the time, "bandy" and "hockey on the ice" were used interchangeably to designate exactly the same game. Would anyone buy a book called *A Handbook of Baseball; or, Curling*? Or maybe this example is too extreme. Would a book titled *A Handbook of American Football; or, Canadian Football* stand a good chance of making the best-seller list? What about *A Handbook of 15-Player Rugby; or, 13-Player Rugby*?

The Encyclopaedia of Sport, 1897

This major work of almost 1,300 pages, divided into two volumes, was edited by the Earl of Suffolk and Berkshire, Henry Charles Howard (1833–1898), Hedley Peek (1858–1904) and Frederick George Aflalo (1870–1918). The chapter about bandy was written by Arnold Tebbutt, whom we know well by now. It is not surprising that Arnold also presents "bandy" and "hockey on the ice" as synonyms here. The beginning of the article on bandy is as follows:

> Bandy, or Hockey on the Ice, is a similar game to hockey on the land. It is played by skaters upon broad sheets of ice between goals, with curved sticks called 'bandies', and a ball or 'cat'.[15]

There is not much to add here that hasn't already been mentioned. Of interest is, further in the article, the mention of the number of players and the description of the stick:

> NUMBER OF PLAYERS — The players are eleven a side, but if the field is smaller than 100 yards x 50 yards it is better to reduce their number; thus, six a side make a good game on a field of 75 yards x 35 yards.
> THE BANDY — The bandy used is a curved ash stick of about 1½ inches diameter and 3½ feet long. It is very similar to the stick used in hockey on land, except that the blade is not so curved, and is not, as in that game, rounded on one side, but has both sides flat.[16]

So we know that the game played on ice, whether called "bandy" or "hockey on the ice"; had an angled stick (like today's ice hockey sticks), not a curved one (like field hockey's sticks); allowed backhand shots; and was best played with six players (like today's hockey) if the field length did not exceed 75 yards (or 225 feet, just 25 feet more than today's standard NHL rinks). We also notice the use of the expression "hockey on land," which we might say is to "field hockey" what "hockey on the ice" is to "ice hockey"—that is, exactly the same thing.

Perhaps of even more interest is the following paragraph, found further still in the text:

> The game has been described as played in accordance with the rules of the National Bandy Association which are given below. But where the field of ice is very small a plain cork bung, covered with leather or bound with string, may be used with advantage; and in some places the thin hockey-stick with bent end of about six inches, formerly used by the Virginia Water and other clubs, is still preferred. On the artificial ice at the Ice Palace (Regent Street), where the space is of course extremely limited, a fairly good game is obtained by using a flat india-rubber disc (3 inches diam. x 1 inch thick) as the cat, and by prohibiting the bandy when used in hitting from being raised from the ice.[17]

So according to this, bandy—a.k.a. hockey (on the ice)—can be played outdoors or indoors, on a large or a small surface, and with a ball or a puck-like india-rubber disc of exactly the same dimensions as today's hockey puck.

Let us very quickly go over more references from the same years.

Skating, 1897
This is not to be confused with the book of the same name issued by a different publisher in 1892, 1894 and 1902. This time, the author of the article on bandy is Arnold Tebbutt, who kept finding slightly different ways of telling the same story. The article on bandy begins as follows:

> THE game of Bandy, or, as it has so often been called, Hockey on the Ice, is one of the oldest and yet at the same time one of the most modern of games. Oldest it can claim to be in respect to one small district of which the Bury Fen is the centre, for the records of matches played by the Bury Fen Club extend back some 80 years, and there is but little doubt it was played long before that date.[18]

The "House" on Sport, 1898

Gilbert Edward Birkett Kennedy (1866–1921) was a well-known all-round athlete, born in Hampton Court, in the London borough of Richmond-upon-Thames (historically a part of Middlesex). As a member of Molesey Hockey Club, Kennedy played hockey on the ice for the Virginia Water Combo team against the Bury Fen team in 1891. He later captained the Thames Valley Club and in the mid-1890s played for the Virginia Water Club. He was one of the founders of the Bandy Association in 1891 and was part of the committee that drew up the first unified rules for the game.

The second paragraph of the book's article about "Skating—Bandy" is of much interest:

> Hockey on the ice is all very well in its proper place, and that place is where the area of the ice is considerable, giving room for everyone to indulge in his or her own particular kind of exercise, whether figure skating, hand-in-hand, or hockey. On such a piece of ice, where there is no difficulty in monopolizing a large piece for the game, hockey, or 'Bandy' as we shall henceforth call it, is one of the very best of games, both from a scientific and from an athletic point of view. Bandy, as perhaps everybody is not aware, is the name given to 'Hockey on the ice' (rather a mouthful) by the skaters of the Fen districts, who we may consider are the great enthusiasts at the game. The name has been definitely adopted by the metropolitan players. There is now in existence a 'Bandy Association', formed some seven years ago, with rules and regulations as to the size of sticks, balls, etc.[19]

So, while Kennedy (a Londoner) agrees with the Tebbutt brothers (Fenmen) that bandy and "hockey on the ice" are synonyms, he differs with them as to which term is the primary one, suggesting in particular that not everyone knows what bandy is. This establishes with further certainty that *bandy* was the primary term used in the Fens, while *hockey* was preferred by the Metropolitans.

Hockey Historical and Practical, 1899

This book examines the roots of hockey, including the ancient ones, in addition to the then-current form. Chapter 1, entitled "Early History," includes the following sentences:

Various names have been given to hockey in different parts of the British Isles, of which hurley, bandy, and shinty are the best known. Its Scotch designation is shinty, hurley its Irish, and bandy its Welsh.[20]

This is in reference to the version of the game played on the ground, but the synonyms are much the same as for ice hockey.

At this point, if the reader is not convinced that bandy and hockey were completely interchangeable terms, both for the ground and ice versions — with regional preferences for one term or the other — then it is hard to see what more could be done to persuade him or her, short of transporting a 19th-century bandy/hockey player into the present and getting him to testify under oath to this effect.

You probably saw this coming — we have that!

The Tichborne Trial, 1873

Sir Roger Charles Tichborne (1829-1854) was born in Paris and went to England in 1845. He began his studies at Stonyhurst College in July the same year; after three years, in October 1848, Roger left the College and proceeded to Dublin, where he joined the Dragoon Guards. Having resigned from this post, in 1853 he left for a tour of South America.

In April 1854, while Tichborne was headed to Jamaica from Rio de Janeiro, his ship was lost at sea with all hands, and he was pronounced dead the next year. On learning the news of her eldest son's passing, Sir Roger's mother refused to admit that he was dead. She sent inquiries all over the world, and promised rewards for help in finding her son. In November 1865, she received a letter from a lawyer in Sydney who claimed that a man supposedly fitting the description of her son was living as a butcher in Wagga Wagga, New South Wales, Australia.

The supposed Sir Roger was actually Arthur Orton (1834-1898), who at the time used the name Tom Castro. Aside from some facial resemblance to Tichborne, he did not fit the physical description at all and did not even speak French — Tichborne's mother tongue. However, Lady Tichborne was desperate enough to accept him as her son and sent him money to come to her.

After some reluctance, Orton was persuaded by "associates" (including an old friend of Tichborne's father) to travel to Britain. In January 1867, he travelled to the Paris hotel where Lady Tichborne was living, and the desperate lady "recognized" him instantly as her son. The fact that Orton did not understand a word of French did not bother her, and she gave him an allowance of £1,000 a year. Orton researched Sir Roger's life to reinforce his imposture. When Lady Tichborne died in March 1868, however, Orton lost his most prominent supporter. Other family members took him to court to establish his inheritance on May 11, 1871. The trial lasted 102 days and involved many aspects: the inability to speak French, tattoos, the testimony of Orton's former girlfriend and... bandy/hockey, which was Tichborne's favourite game, but was unknown to Orton.

The prosecutors called several witnesses who had played bandy and hockey at Stonyhurst between 1845 and 1848. The examination showed that hockey was played on the ice with thin sticks and a large cork bung or a small ball— bandy, on the other hand, was played on the ground with much larger sticks and a big ball of leather stuffed with hay (compare with the game of bandy played at Oscott College). Skates were never mentioned, and it is likely that the games on ice were played without skates.

Below are extracts from interrogations of the defendant and witnesses at the trial. Note that Stonyhurst College was founded in 1593, and is located in rural Lancashire.

On the 12th day of the trial, May 7, 1873, the prosecutor, Henry Hawkins, questioned the defendant.

> What games did you play?
> —*I played cricket.*
> What else?
> —*Sometimes we played hockey.*
> Where did you play that? In the cricket-field?
> —*No; a piece of ground off the cricket-field and forming part of the same green.*
> I suppose you played cricket in summer. When did you play hockey?
> —*I don't remember.*

Later the same day:

> Did you ever hear of "Bandy?"

—*Do you mean the nickname of a person?*
Never mind what I mean; I will tell you by-and-by. Did you ever hear of "bandy?"
—*Yes, I think I have.*
What is "bandy?"
—*The name is very familiar to me, but I don't know what it is.*
What does "bandy" mean?
—*To the best of my recollection, it strikes me part of Stonyhurst was called "bandy".*
Can you swear it?
—*No.*
Is it a dog or a cat, or a woman, or what is it?
—*I believe it is part of the building.*
Does "bandy" come with a Stonyhurst sort of flavour to you?
—*I have no recollection. I don't know what you mean by flavour.*
I beg your pardon. Does it come with Stonyhurst recollections?
—*Yes it does.*
What was there connected with "bandy?"
—*I don't know.*
Would it surprise you to learn that "bandy" was a game played with balls by the Philosophers at Stonyhurst, and in which ROGER CHARLES TICHBORNE was a great proficient?
—*I wasn't a proficient at it.*
Do you recollect anything about it?
—*My memory isn't correct enough to enable me to speak of it.*
Well, there is a difference between a game and a part of a building you know.

On the trial's 29th day, May 31, 1873, the prosecutor interrogated a witness, Sir John Lawson.

There was a game of bandy, I think?
—*That was played by the philosophers only.*
Was that a name always applied to that game?
—*Always.*
You say that was played by the philosophers?
—*Yes.*

Was that a game peculiar to Stonyhurst?

—*I never saw it anywhere else.*

How was that played?

—*There was the same object as football to drive the ball between two goals which were marked by upright posts, one on each side of the ground, and the players were divided into two parties, each trying to defend their own goal and force the ball through the goal of the opposite party. It was played with sticks with a crook at the end, not exactly at right angles, but very near it, and played with sticks entirely; we were not allowed to kick the ball.*

Like hockey?

—*We used to make the distinction of hockey on the ice, and bandy on the ground.*

The same thing otherwise? I do not know whether the same sticks were used?

—*Oh, no; much larger sticks were used for bandy than for hockey. We were used to play hockey with walking sticks with a round handle.*

And you had them made on purpose?

—*We used to cut them out of wood whenever we could find them.*

Different in form from hockey sticks?

—*Quite different in form from hockey sticks.*

And a different ball?

—*Hockey was played with a large cork bung, but the bandy-ball was a leather case stuffed with hay.*

So that at Stonyhurst there was a clear distinction between bandy and hockey?

—*Oh, yes.*

You have described bandy, where was bandy played?

—*When the philosophers were at St. Mary's Hall the bandy-ground formed part of the garden in front of the seminary—It was not quite in front, a little to the north-east; afterwards we used to play in the ground that is, the cricket-field.*

Hockey, as I understand you, was played on the ice?

—*On the ice.*

The same day, the prosecutor questioned a second witness, Walter Strickland Mannock.

Do you remember your games, what games had you there?
—*Bandy.*
That is a game we have heard described; I dare say you are aware how it was played?
—*With a crooked stick and a ball.*
What sort of a ball, and what size was it?
—*I suppose about as big as three oranges put together.*
How was the ball made? Did the students make it themselves?
—*I do not remember.*
Do you recollect whether hockey was played also?
—*That is the same thing.*
It is?
—*Yes.*
Are you sure?
—*Yes.*
Is it the same thing as hockey?
—*That is the impression I have always had, that hockey and bandy were the same.*
Is not hockey played with a bigger ball? [Asked by the Lord Chief Justice]
Was hockey played with the same sort of ball as bandy, or was it the same thing—knocking about—do you remember?
—*I took it to be the same.*

On the 30th day of the trial, June 4, the prosecutor interrogated a third witness, Robert Humphreys. His testimony was similar to that of the first witness, in that he considered bandy a summer game, played on the ground, and hockey a winter game, played on the ice.

On the 32nd day of the trial, June 6, a fourth witness, Lord Bellew, spoke about Tichborne's fondness for bandy, but was not asked about the difference between it and hockey.

On the 39th day, June 17, the defender, Hardinge Giffard, questioned Rev. Thomas Meyrick.

They had their games, I suppose...What would a Stonyhurst boy call it?
—*A Stonyhurst boy would, I have no doubt, call it "bandy."*

What do you think a boy who came to Stonyhurst scarcely able to speak English would call it, in candour?
— *Well, I think, as I called it hockey, and never could bring myself to call it bandy, a Hampshire man would have called it hockey.*[21]

So the final score is:

- Two witnesses indicated that "bandy" was the name for the game played on the ground, and "hockey" (unqualified) was used for the same game—though using a different stick and a different ball—played on the ice.
- One witness was certain they were the same: same game, same ball (he was not asked about the stick). He also said he was sure.
- One witness acknowledged that, while players at Stonyhurst would call the game (presumably the ground version) "bandy," he himself called it "hockey" and would expect someone from Hampshire (about 400 kilometres south of Lancashire) to also call it "hockey."

And this is the point we have been making: "bandy" and "hockey" were interchangeable terms, though some regions preferred one over the other, with each name being in some places used for the game played on the ground, and in other places being preferred to designate the game played on ice. Eventually the games became different, but it was a slow process. For example, the absence of a stick for the goalie only came about around the mid-1910s, when the innovative goalkeeper Gösta Berendt (1893–1970) of AIK Stockholm decided in 1913 to do away with his stick, feeling he could better catch the ball without one. Within a few years, all bandy goalkeepers in Scandinavia had followed his lead.[22]

Having established that the name *bandy* cannot be used as a valid reason to write off a game as not being hockey, let us provide some more examples of organized hockey, these ones going by the name "bandy."

Bluntisham-cum-Earith, Huntingdonshire (Cambridgeshire), 1870

This detailed game report appeared in the *Cambridge Independent Press* on Saturday, December 31, 1870:

Hockey Match at Earith

On Wednesday afternoon a very interesting match, at the fine old game of bandy or hockey, took place on Bury Fen, near Earith, between sixteen players from Over and Swavesey, and an equal number from Bluntisham and Earith.

The players on the Over side were selected by Mr. Charles Robinson, who had Mr. Neville Goodman, of Cambridge, by agreement, on his side, and the players on the opposite side by Mr. C. P. Tebbutt, of Bluntisham.

The prize was a cricket ball, and was won by the Bluntisham and Earith players, who kept up their long-standing reputation as excellent bandy players.

On the side of Over a great deal of spirit was shown in the game, and Mr. Goodman and a young player from Swavesey played very well. On the opposite side, Mr. Headley, of Earith, and Mr. Archer, of Bluntisham, played admirably, and we were glad to see a young player, son of Mr. Tebbutt, who also was also very useful to his side.

The most excellent and friendly feeling was shown by both sides, and the Over and Swavesey players have by no means given up the hope of bringing a stronger team on some other occasion for another friendly contest.[23]

The reporter takes no chance and calls the game "bandy or hockey," so as to be understood by all readers. The end of the report shows that here is clearly a rivalry between the two teams.

Colne, Huntingdonshire (Cambridgeshire), 1831

This is the oldest known contemporary report of an actual match between two identified teams, some 44 years before the first Montreal game! Skates are not mentioned, but we've seen from the history of bandy written by Arnold Tebbutt that, in the Fens, bandy designated a game played on ice, with skates.

From the *Huntingdon Bedford and Peterborough Gazette* of Saturday, February 5:

On Friday se'nnight [January 28] a bandy match was played off, between nine young men of Bluntisham, and nine of Colne, upon a fine field of

> On Friday se'nnight a bandy match was played off, between nine young men of Bluntisham, and nine of Colne, upon a fine field of Ice on Colne Fen. The gallant sons of Bluntisham were all confident of success, having ordered a large room at the White Horse Inn to be prepared for them on their return; as they intended to celebrated the expected triumph by a convivial evening. But lo! unfortunately they left not only the laurels behind them but their money also, proving themselves unable to compete with "*noodles*."

Ice on Colne Fen. The gallant sons of Bluntisham were all confident of success, having ordered a large room at the White Horse Inn to be prepared for them on their return; as they intended to celebrated [sic] the expected triumph by a convivial evening. But lo! unfortunately they left not only the laurels behind them but their money also, proving themselves unable to compete with "*noodles.*"[24]

The word *se'nnight* is a contraction for "seven nights," meaning a week. This was a game planned quite some time in advance, as a large room had been prepared for the celebration — though the team that expected to celebrate was handed a loss.

Old West River, Willingham, Cambridgeshire, c. 1827

This represents the oldest game to have been reported, though the report is not contemporary, as it appeared in the 1892 book *Skating,* whose chapter on bandy was written by Charles Goodman Tebbutt, as seen in chapter 7. Tebbutt is not certain of the exact year, but based on reports of the time, the winters that allowed skating would have almost certainly been 1826 or 1827.

Tebbutt writes the following about this game:

> The first particulars of a match come from Mr. Richard Brown [1803–1897], who umpired on the occasion. It was about 1827, and is typical of the class of matches then held.
>
> William Leeland [1804–1891] was captain. It was a match between Willingham and the Bury Fen players of Bluntisham-cum-Earith, and was fought out on a wash along the Old West River near Willingham.

The game was for a leg of mutton, which all afterwards enjoyed at the expense of the Willingham team at a neighbouring inn.

After play it was usual to have what was called a 'randy', when good healths were drunk, defeat and hard luck forgotten, and fresh matches arranged.

Until well into 1850 Leeland captained the Bury Fenners, and only died in the autumn of 1891, in his ninetieth year [87th]. An interview with this fine old player was made specially interesting by his pleasant memories of matches won at bandy. He delighted to the last in telling how they journeyed up the main river and defeated their most redoubtable foes, Swavesey and Over; how they skated along the Old West River and lowered the colours of Willingham and Cottenham; how, on the frozen expanse of washes between the Bedford rivers, they played for and enjoyed legs of mutton at the expense of Sutton and Mepal; and how, at various times, on their own fen, besides meeting all these teams, they beat Chatteris, Somersham, and St. Ives. The game old captain never forgot to add that they 'never was beat by any town and could do it with ease'.

The renowned team consisted of William Leeland (capt.), a boatwright and right-handed player; Phil Bedford, a lighter-man, 'that marvellous dribbler', whose only fault was, that he kept the ball too long, and who, with his light short one- handed bandy, threaded his way through all opposition, lifting up the big bandies of his opponents when in his way; Hodgson and John Jackson, sure goal-keepers—the latter's bandy, well past its jubilee, was used by his grandson, Murphy, in the game played last winter against Virginia Water; John Aubrey, a labourer, and second only to Phil; Bill Ayres, a famous skater, the fastest half-miler in the Fens; Bill Christmas, a bandy-legged man; John Rawling, the big man of the team; William and John Large, brothers, who emigrated to America; Jos. Edwards, who acquired a knack of getting the ball between his feet and carrying it along; Mr. R. Brown, and Mr. Jonas Tebbutt; Rob. Headley, Jas. Searle, and Thos. Mehew. Of these only Mr. R. Brown (88), Jas. Searle (75), and Bill Christmas (71), still live at the time of writing (Christmas, 1891).

Next to the Bury Fen players those of Swavesey were considered 'the most deadly'.

The 'cat' or 'kit' was generally a ball, but often a bung of cork or wood did service, sometimes a cricket ball, and more recently an indiarubber ball was used. The bandies were curved sticks often cut from the lower branches of the pollard willow-trees which abound in the Fens. The lower branches grow in a curve upwards until clear of the upper branches which surround the topped head of the tree, and thus are often naturally just the right shape for bandies.

A good bandy was eagerly looked after; once possessed it was carefully preserved, and became the pride of the owner. As it hung up in the cottage it recalled many an exciting game, and started many a fireside talk of how matches were lost and won; thus stimulating the young to become players. No one who has not talked to the superannuated players can realise how intense was the interest in bandy fifty years ago in Bluntisham-cum-Earith.

A generation later, when Leeland's playing days were over, we still find the game in full swing during those winters when frost made the Fen waters bear. The improvement in agriculture and drainage of land, and enclosure of open fields, had deprived some villages, like Cottenham, of their bandy ground, but whenever possible, Bury Fen, Swavesey, Over Chatteris, &c., played matches. Messrs. Charles Prentice Tebbutt [1824–1910], Neville Goodman [1831–1890], and William Loveday Meadows [1820–1910] captained the Bury Fen teams.[25]

The profiles and birthdates of most of these players are known and make it completely plausible that they could have participated in a bandy/hockey game in 1827, almost half a century before the first Montreal game.

Of interest is the existence of a name other than "ball," "puck" or "bung" to designate the object of the play; it was seemingly called "cat" or "kit" at some point.

Is "Hockey" Just Field Hockey, and Is "Hockey on the Ice" Not Ice Hockey?

We all know it: internationally, the short form "hockey" primarily means "field hockey." So much so that the International Olympic Committee only ever uses the term "hockey" to designate the game played in its Summer Games[26] (and "ice hockey" for the winter version),[27] even though there can be no doubt that the winter ice version gets a few orders of magnitude more TV revenue than the summer grass version does, and thus might feel that *it* should have first dibs on the non-qualified term.

But in the 19th century, would a typical English person have always meant "field hockey" when saying just "hockey"? Is it all right to dismiss all references of "hockey" as being field hockey (possibly on ice, but definitely without skates) because this is what the term currently means? Obviously not. We have already covered numerous examples in the previous chapters:

- The Croxby Pond references from 1838 both only use *hockey.*
- The Bowood reference from 1859 writes just *hockey.*
- The Aspatria references from 1861–1865 always only use *hockey.*
- The royal Virginia Water reference from January 1864 uses the term *hockey* three times, none of them qualified with the prefix *ice* prefix or the "on the ice" suffix, even though the illustration attests that it was on ice and with skates.
- Not previously mentioned, the *Ipswich Journal* of Saturday, February 19, 1870, saw the bright side of recent frosts: "The late severe frosts have given the skaters such an opportunity for their pastime as they have not enjoyed for several years. The fish pond has been attended by a large number; the ice being in very good condition has afforded excellent sport in the game of hockey. No accident of any serious nature has occurred."[28]
- The 1871 Elsham reference from the *Stamford Mercury* uses "hockey on the ice," but the ones from the *Bell's Life in London, and Sporting Chronicle* and the *Hull Packet and East Riding Times* are content with *hockey.*
- Also from 1871, the Bluntisham-cum-Earith game announcement and report both only use *hockey.*
- And still that same year, the game in Moor Park described the activity as "hockey."

We've seen, from the Tichmore Trial in particular, that words tended to have regional meanings, but even that is not entirely clear, as it is likely that the word used in one region, or even just one village, evolved through contacts with the outside. It does not seem an achievable goal to try to draw a map of England showing the name given to each activity per region.

In the same way, the term *hockey* itself is used with different variations. Should we consider "hockey on the ice" as different from "ice hockey"?

There seems to be no basis for believing that various terms were intended to carry different meanings; it just took some time for a consensus to emerge, just as hockey was, on occasion, spelled "hocky" or bandy spelled "bendy," both examples having been seen earlier in this chapter.

"Hockey"

As shown above, the simple term *hockey* often meant the game played on the ice with skates. It may no longer be the case in England, but a hundred years ago and more, it clearly was.

"Hockey on the Ice"

This was the first attempt to describe the game of hockey played on ice. The term does not imply the use of skates, but more often than not, they were used, as in these examples.

From the *Preston Chronicle* of Saturday, January 19, 1850:

> JUVENILE DISASTER — TRUANTS IN TROUBLE
> On Tuesday, near Shields, a 'parcel of lads' were playing at hockey on the ice. Three of them came skating up to each other; and just as another hit was joyously proclaimed, the ice went 'c-r-c-k, cr-ack, crack'. The next moment the trio were over head and ears in the pond.[29]

Two of the "truants" nearly drowned but managed to escape alive. From the 1919 book *Memories of an Old Etonian, 1860–1912:*

> In winter, if we happened to have a frost hard enough to make Virginia Water safe for skaters, we used to be taken there by Mr. James to skate and play hockey on the ice, a game in which my tutor always took part himself.[30]

It is not known if the author intended to use the terminology familiar to him at the time of writing the book, or the one used when he was playing the game (1866–1870), but either way, the example shows that "hockey on the ice" was commonly played with skates.

The term has even been used in Canada, if not often. *The Gazette*'s report of the game played in Montreal on Saturday, February 5, 1876, had the headline HOCKEY ON THE ICE, and started with the words "A game of hockey was played on the ice at the Victoria Skating Rink . . ."[31] So not only could "hockey on the ice" be used in Montreal, it would even seem that the unqualified term *hockey* itself might have possibly been ambiguous as to the type of surface on which it was played. The next year, the report of the February 26, 1877, game appeared in *The Gazette* under the title HOCKEY ON ICE,[32] a very slight variant of the same name.

"Ice Hockey"

This is the current, internationally agreed-upon term for the sport played on ice with skates. It was rarely used in England prior to hockey taking hold in Montreal, but there are some instances, as in the following quote from the 1869 book *A System of Figure-Skating, Being the Theory and Practice of the Art as Developed in England, with a Glance at Its Origin and History,* by Henry Eugene Vandervell and Thomas Maxwell Witham.

> It is a rapid rotary pirouette, not very graceful, but showing the great powers of a strong skater. The body from the hips is leaned forward, and the balancing leg off the ice raised almost horizontally, the hurley (ice hockey) stick often tucked under the arm—sometimes as many as ten or a dozen or more revolutions being turned.[33]

The Vandervell-Witham "ice hockey" reference is the earliest contemporary use of the term "ice hockey" that the authors have come across so far.

"Bung and Hockey"

Rarely used, this term did appear in *Jackson's Oxford Journal* on Saturday, February 18, 1860, to describe a game in which the Prince of Wales (Albert Edward) participated:

> On the following afternoon [February 15] the Prince again skated for some hours on Long Meadow, and appeared much to enjoy the game of 'bung and hockey', entering as he did into competition with all engaged in the same pursuit, and delighting every one with his affability.[34]

The term even made its way into Joseph Wright's *English Dialect Dictionary* (Volume VI, 1905):

BUNG-AND-HOCKEY, *sb.* Oxf. A game of hockey played with a 'bung'
instead of a ball. (G. O.)[35]

So, according to the entry, this peculiar designation for the game played
with a bung was used in the county of Oxfordshire, as attested by "correspondent" George Ostler.

"Skating Hockey"

If we were to start from scratch, maybe *this* is the term that should have
been adopted from the beginning, seeing that it is fully unambiguous (assuming everyone agrees that "skates" have blades, while the type with wheels
is always called "roller skates"). The good people from Bluntisham and
Earith must have made that very reflection as they named their club
"Bluntisham and Earith Skating Hockey Club," as seen in chapter 7, but
the name never really caught on.

In the end, the authors could not find any pattern as to some names designating a different method of playing the game than other names, save for
the fact that "bung and hockey" was of course always played with a bung.
We know that the National Skating Association had two sets of rules, one
for the Fens, where the players tended to call the game "bandy," and one
for the Metropolitan District, where the players tended to call the game
"hockey," but the NSA itself, in its publication of the rules, does not make
that distinction, so it would appear foolhardy to try and make it now, over
130 years later.

Chapter 8 Notes

1. J. W. (Bill) Fitsell, *How Hockey Happened* (Kingston, Ont.: Quarry
    Press, 2006): 52.
2. John Trotter Brockett, *A Glossary of North Country Words, in Use*
    (Newcastle upon Tyne: Emerson Charnley, 1829): 72, 99, 156, 266.
3. N. W. (signature), "The Ice," *The New Sporting Magazine* XIV, no.
    83 (March 1838): 153–156.
4. "Holyrood Gymnastic Club and Wolfhounds," *Edinburgh Old Town
    Association Newsletter,* April 2012: 3.
5. Henry D. Richardson, *Holiday Sports and Pastimes for Boys* (London:

William Somerville Orr & Co., 1848): iv.
6.   Ads appeared in *The Daily News* (London), 24 Nov. 1847; *Manchester Courier and Lancashire General Advertiser,* 8 Dec. 1847; *Liverpool Mercury,* 10 Dec. 1847, and Leeds Intelligencer, 11 Dec. 1847.
7.   Richardson, 62–63.
8.   John Moyer Heathcote, Charles Goodman Tebbutt and Thomas Maxwell Witham, *Skating* (London: Longmans, Green & Co., 1892): 429.
9.   Ibid., 435.
10. Ibid., 436.
11. Sydney Charles King-Farlow, "Bandy, or Ice Hockey" in *Ice-Sports* (London: Ward, Lock & Co., 1901): 199–231.
12. *The Field* (London), 17 Apr. 1897.
13. The little-known rules of "The Rink Hockey Association":

Rules of the Rink Hockey Association
Formulated at the founding meeting of the Association on March 26, 1897;

1.   A hockey skating team shall consist of five or six players.
2.   The hockey stick shall be of wood, not to exceed in width in any part, nor more than 4 feet long, as measured along the handle and round the curve, and shall have no metal fittings or sharp edges.
3.   Players must in all matches wear the colours of their club.
4.   The putt shall be of rubber. In roller hockey the game shall be played with a composite ball.
5.   The goal shall consist of cages, the height of which shall be 3 feet, the depth 3 feet, the width 5 feet, for ice rinks, and 4 feet for roller rinks. They shall consist of wooden frames clamped together at the joints, and the backs and sides shall be covered by hemp netting.
6.   The choice of goals shall be tossed for at the beginning of a game by the captains of the competing teams, and at half time only shall the teams change ends. The time of the match shall be thirty minutes, exclusive of three minutes interval, which shall be allowed after fifteen minutes play.

7. The game shall be started by the centre forwards of each team bullying the putt or ball in the centre of the rink, and after each goal and after half time—The bully shall be played as follows: Each player is to strike the ground on his side of the putt or ball and his opponent's stick three times over the ball alternately, after which either of the two players only shall be at liberty to strike the putt or ball.

8. An umpire and two goal judges shall be appointed, each captain appointing a goal judge, who shall stand immediately behind the cage, one to each goal. The decision of goal judges may be referred to the umpire, but his decision is on all occasions final.

9. A goal is scored when the putt or ball has passed within the mouth of the cage.

10. When playing the putt or ball the player shall not raise his hockey stick above the elbow during any part of the stroke.

11. The putt or ball may be stopped with any part of the body or hockey stick, but not with the hand, except in the case of the goal keeper, nor must it be picked up, carried, kicked, thrown, knocked on except with the hockey stick. No charging, kicking, collaring, shinning, tripping, or throwing the hockey stick, or rough play shall be allowed. Fencing or hooking the sticks under no circumstances shall be allowed.

12. On the occasion of a free hit no member of the offending team shall be within three yards of the spot where such a hit is made, but he shall not be compelled to go behind his own goal line. A goal cannot be scored from a free hit unless the putt or ball is first touched or hit by another player.

13. On the occasion of a free hit, or when the putt or ball is hit off from the goal line or from the touch sides of the rink, the striker shall not touch the ball again until it has been touched or hit by another player.

14. No player shall be allowed to touch the putt or ball, or interfere in any way with the players while either one, or both, of his skates are off, or if his stick is not in his hand.

15. The goal keeper shall be allowed to stop the putt or ball with any part of his person. He may kick, hit, or catch it, but in

the event of his catching the putt he shall not be allowed to throw it out or carry it, but must immediately drop the putt and either kick or hit it into play. Should the goal keeper retain the putt or ball longer than five seconds in his hand, then his opponents may claim a penalty bully, from which a goal may be scored direct.

16. When the putt or ball has passed into touch it shall be immediately struck or hit in from where it left the surface in any direction, by one of the opposite team to that of the player who last touched it. No other player shall approach within three yards of it.

17. The penalty for a breach of any of these rules shall be a free hit by one of the opposite team from the spot where the rule is broken.

18. In the event of any appeal for any supposed infringement of the rules, the ball or putt shall remain in play until decision has been given.

19. The umpire shall have power to stop the game at such times as he may think fit whenever he may deem it necessary to do so, and he shall deduct any time which he considers has been wasted, either owing to an accident or other causes. In the event of a temporary suspension of play from any cause, the putt or all not having gone into touch or behind the goal line, the game shall be re-started by a bully at the spot where play was suspended.

20. "Touch" is outside the boundary of the field of play.

14. Arnold Tebbutt, *A Handbook of Bandy; or, Hockey on the Ice* (London: Horace Cox, 1896): 1.

15. Arnold Tebbutt, "Bandy, or Hockey on the Ice," *The Encyclopaedia of Sport,* vol. 1 (London: Lawrence and Bullen, 1897): 71.

16. Ibid.

17. Ibid.

18. Charles Goodman Tebbutt, Archibald Read and Arnold Tebbutt, *Skating* (London: George Routledge and Sons, 1897): 129.

19. Gilbert Edward Birkett Kennedy, "Skating—Bandy," in *The "House"*

on Sport, by Members of the London Stock Exchange (London: Gale & Polden, 1898): 350.

20. J. Nicholson Smith and Philip A. Robson, *Hockey Historical and Practical* (London: A.D. Innes & Co., 1899): 1.

21. Edward Vaughan Hyde Kenealy, ed., *The Trial at Bar of Sir Roger C. D. Tichborne, Bart., in the Court of Queen's Bench at Westminster, before Lord Chief Justice Cockburn, Mr. Justice Mellor, and Mr. Justice Lush, for Perjury* (London: "Englishman" Office, 1876): vol. I: 80–390 and vol. II: 141.

22. Eric Sköld, ed., *Boken om Bandy*, vol. I (Uppsala, Sweden: Bygd och Folk Förlag, 1948): 235.

23. *Cambridge Independent Press*, 31 Dec. 1870.

24 *Huntingdon Bedford and Peterborough Gazette*, 5 Feb. 1831.

25. Heathcote, Tebbutt and Witham, 431–433.

26. "Hockey," Olympic.org: Official Website of the Olympic Movement, n.d., web, 3 Apr. 2014, <http://www.olympic.org/hockey>.

27. "Ice Hockey," Olympic.org: Official Website of the Olympic Movement, n.d., web, 3 Apr. 2014, <http://www.olympic.org/ice-hockey>.

28. *Ipswich Journal*, 19 Feb. 1870.

29. *Preston Chronicle*, 19 Jan. 1850.

30. George Greville Moore, *Memories of an Old Etonian, 1860–1912* (London: Hutchinson & Co., 1919): 85–86.

31. *The Gazette* (Montreal), 7 Feb. 1876.

32. *The Gazette* (Montreal), 27 Feb. 1877.

33. Henry Eugene Vandervell and Thomas Maxwell Witham, *A System of Figure-Skating: Being the Theory and Practice of the Art as Developed in England, with a Glance at Its Origin and History* (London: MacMillan and Co., 1869): 258-259. The passage referenced was itself quoted from the *Field* of January 18, 1868, and the mention of "ice hockey," in parentheses, was almost certainly added by the authors Vandervell and Witham for clarity to their readers, as many other terms from the *Field*'s quote were "translated" in the same way.

34. *Jackson's Oxford Journal*, 18 Feb. 1860.

35. Joseph Wright, *The English Dialect Dictionary: Being the Complete Vocabulary of All Dialect Words Still in Use, or Known to Have Been in Use During the Last Two Hundred Years*, vol. VI supplement,

(Oxford, U. K.: Henry Frowde, 1905): 52. The initials G. O. stand for George Ostler (1863–1929), the contributor to this reference. Ostler was a printer/compositor at Oxford University Press, who later compiled *The Little Oxford Dictionary,* published in 1929.

CHAPTER 9

Any Way You Look at It

As much as the authors would like to think they are very persuasive, they also know that the idea of ice hockey being played in England for decades before making its way (permanently) to Canada could be greeted with a certain amount of disbelief. If it were true, after all, surely a lot of people would have known about it already.

In a way, they did, and for those who have ever heard the expression "stick and ball games," this is what those English hockey games have often been passed off as, with the implication that a "stick and ball game" is never hockey—not even, somewhat amazingly, when it is *called* hockey. Chapter 3 showed that those games passed the six-point definition test. Chapter 4 showed that they also passed the test of what the Society for International Hockey Research Origins Committee report identified as unique to the first Montreal game. Chapter 5 showed that, in fact, some game reports (from England) were every bit as detailed as those for that first Montreal game. Chapter 6 showed that the distinction between "real, modern" hockey and 19th-century English hockey could not be linked to whether they were played indoors or outdoors. Chapter 7 showed that, before there were rules in Montreal, there were also rules in England, and provided a reminder that the first Montreal rules were a barely amended version of English rules, albeit rules for field hockey.

But there could still have been some fundamental differences between the type of hockey (sometimes called bandy or even other names) played in England, and the type played in Montreal—and eventually all over Canada.

We have tried to think of all possible singularities that would make the first Montreal game, and the subsequent ones, clearly distinct from all previous games played in England.

Montreal's Games Were Played by Adults

Indeed, the first Montreal game, and the subsequent ones that were reported in the press, were played by adults—typically young ones—whereas books in England describing hockey had names like *A History of the Juvenile Sports, Every Boy's Magazine, The Boy's Handy Book of Sports, The Boy's Own Book,* and so forth.

Yet there is a critical mass of evidence that the game in England was played by adults as well. Several such examples have already been shown—in particular, involving royalty (the Prince was not only married, but his wife was only hours from giving birth!), but also including all games where the names of the participants or, as a minimum, of the captains were provided.

Incidentally, for aficionados of the monarchy, here is one more report, from the *Derby Mercury* (Derbyshire) of Wednesday, February 17, 1864:

> COURT AND OFFICIAL
>
> On Wednesday the Princess of Wales drove in a closed carriage to the Balaklava Pond, in the Home Park, to see the Prince and a number of gentlemen skate, several of whom, with the Prince, were let into the water, about knee-deep, in consequence of the thinness of the ice. This, however, did not prevent their game of hockey, which was continued with much spirit till rather a late hour in the afternoon.[1]

And for anyone who believes that the grown men who participated in hockey games might have been boys in men's bodies or that, even when practised by adults, hockey was still not a manly activity, here is a rebuttal, courtesy of *Jackson's Oxford Journal* on January 19, 1861:

> FARINGDON
>
> EIGHTH BERKS RIFLES —
>
> Our Rifle Corps assembled for drill on Thursday last, being the first time since the Christmas holidays, when, after being inspected by the Commanding Officer (D. Bennett, Esq.), and about half an hour's drill, the

greater part of the members adjourned, skates in hand, to the fish pond in the park, where a very spirited game at hockey was joined in by all present. Drill takes place every Monday, Wednesday, and Friday evenings at eight o'clock, and on Thursdays at four o'clock.[2]

The Puck!

We all know it. Prior to the first Montreal game, the announcement in *The Gazette* reassured those considering attending the novelty being offered that "Some fears have been expressed on the part of intending spectators that accidents were likely to occur through the ball flying about in too lively a manner, to the imminent danger of lookers on, but we understand that the game will be played with a flat circular piece of wood, thus preventing all danger of its leaving the surface of the ice."[3]

So the flat, circular piece of wood, for (temporary) lack of a catchier name, was invented right there and then on the spot. It would go on to be christened "puck" (nobody really knows why, though one possible explanation is from the Irish verb *to puck,* meaning "to hit")[4] in the report on the third Montreal game[5] (the first of the second season, played February 5, 1876) and, as legend has it, forever replace the utterly spherical ball that had been used until then for all hockey games ever played anywhere.

(Left) The bung described (and shown) in an 1862 issue of Every Boy's Magazine,[7] *as seen in chapter 7. (Right) The bung used for the hockey game on the Thames at Richmond in 1855, as shown in* The Illustrated London News[8] — *the full illustration is seen in chapter 5.*

(Left) A detail of "Skaiting Dandies, Shewing Off," a print made c. 1818 by Charles Williams.[9] The bung is not particularly visible, but the description by the British Museum leaves no doubt: "Men in the distance skate with ease; some play hockey with sticks and a cork." (Right) A detail of the bung.

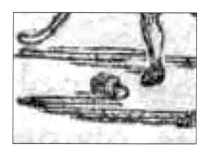

Of course, this is not a particularly accurate description of how hockey had been played. Unless the reader has skipped the majority of chapters to this point, he or she will have noticed many references to a "bung," which is a type of cork used to plug barrels. One benefit of using such an implement—besides the fact that they was easily obtained, seeing how much beer was consumed in those days (more than water, we are told),[6] is that these objects were relatively light, and the pain inflicted when one struck a player was considerably less than that caused by a wooden ball, for example. You will have seen some of these already, but on the following pages is a collection of illustrations of puck-shaped bungs mentioned in references to hockey played in England, prior to the first Montreal game—note that some of them were described for use in field hockey.

Maybe the Stick?

We know what a hockey stick looks like: a shaft and a blade, though in the old days a stick came from a single piece of wood. Sticks in England, where hockey on the ice derived from field hockey, had to look more like a shepherd's crook, no? After all, that is—reportedly—how hockey gets its name.

Nice try. In his 1911 letter to the editor of the *Eton College Chronicle*, Rev. Alfred Guy Kingan L'Estrange (1832-1915) remembered hockey sticks from his time at the school (1846-1851): "The blades of the sticks we used

---

(Opposite page, top left) This bung appears in an illustration in the 1805 Book of Games *(the full illustration is in chapter 7). It is used to play on the ground.*[10]

(Bottom left) Before the game took to the ice, bungs were used in field hockey, as illustrated in Richard Johnson's Juvenile Sports and Pastimes, *published in 1773 (the full illustration was shown in chapter 3). The drawing does not show the bung very clearly, but the author's description is unambiguous: "The kockey must be made of the largest cork-bung you can get. Cut the edges round, and then it is prepared for use."*[12]

(Right) This bung (seen in a detail from this book's cover picture) appeared in an engraving published by Joseph Le Petit Jr. in 1797—which was 78 years before the first Montreal game![11]

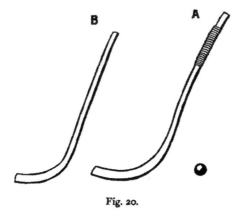

Fig. 20.

The two models of hockey sticks recommended by the NSA in 1882.

were not curved, but lay straight on the ground at right angles to the handle, and were about a foot long."[13]

The concept of a hockey stick whose blade lies flat on the ground, rather than being curved, seems quite revolutionary for the early 1850s. Granted, L'Estrange was describing field hockey. Was anyone playing ice hockey with field hockey sticks at the time? Surely some people were, if one is to believe the description of *The Boy's Own Book* (from the 1849 edition and all subsequent versions):

> It is an amusement for all seasons, — in the summer on the turf, in the winter on the ice.
>
> Sides are to be chosen by the two best players, selected alternately. Every player must be provided with a good strong tough stick, hooked or turned up at the end in an oblique angle, so that when held by one or both hands in a slanting position, the end lies flat on the ground. A cork bung is usually the object of contention.[14]

So this also answers the question of whether the sticks were held with one or both hands. Seemingly both were done.

 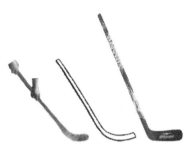

(Left) The stick used by the first McGill University team, in 1881.[16]
(Right) Comparing them side by side (after inversion so they all point the same way), one sees that, in fact, the blade angle and length of the NSA stick look quite a bit more like a modern hockey stick than the McGill one does!

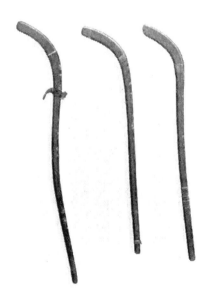

The stick on the left was used at the beginning of the 19th century by John Jackson (1798–1872), of Earith, and was later owned and used by his grandson Thomas Murphy (1857–1925). For more details, see the section on goalkeepers beginning on page 173. The middle stick was a willow bandy stick used by C.G. Tebbutt in 1875, while the stick on the right was, in 1905, a regulation ash bandy stick.[17]

In 1882, the chapter about "The Game of Hockey" in the *Handbook of Fen Skating* (discussed in chapter 7), featured an illustration of two different models of hockey sticks (seen again on page 171) with the following description:

> In default of obtaining such a one as we have described an ordinary strong walking stick may be played with, but it will be at a great disadvantage, when used against other bandies of the more suitable shape. A stick such as is shown in Fig. 20 A, may to the uninitiated, appear a dangerous weapon, but in practice it is not so, for in the hand of a skilful player, it is used for carrying on the ball by shoving and guiding, and only occasionally is it used for hard knocking. It is needless to fix any limit to its length or thickness, because excess in either of these respects, is a disadvantage to the player himself. Older and less active players will prefer the bandy of the full length of about 39 inch, as is shown in the picture A, which would weigh about one lb.; but a younger and more active player bends down closer to his work, and would thus find the extra length interfere with the movement of his limbs, he would therefore cut it about 3 inches shorter at each end, and as he is continually changing it from hand to hand as occasion requires, he often prefers it of a less crooked form as shown at (B.), the weight would thus be reduced to little more than three-quarters of a pound.[15]

So in fact, the model that resembles most the current ice hockey stick (model B, on the left) is recommended for "younger and more active players" (read, the better ones). Compare it with the sticks used by the first McGill University team in 1881.

Goalkeepers

No goalkeepers were mentioned in the first Montreal game, but it did not take long. The next reported game, played just two weeks later (March 16, 1875) did mention that "Mr. Henshaw" was "a most wary and valuable goal keeper."[18] There is probably a good chance that the first game also featured netminders. But what about England?

We have mentioned Sir John Dugdale Astley ("the sporting baronet") in chapter 4, as well as his 1894 book on his "life in the world of sport." In it, he remembers a very special game from December of 1853:

The Prince Consort—who was a beautiful and graceful figure-skater—
kept goal for the opposite side, and Lord Listowel (father of the present
Earl) kept ours. I don't think that I ever enjoyed a game more, and it
was that day I first had the honour of making the acquaintance of the
Prince of Wales.[19]

Of course, Montreal has the upper hand on this one, as it had a "Roy"
(French for "king") as its goalkeeper for several seasons, while the Windsor
team had to settle for a Prince Consort.

In chapter 7, we discussed the 1892 *Skating* book and its chapter on
bandy by C. G. Tebbutt. In it, he describes a game played c. 1827 and lists
every player involved, including a mini-biography of each:

> Hodgson and John Jackson, sure goal-keepers—the latter's bandy, well
> past its jubilee, was used by his grandson, Murphy, in the game played
> last winter against Virginia Water; . . .[20]

"Hodgson" was Frederick Aemilus Hodgson (1790–1858), a goalkeeper
who was in the shadow of the more famous John Jackson (1798–1872), a
legendarily "sure" goalkeeper from Earith.[21] As noted previously, his stick,
used in the early 1800s, was also later used—well past its jubilee—by his
grandson, Thomas Murphy (1857–1925) in a game played by Bury Fen in
1891 against Virginia Water.[22] This bandy stick is probably the oldest known
stick associated with a specific player, having been used at least as far back
as the late 1820s.

Small Goals

We have seen in previous chapters that the playing surface in England was
often considerably larger than typical ice rinks of today—or than the Victoria
Skating Rink of 1875, for that matter. It perhaps followed that the goals
themselves were also considerably larger than the now-standard six feet wide
and four feet high. The NSA rules stipulated a width of 15 feet for hockey
"as played in the Fens"[23] and 10 feet for the variety "as played in the Metropolitan District."[24]

Michel Vigneault, in his article "Out of the Mists of Memory," which
appeared in the first edition of *Total Hockey*, writes, "Also, the game introduces goals like lacrosse (two sticks in the ice, eight feet apart and six feet

tall)."[25] In chapter 4, we observed that there may be some ambiguity as to whether *The Gazette*'s article really meant that the figure (eight feet) represented the distance between the goal posts at the game, or simply stated that it was the usual distance, and that the goals used in the game appeared to be similar.

So it may be that what distinguishes the Montreal game from all its English predecessors is the presence of small goals.

But, in fact, that is not the case.

In chapter 8, we encountered Henry D. Richardson's 1848 book *Holiday Sports and Pastimes for Boys.* It describes in sufficient detail how the goals should be set up:

> The game is as follows:—two long and upright poles are stuck into the ground in a conspicuous part of the field, and about two hundred yards from them, and as nearly opposite to them as possible, two other sticks are planted; each pair of posts are about six feet apart.[26]

So here we have exactly the NHL width, though no height is specified. For that, we turn to *Every Boy's Magazine,* with its 1862 article on hockey by John George Wood:

> The same goals indeed will answer as for that game, only the cross pole should be lashed to the uprights at a much lower elevation, say three feet six inches or four feet from the ground, and the uprights should be within six feet of each other. Very good and simple goals can be made by taking long osiers, willow branches or brambles, pointing the two ends, bending them over and sticking the pointed extremities into the earth, so as to make an arch.[27]

And now we have exactly the NHL dimensions, both in width and height. And we even have the crossbar, whose appearance in Canada will be simultaneous with the arrival of the goal net—sometime between about 1897 and 1900,[28] depending on the league.

For those who consider that "bent over willow branches or brambles" barely qualify as crossbars, we offer perhaps something more acceptable, from an 1868 issue of a magazine called *The Popular Educator* edited by Francis Chilton Young (1827–1898).

The players are divided into two parties, each of which has its *goal,* the goals being fixed towards either end of a tolerably spacious ground. They consist, as at Football, of two upright posts, about six feet apart, but the cross-pole is almost invariably employed at Hockey, and is usually placed at a height of about four feet from the ground. Through these goals the ball has to be driven; and the space through which it has to pass at either end, before the game is won, is therefore a space of about six feet by four.[29]

Granted, all three examples provided above refer to field hockey, not ice hockey, but we have seen previously that the two were commonly played with exactly the same rules, except in some cases for the stick and the ball/bung. If the goal was defined as above for field hockey, then it is unlikely it was given a different design for playing on the ice.

Referees or Umpires

Referees (or, rather, umpires) were first mentioned in Montreal in *The Gazette*'s report of the third known game played at the Victoria Skating Rink, which took place on February 5, 1876: "The game was conducted under the 'Hockey Association' rules, Messrs. W. Hutton, President of the Rink, and Philip Cross acting as umpires."[30]

Thus, from very early on, the Montreal game made use of umpires. Would that confer to the Montreal games an aura of respectability missing from the English games? Not according to George Frederick Pardon (1824–1884), journalist and compiler of books on games. His 1858 *Games for All Seasons* contained an entry about hockey:

THIS capital game is not unlike Golf, only instead of a ball it is usually played with a bung. Two or more persons may play at it, and the object of the game is to drive the hockey over a bound set on either side.

It is a good game to play on the ice; and, with a good ash or oak stick, hooked at the end, much amusement may be found in striking the ball whenever it comes in your way.

As soon as the sides are arranged, and the goals fixed, chances are taken for the first stroke, and the umpire calls Play! The first player strikes the bung forcibly with his stick, and it is then the business of his antagonists to strike it back again as soon as it reaches the ground.

This alternate striking the hockey forward and backwards is the whole art of the game, and the side that succeeds in forcing it over the boundary, wins. Hockey, Golf, and Mall, have all family likeness.³¹

We presume that calling "Play!" was not the umpire's only duty and that he was also charged with regulating the game to some extent.

We also have the description of the bandy game in the Fens in 1826 or 1827, which appeared in the 1892 book *Skating*. The account provided the identity of the game's umpire:

> The first particulars of a match come from Mr. Richard Brown [1803–1897], who umpired on the occasion. It was about 1827, and is typical of the class of matches then held.³²

According to this passage, it was in fact Mr. Brown himself who provided the information that Tebbutt used for the description of the game.

The Faceoff
In Canada, the faceoff (at first called the "bully") was not defined before its appearance in the Ontario Hockey Association rules of 1891, in which it is known as the "face," and was defined exactly as in *Games for All Seasons*.³³ How bullies were conducted in Montreal's early hockey days is thus not known, but Iain Fyffe suggests it might have been in the old field hockey style, with players tapping their sticks before going for the puck. That method even appeared in the first ice hockey cartoon, Disney's 1939 *The Hockey Champ*, featuring Donald Duck.³⁴ Field hockey abandoned, for most purposes, that method in 1981.³⁵ The current method for ice hockey was "invented" by Fred Waghorne in 1904.³⁶

But that method had been used in England for a long time, at least in some circles, as the Aspatria 1865 reference introduced in chapter 3 describes: "About two o'clock sides are generally chosen, and the ball is thrown down for a game of 'hockey.'"³⁷ The 1829 *Glossary of North Country Words, in Use,* mentioned in chapter 8, explains: "A piece of globular wood, called an *orr* or *coit,* is thrown down in the middle of the field, . . ."³⁸

Throwing the ball "up" was also used, and so was the stick-tapping method, to be sure. But in England, Mr. Waghorne would not have been able to patent his "invention," as it was already in the public domain, so to speak.

Thanks to the *Glossary*, Bobby Orr should be thrilled to learn that his name was once used to designate the object of play in hockey.

Having covered most aspects of what defines hockey, the authors expanded their horizons and found probably unexpected aspects of 19th-century English hockey that resembled current North American ice hockey.

Exporting the Game

Canada exported its game in more ways than one, something we will address in greater detail in chapter 13. In addition to postseason tours[39] involving exhibition games in Europe in 1938 and 1959[40] and preseason games in the 1980s and 1990s,[40] the NHL since 2007 has often started its regular season overseas, showing the rest of the planet what the "best hockey league in the world" is all about. But ice hockey had been exported before, long before.

Tehran, Persia (Iran), 1865

At the beginning of 1866, an unnamed correspondent for the *Levant Herald*—the first English-language newspaper published in Istanbul, Turkey—wrote a letter to his newspaper from Tehran, describing the events in the Persian capital during the Christmas holidays of 1865. The letter was eventually published in two English newspapers, the *Daily News* (March 5) and the *Leeds Mercury* (March 6).

The letter mentions a "hard frost" that had set in on the morning of Christmas Day, so that "the ice upon the reservoirs outside the town was in capital condition for skating." The letter later describes how "Mr. Alison" (Charles W. B. Alison [1811–1872], the British minister in Tehran between 1860 and 1872, "host" of the British colony and the foreign missions at the "Kasr Kajar") was treating its (British) guests particularly well. The letter then continues to discuss the skating:

> After breakfast skating was the order of the day, and the magnificent reservoir in the palace garden—of which the room where we breakfasted commanded a fine view—was well adapted for the purpose.
>
> The British Minister was foremost in the field, and several other Englishmen followed his example. Amongst the foreigners, the members of the Turkish mission were by far the most enterprising; they showed an amount of pluck which excited general admiration, and acquitted

themselves with great credit, considering that they had never before adventured on skates. Intelligence of this sport soon reached the Shah, whose son-in-law, indeed, as well as the son of the Turkish minister, had distinguished themselves in it, and having learned that two English engineers, the Messrs. Stantley, were accomplished skaters, next only to the minister himself, they were summoned to the Royal presence.

There on the ice they astonished the wondering eyes of Nasr-Eddeen [the Shah] with astounding evolutions, and the 'Pole of the Universe' was convulsed with merriment during the whole hour. The 'Ice-devils' were then dismissed with honour, and twelve pairs of the wonderful 'iron wings' were ordered on the spot. His Majesty's Ministers are said to be in great trepidation lest they should be called upon to emulate those achievements for the delectation of the King of Kings. Several of them, indeed, already complain of chronic rheumatism.

We are now looking forward to a grand hockey match on the ice next week, at which Mr. Alison has promised to preside.[41]

Whether the "grand match" did take place, we cannot say.

Ningbo [Ningpo], Zhejiang Province, China, 1862
Yes, China!

Arthur Evans Moule (1836–1918) was an English missionary who arrived in China in 1861, where he served continuously until 1896. The Taiping Rebellion was a massive civil war in southern China from 1850 to 1864, against the ruling Manchu-led Qing Dynasty. From December 1861 until May 1862, the Taiping rebels controlled the city of Ningpo, located south of Shanghai.

Based on his own journal, Moule described, in *Half a Century in China: Recollections and Observations,* published in 1911, the life of the British contingent stationed close to the city during that winter:

> The weather was intensely cold, the thermometer standing at only thirteen degrees above zero in my room, with a fire burning all night.
>
> The severity of the weather kept the T'aip'ings quiet for a time, but they observed the 20th of January, Hung Siu-ts'iian's birthday, with great noise and display.

The weather could not numb English energy, for we played hockey on the ice which covered the broad moat near the north gate.[42]

Whether the local population witnessed the game appears doubtful. England and China would eventually meet for the first time in an ice hockey game in 1973, at the 1973 World Championship Group C. On March 17 in Rotterdam, the Chinese team walloped the particularly weak British representatives by a score of 7-1 in what was one of the "better games" for the Brits, who had a particularly difficult tournament, with an overall goal difference of minus-42 over their seven games, en route to a last-place finish in the International Ice Hockey Federation's lowest division.[43]

Just How Familiar Was It?

While we have seen many examples of hockey being played in England, and being reported, can we conclude that ice hockey was familiar to most people, that it was a widely known activity in days where games rarely benefited from the exposure of TV broadcasts? Or was knowledge of the activity limited primarily to those who took part in it?

Allow us to present various excerpts of authors or reporters using the word *hockey* and seeming not to be concerned that their readers might not understand what it means. Many of these references, in fact, show the author using the term *hockey* to *describe* an object or an activity to his intended audience.

During the 1790s, someone under the pseudonym "Master Thomas Plumb" wrote a great number of satirical essays for the *Whitehall Evening Post*. His identity is unknown, but his "signature" usually mentioned Berkshire, a county just west of London. On August 16, 1791, one of his poems contained the following two lines: *At nine-pins play, at tennis, and bonace, / Hop-scotch and hockey, trapstick and cock-all!*[44]

Major Alexander Gordon Laing (1793-1826) was born in Edinburgh. In 1809, he volunteered for military service, becoming an ensign in the Prince of Wales Volunteers. From February to October of 1822, Laing travelled throughout the Mandingo, Timannee, Kooranko and Soolima territories of Sierra Leone. After returning to England in 1824, he prepared a narrative of his earlier journeys, published the following year as *Travels in the Timannee, Kooranko and Soolima Countries, in Western Africa*. About the Timannee people, he writes, "The hoe with which they turn up the ground, is made of hard wood; and the instrument for clearing the grain from the husk is

Banner of the Whitehall Evening Post *in 1791.*

merely a small hooked stick, like that used by boys in England at the game of hockey."[45]

As we have seen in chapter 1, Sir John Franklin, in his expedition of 1825–1827 to what are now the Canadian Northwest Territories, wrote to his niece and to a geologist friend[46] and mentioned to both about hockey being played, without needing to describe what it was. Of interest is that Franklin was born in Spilsby, Lincolnshire, and went to school in both St. Ives, Huntingdonshire and Louth, Lincolnshire; all these places are part of the region known as The Fens, St. Ives being in the middle of it and the other two towns being on its edge.

Frederick William Beechey (1796–1856) was born in London. With apparently no formal schooling, in 1806 he entered the Royal Navy, being rated as a midshipman the following year. In 1818 he served under Lieutenant John Franklin in David Buchan's Arctic expedition. After other expeditions, in 1825 he was made commander of the sloop HMS *Blossom* and instructed by the Admiralty to explore uncharted areas of the Pacific. Over three years, he discovered several islands in the Pacific, and an excellent harbour near Cape Prince of Wales. In 1831, he published *Narrative of a Voyage to the Pacific and Beering's Strait,* in which he wrote of the "Tooleerayos," natives he encountered in 1826 who lived near Tulare Lake in California's San Joaquin Valley. "Another party were playing at a game resembling hockey, and in various parts of the plain adjoining the mission many others were engaged in pleasant recreations, passing their day in exercise, content, and enjoyment."[47]

George William Traill (1792–1847) descended from a landowning family in Rousay in the Orkney Islands, Scotland. He entered the Indian Civil Service and served as the 2nd British Commissioner of Kumaon (a mountainous region of northern India) between 1816 and 1836. Not generally

Ads blues and cockle-shells! that handsome face,
- On whose rare features Cupids great and small
At nine-pins play, at tennis, and bon-ace,
Hop-scotch and hockey, trapstick and cock-all!

From 1791, the oldest known mention in a newspaper of the game of (field) hockey, and the second-oldest mention overall.

known for his benevolence, he made an ample fortune in India and became known as the "King of Kumaon." In 1828, he wrote about the inhabitants of his "kingdom," in *Statistical Sketch of Kamaon:* "The mountaineers are of a lively disposition much inclined to singing, dancing and sports; they are also fond of hearing and relating tales, and of puzzling one another with riddles; games of ball are prevented by the nature of the country, but sports of other kinds are numerous; and among them the Englishman will recognize Hocky, and many other games familiar to his youth."[48]

Sir Grenville T. Temple, 10th Baronet of Stowe, Buckinghamshire (1799–1847), visited Algeria and Tunisia in 1833 and afterwards published *Excursions in the Mediterranean: Algiers and Tunis, by Major-General Sir Grenville T. Temple,* based on his diary. Visiting the small town of Sidi Maharess, located on the island of Djerba, he noted: "On the beach I observed several young men and boys playing at a game perfectly resembling hockey or goff. Spinning-tops are also much in fashion with Tuniseen boys as in our English schools."[49]

Vice-Admiral Robert FitzRoy (1805–1865) was born in Ampton Hall, Ampton, Suffolk, into the upper echelons of the British aristocracy and a tradition of public service. He achieved lasting fame as the captain of HMS *Beagle* during Charles Darwin's famous circumnavigation of the world between 1831 and 1836. As the ship reached Patagonia in 1834, he noted: "There are meetings held among the Patagonians which might be termed 'courts of justice'. One such meeting was described to me by an eyewitness... The same individual told me that the Patagonians often played at a game like hockey."[50]

All these references above contain an implication that the author expects the reader to already know about hockey. This next author is explicit on the subject.

George Christopher Davies (1849–1922) was born in Oswestry, Shropshire. He wrote about 15 books on fishing, sailing, and outdoor recreations, as well as one novel, *The Golden Shaft* (1875), a three-volume autobiographical piece set in Wales, about a sportsman and novelist. The following passage describes a winter day in January:

> They descended the hill, and passed through the sleepy, pretty little village of Ellerslie with its pride, the mere, nestling among the trees, and nursing its islands with a jealous care . . .
>
> The putting on the ladies skates was a pleasant operation, as it always is where feet are small and ankles are taper . . .
>
> When, however, ladies can skate well, it is a pleasure and a luxury to see them, and to skate with them . . .
>
> As the day advanced the number of the skaters increased . . .
>
> By-and-by people began to play hockey on the ice, and as this was rather dangerous to the lady skaters, and they were becoming tired, they left the ice, Harold and a few of the other men remaining. A proper game of hockey was then organized, the curate of the parish taking the leadership of one side, and Harold of the other.
>
> I am not going to describe a game of hockey. Everybody knows what it is like. The two leaders and their principal backers up threw themselves into it like Englishmen, that is with a will, and many a severe fall they got, and many a hit upon the shins.
>
> One of Harold's men hit the ball to one side, and it went speeding along the ice among the spectators, and both sides, to the number of about fifty, rushed helter skelter after it, scattering the lookers on right and left.
>
> One girl, in her haste to get out of the way of the charging host, fell, and Harold being one of the foremost, was upon her before she could get up. At the pace he was going it was impossible to stop or turn, he was so close to her, so making an effort he jumped over her, losing his balance in the attempt, and coming a cropper directly afterwards, tripping up half a dozen more as he slid anyhow over the ice. As soon as he regained his legs, he hastened back to inquire if she were hurt . . .
>
> 'You are neglecting your game', she said.
>
> 'Oh, they will get on well enough without me. I am rather tired of it too' . . .

'Let me skate you about. Put your feet close together and stand stiffly. I will get behind you and put my hands on your waist, so', and starting off with her, at first gently, but quickening his pace he whirled her along at the top of his speed . . .[51]

So in 1875, Montrealers were getting their very first exposure to ice hockey. In England, in that same year, "Everybody [knew] what it is like." This perfectly summarizes the message that the authors have been trying to convey throughout this book.

Lamenting the Lack of Hockey

It is one thing to know what hockey is; it is another to become passionate about it. In Canada, the NHL can go nearly 16 months without staging a single game (as between June 7, 2004, and October 5, 2005), and the sports— and even financial—pages of newspapers will still be filled with information about it, including many complaints about the lack of hockey.

The latest NHL lockout (2012/13) only shortened the season by about half, and once again, everyone was talking about how badly missed hockey was. In Montreal's *Gazette* alone, you could find an article detailing the financial cost to the businesses operating near the Bell Centre,[52] a blog entry wondering whether the fans should forgive this fourth labour conflict in just a little over two decades,[53] and a hockey reporter (Pat Hickey) seemingly so desperate that he started reporting on a virtual season played on EA's video game *NHL 13,* with made-up quotes and all. One of his write-ups reportedly ranked among the most popular on *The Gazette*'s website.[54]

What if England's hockey fans had been deprived of hockey? Would *they* have taken the time and filled newspaper space with complaints about the situation?

Well, on occasion they were, and they did. One of the most poignant stories appeared in *The Standard* (London) on December 29, 1873:

> There is no ice at present, so that hockey, one of the best games imaginable on skates, has had no trial this year. In the fen country, when there is frost of any duration, skating races and handicaps are of frequent occurrence, . . . Unluckily for this our winters are so uncertain and short that skating will never be able to take its proper place among our sports unless the Yankees cut through the Isthmus of Panama in a fit of spite and divert

the Gulf Stream into the Pacific; then we might get some winters like they have at Moscow.[55]

But Londoners were not the only ones to feel the pain. Such hardship also occurred elsewhere—in Worcestershire, for example. Witness this quote from *Berrow's Worcester Journal* of December 19, 1868:

> We have always been led to associate the month of December with frost and snow—with the ponds and rivers hard-frozen with black ice over which the skates ring cheerily, from which the hockey-stick echoes through the quiet lanes, and the skaters' and sliders' merry voices resound until the villagers congregate to see the fun. But alas! for Tradition. The jolly old monarch—a veritable "shadow in outline"—is even at our thresholds, and yet there is a lamentable lack of seasonable weather; while, as for skating, who can think of it when the rain is drip, drip, dripping, and the streets are in a state of hopeless mud? It is dolorous; but we shall have another "green yule," which proverbial philosophy has inseparably associated with "a fat kirkyard." [56]

But the saddest story of all is that of Henry Morgan-Clifford (1806–1884), a British Liberal Party politician, born at Welsh Park, County Tipperary, Ireland. When his father died in 1814, Henry and his mother settled at Perristone, Herefordshire, from where the father's family originated. He attended the now-familiar Eton College from September 1819 to April 1825. His autobiography, *Reminiscences of His Life,* edited by his wife, Catherine Harriette (d. 1898), and published in 1893, spoke of his years at Eton:

> My other and winter amusement was 'Hockey'; here too, I worked hard, and obtained the second place of my day. To me it was the most fascinating of all games; and I have longed for it again all my life!
>
> I went to Eton in September 1819, and left it in April 1825. The boy had almost grown into the man. There were no home restrictions or discipline in my case to restrain such development.
>
> I arrived at Ch. Ch. [Christ Church, Oxford University] during an unusually severe frost, about the middle of January 1827. There were no outdoor amusements except skating, which was not in my way . . .[57]

So this poor man waited, in vain, all his life to play hockey again! His plight may seem familiar to fans of the Toronto Maple Leafs, some of whom have waited all their lives to *see* hockey again. Even the lamenting of skating not being in their way will hit home as well, though for Morgan-Clifford, it was explained by his being a hockey player of the "field" type.

Chapter 9 Notes

1. *Derby Mercury,* 17 Feb. 1864.
2. *Jackson's Oxford Journal,* 19 Jan. 1861.
3. *The Gazette* (Montreal), 3 Mar. 1875.
4. Thomas Crofton Croker, *Legends of the Lakes; or, Sayings and Doings at Killarney, Collected Chiefly from the Manuscripts of Robert Adolphus Lynch, Esq.,* vol. 1 (London: John Ebers & Co., 1829): 16. The book was actually published on December 22, 1828, according to an advertisement in the London *Morning Chronicle.* The part describing a game of hurley includes the first found reference to the Irish expression *puck* in the sense of "hit a ball."

   "But as I was saying, there was Darby Minehan whistling away like a blackbird in a summer's morning, only 'twas night at the time he was on the bridge, just where we are standing now, and the moon shining bright as day, when what would he see but a parcel of *by's* playing hurley on the mall. 'Hurrah', says Darby, 'hurrah, *by's,* says he, 'here's the *lauve laider* (strong hand) for you', — making over to join the fun, for he was mortal fond, of that same hurley. But when he came up to them, the Lord *presarve* us, who should they be but a parcel of dead people, and O'Donoghue's fetch in the middle of them all, <u>pucking the ball</u> about like a May-boy. . ."

   A second early reference, uses the same terminology:

   "HURLING ...All preliminaries being adjusted, the leaders take their places in the centre. A person is chosen to throw up the ball, which is done as straight as possible, when the whole party, withdrawing their hurleys, stand with them elevated, to receive and strike it in its decent; now comes the crash of mimic war — hurleys rattle against hurleys — the ball is struck and re-struck, often for several minutes, without advancing much nearer to either goal; and when some one is lucky to <u>get a clear 'puck' at it,</u> it is sent flying over the field." (Samuel Carter

Hall and Anna Maria Hall, *Ireland: Its Scenery, Character &c.*, vol. I [London: How & Parsons, 1841]: 257–258.)

5.   *The Gazette* (Montreal), 7 Feb. 1876.

6.   From the following quote, for example: "Would you believe it, though water is to be had in abundance in London, and of fairly good quality, absolutely none is drunk? The lower classes, even the paupers, do not know what it is to quench their thirst with water. In this country nothing but beer is drunk, and it is made in several qualities . . ." (Madame Van Muyden, ed., *A Foreign View of England in the Reigns of George I and George II: The Letters of Monsieur César de Saussure to His Family* [London: John Murray, 1902]: 157-158.)

7.   George Forrest (John George Wood), "Hockey," *Every Boy's Magazine*, no. 3 (April 1862).

8.   "The Thames frozen over at Richmond," *Illustrated London News*, 3 Mar. 1855: 197.

9.   Charles Williams, *Skaiting-Dandies, Shewing Off*, c.1818, British Museum.

10. Richard Phillips, *The Book of Games, or, A History of the Juvenile Sports, Practised at the Kingston Academy; Illustrated with Twenty-four Copper Plates* (London: Tabart & Co., 1805): 8-9.

11. Benedictus Antonio Van Assen, untitled hand-coloured stipple engraving, 1797, Blyberg-Lefever Collection.

12. Master Michel Angelo (Richard Johnson), *Juvenile Sports and Pastimes, to Which are Prefixed, Memoirs of the Author: Including a New Mode of Infant Education* (London: Thomas Carnan, 1773): 92.

13. Alfred Guy Kingan L'Estrange, "Hockey at Eton," *The Eton College Chronicle*, 16 Nov. 1911: 44.

14. "Hockey," *The Boy's Own Book: A Complete Encyclopedia of All the Diversions, Athletic, Scientific, and Recreative, of Boyhood and Youth* (London: David Bogue, 1849): 41.

15. Neville and Albert Goodman, *Handbook of Fen Skating* (London: Sampson Low, Marston, Searle, and Rivington, 1882): 139–140.

16. *McGill University first hockey team 1881, at the Crystal Palace skating rink*, 1881, photograph, McGill University Archives.

17. Charles Goodman Tebbutt, "Bandy, or Hockey on the Ice," *The Sports of the World, with Illustrations from Drawings and Photographs* (London: Cassel and Co., 1905): 237.

18. *The Gazette* (Montreal), 17 Mar. 1875.

19. John Dugdale Astley, *Fifty Years of My Life in the World of Sport at Home and Abroad,* vol. I (London: Hurst and Blackett, 1894): 30.

20. John Moyer Heathcote, Charles Goodman Tebbutt and Thomas Maxwell Witham, *Skating* (London: Longmans, Green & Co., 1892): 432.

21. Ibid., 432.

22. Ibid., 432.

23. National Skating Association of Great Britain, "Hockey on the Ice. Rules," *Rules of the National Skating Association of Great Britain* (Cambridge, U.K.: Digby and Son, 1883): 15.

24. Ibid., 17.

25. Michel Vigneault, "Out of the Mists of Memory," *Total Hockey,* 1st ed., (Kingston, New York: Total Sports, 1998): 10.

26. Henry D. Richardson, Holiday Sports and Pastimes for Boys (London: William Somerville Orr & Co., 1848): 62.

27. George Forrest (John George Wood), "Hockey."

28. Paul Kitchen, "Early Goal Nets — The Evolution of an Idea," *Hockey Research Journal V* (2001): 12–14.

29. "Hockey," *The Popular Educator,* no. 13 (January 1868): 207.

30. *The Gazette* (Montreal), 7 Feb. 1876.

31. G. F. P. (George Frederick Pardon) *Games for All Seasons* (London: James Blackwood, 1858): 20.

32. Heathcote, Tebbutt and Witham, *Skating,* 431.

33. Iain Fyffe, *On His Own Side of the Puck — The Early History of Hockey Rules* (San Francisco: Blurb Inc., 2014): 98.

34. *The Hockey Champ* Walt Disney Productions, 1939.

35. Errol D'Cruz, "New hockey laws ended India's rule," *The Times of India,* 27 Feb. 2010, web, 7 Apr. 2014, <http://timesofindia.india-times.com/sports/tournaments/top-stories/New-hockey-laws-ended-Indias-rule/articleshow/5623020.cms>.

36. Scott Young, *100 Years of Dropping the Puck: A History of the OHA,* (Toronto: McClelland & Stewart, 1989): 87.

37. *Carlisle Journal,* January 27, 1865.

38. John Trotter Brockett, *A Glossary of North Country Words, in Use* (Newcastle upon Tyne: Emerson Charnley, London: Baldwin and Cradock, 1829): 99.

39. *The Gazette,* 24 May 1938: 12.

40. *Milwaukee Journal,* 27 Apr. 1959: 28.
41. *Daily News* (London), 5 Mar. 1866, and *Leeds Mercury,* 6 Mar. 1866.
42. Arthur Evans Moule, *Half a Century in China: Recollections and Observations* (London: Hodder and Stoughton, 1911): 55.
43. *WK '73 IJshockey Holland* (Eindhoven: Nederlandse IJshockey Bond, 1973).
44. *Whitehall Evening Post* (London), 16 Aug. 1791.
45. Alexander Gordon Laing, *Travels in the Timannee, Kooranko, and Soolima Countries, in Western Africa* (London: John Murray, 1825): 103–104.
46. John Franklin, Letter to Mary Anne Kay, 8 Nov. 1825, John Franklin papers, GB 0064 FRN/1/8, National Maritime Museum, London. Augustus Henry Beesly, *Sir John Franklin* (London: Marcus Ward & Co., 1881): 131.
47. Frederick William Beechey, *Narrative of a Voyage to the Pacific and Beering's Strait, to Co-operate with the Polar Expeditions: Performed in His Majesty's Ship* Blossom, *Under the Command of Captain F. W. Beechey, R. N., F. R. S. &c. in the years 1825, 26, 27, 28,* vol. II (London: Henry Colburn & Richard Bentley, 1831): 52.
48. George William Traill, "Statistical Sketch of Kamaon," *Astatic Researches,* vol. 16 (Calcutta, India: Government Gazette Press, 1828): 219.
49. Sir Grenville Temple, *Excursions in the Mediterranean: Algiers and Tunis,* vol. II (London: Saunders and Otley, 1835): 120.
50. Robert FitzRoy, *Narrative of the Surveying Voyages of His Majesty's Ships* Adventure *and* Beagle *between the Years 1826 and 1836, Describing Their Examination of the Southern Shores of South America, and the* Beagle's *Circumnavigation of the Globe,* vol. II addenda (London: Henry Colburn, 1839).
51. George Christopher Davies, *The Golden Shaft* (London: Richard Bentley and Son, 1875): 86–92.
52. Jeff Heinrich, "Asserting the NHL lockout fallout," *The Gazette* (Montreal), 13 Nov. 2012, web, 7 Apr. 2014. <http://www.montrealgazette .com/entertainment/Assessing+lockout+fallout/7526442/story.html>.
53. James Mennie, "NHL lockout: Should fans forgive?," *The Gazette* (Montreal), 8 Nov. 2012, web, 7 Apr. 2014, <http://blogs.montreal-gazette.com/2012/11/08/nhl-lockout-should-fans-forgive/>.
54. Donald Melanson, "NHL lockout prompts Montreal sports writer to

chronicle virtual hockey season," *Engadget.com,* 29 Nov. 2012, web, 7 Apr. 2014, <http://www.engadget.com/2012/11/29/nhl-lockout-virtual-season/>.

55. *The Standard* (London), 29 Dec. 1873.
56. *Berrow's Worcester Journal,* 19 Dec. 1868.
57. Henry Morgan-Clifford, *Reminiscences of His Life,* ed. Catherine Harriette Morgan-Clifford (printed for private circulation), 1893: 34, 71.

"As We Know It Today"

I N 2003, LIBRARY AND ARCHIVES Canada launched a virtual exhibit called "Backcheck: A Hockey Retrospective." It consisted of many web pages describing various aspects of hockey, from a historical perspective. On its origins page ("The Origins of Hockey"), Backcheck confesses that, as its creators "value life and limb as much as our gentle readers will surely do," they will not take sides.[1] This is a reasonable approach and certainly the right one to take under such circumstances.

Yet it does appear to take something for granted. "Research points to North America as the region where the idea of a contest on ice took hold and led to the sport we know today." It is not even the part about North America that draws our attention; it is the last part of the sentence: "the sport we know today."

This expression is often rendered in a different form, designating more specifically which sport is being referred to. This is the form that we will examine next.

Hockey as We Know It Today

The International Ice Hockey Federation used this phrase when it announced in a press release that it would recognize the Victoria Skating Rink as the birthplace of organized ice hockey (though the headline surprisingly shortened this to "birthplace of hockey"): "No other cities or places, which might claim to be the birthplace of hockey, can produce the following accurate evidence and proximity to the game of ice hockey as we know it today …"[2]

Prime Minister Stephen Harper of Canada used the phrase in his October 24, 2009, letter honouring James George Aylwin Creighton on the occasion of the unveiling of a monument and plaque at his last resting place: "Hockey as we know it today was formalized by Creighton's innovations."[3]

The late Nick Auf der Maur, columnist at *The Gazette* and elected several times as a city councillor in Montreal, used it in a February 1992 column dedicated to the idea of a "Montreal Hockey Walk of Fame": "[Billy Georgette has] been waging a campaign to have Montreal recognized as the real birthplace of hockey as we know it."[4]

Iain Fyffe, author of *On His Own Side of the Puck — The Early History of Hockey Rules* used it in his blog *Hockey Historysis,* in an entry dedicated to hockey's origins and the need for a proper definition for hockey, before the search for its origins can be launched: "So finding a reference to 'hockey' in the 17th century isn't enough to establish that hockey, as we know it today, was played then."[5]

Emanuel M. Orlick used it as far back as 1943, writing for the *McGill News,* as he was giving advice to hockey researchers who might be looking for the roots of hockey: "The question is not when the games of field hockey, hocquet, hurley or shinney started, but rather, when and where did hurley or shinney develop into the game of Ice Hockey as we know it today."[6]

Bill Fitsell, hockey historian and founding president of the Society for International Hockey Research, also expressed his views on hockey's beginnings in an interview with *Kingstonist:* "In my mind, the debate is settled. When I'm asked the question, 'Where did hockey originate?' I say, 'You tell me what hockey is.' Is it the well-organized, professional, commercial game that we see on television, or is it the freewheeling sort of game that we play on outdoor ice or in shinny matches? If you're talking about the game as we know it today, it tracks right back to Montreal on March the 3rd of 1875, where there is a recorded history of the game, right down to who played and who scored. No other community can actually match that record."[7] (Actually, we do not know who scored in that game.)

The common feature of these six references is that all point either to the first Montreal game, or at least some game or period in Montreal in the decade that followed, as being when "hockey as we know it today" had its start.

Beyond the thousands of words that you have read so far in this book on the English origins of hockey, that is the ultimate question that remains to be answered.

Was It Hockey as We Know It Today?

And our answer to that question, in regards to English hockey played up until 1875—or even a few years later—is simple: absolutely, definitely not.

Hockey as we know it today takes various different forms, depending on the league, the country (even, in Canada, the province), the gender of the players and the age level. Some of the common points, however, include having six players per side, the presence of boards, of a standardized goal (six feet wide and four feet high) and of a rubber puck also of standardized dimensions. A centre red line is used for the icing rule—which varies but always exists (though it is usually inoperative during non-offsetting penalties), and two blue lines are there to enforce the offside rule, which is pretty much universal, save perhaps for the delayed offside sub-rule.

Nearly all games have one or two referees and usually two linesmen. Minor infractions are penalized, with the offending player being sent to the penalty box for two minutes, during which his or her team must play with one fewer player, or two, if two players from the same team are penalized simultaneously. In the event that more than two players of the same team are penalized, some penalties will be delayed so that the offending team cannot have fewer than three skaters and a goalie on the ice. Infractions that involve the loss of a clear chance to score are penalized by a penalty shot, in which a player of the "offended" team tries to score on the goalie of the "offending" team, with no other player involved and no time constraint.

The goalie must wear protective equipment including a face mask and all other players must wear protective equipment including a helmet (and often a visor as well). Teams can dress between about 18 and 20 players per game and player changes can be made on the fly, except for the goaltender.

Nearly all games have a duration of 60 minutes broken into three periods. In case of a tie at the end of regulation time, there is nearly always a period of overtime, of the "sudden-death" type, whose duration varies depending on the league. If there has been no goal after the maximum duration for overtime has elapsed, then there is usually a shootout to designate the winner.

Goaltenders are allowed to assume any position to prevent the puck from entering their goal, and they are also allowed to "freeze" the puck almost at will. Other players may also assume any position to stop a puck anywhere on the ice, and are allowed to touch the puck with any part of their body or equipment, except that they are not allowed to grab it or freeze it deliberately, they may not touch it with their stick above the shoulders, and they may only score with their stick, except for accidental deflections in which the player made no deliberate movement to steer the puck towards the goal. All leagues and all levels of play also have a rule preventing players from interfering with the goalkeeper, and a goal crease in which the rule is applied with more severity, though the exact rule varies.

Nearly all competitive hockey played anywhere in the world today, in 2014, obeys all of the above rules or standards. And save perhaps for the four-inch-diameter, one-inch-thick puck, not a single one of those elements existed in pre-1875 English hockey, at least not as far as we can tell from the knowledge we have today of how hockey was played then. So, no, hockey played in England at the time was absolutely, definitely not "hockey as we know it today."

But guess what: hockey played in Montreal in 1875 or in the decade that followed did not contain any of those elements, either.

In fact, the authors have no doubt that, presented with a film of an 1870s hockey game played in England and a film of an 1870s hockey game played at the Victoria Skating Rink in Montreal, any hockey fan with better than 20/100 vision would conclude that the Montreal game is much more similar to the English game than to "hockey as we know it today."

And how could that *not* be? As we've seen in chapter 7, Montreal hockey in the 1870s and early 1880s was following, almost to the letter, field hockey rules established in England by the Hockey Association, while in England, until the NSA published formal rules for "hockey on the ice" in 1883, ice hockey was played in the same way as field hockey, sometimes with minor adaptations. So the two *had* to be very similar.

The trouble with the expression, of course, is that it is so vague that it can be defined in whichever way supports the thesis that the writer is defending. Between the "freewheeling sort of game" played outdoors and the "well-organized, professional, commercial game that we see on television," where, for example, does pee wee hockey fall? Is it not hockey? Is it not *organized* hockey?

It is the authors' opinion that the phrase "hockey as we know it today" has very little, and perhaps no, value in the debate about the origins of hockey, and the authors humbly suggest that it might best be retired.

Chapter 10 Notes

1. Library and Archives Canada, "The Origins of Hockey," *Backcheck: A Hockey Retrospective,* 28 Jan. 2003, web, 7 Apr. 2014, <http://www.collectionscanada.gc.ca/hockey/024002-2005-e.html>.

2. International Ice Hockey Federation, "IIHF to Recognize Montreal's Victoria Rink as Birthplace of Hockey," *Sport Information Resource Centre Press Release Service,* 5 Jul. 2002, web, 7 Apr.2014, <http://www.sirc.ca/news_view.cfm?id=2192&search=&show=&month=7&year=2002&search_where=&lang=f>.

3. Stephen Harper, "James George Aylwin Creighton Monument and Plaque Unveiling," *James George Aylwin Creighton: Unveiling Ceremony Program* (Toronto: Society for International Hockey Research, 2009), web, 7 Apr. 2014, <http://www.sihrhockey.org/new/pdfs/creighton_booklet_english.pdf>.

4. "The Montreal Hockey Walk of Fame: The Dream," *Hockey Heritage,* n.d., web, 7 Apr. 2014, <http://www.hockeyheritage.org/walkoffame.php>.

5. Iain Fyffe, "Thoughts of Hockey's Origins," *Hockey Historysis,* 22 Dec. 2011, web, 7 Apr. 2014, <http://hockeyhistorysis.blogspot.ca/2011/12/thoughts-on-hockeys-origins.html>.

6. Quoted in Society for International Hockey Research, *Report of the Sub-Committee Looking into Claim that Windsor, Nova Scotia, is the Birthplace of Hockey* (Toronto: Society for International Hockey Research, 2002):15.

7. Harvey Kirkpatrick, "Six Questions for Bill Fitsell," *Kingstonist,* 23 Nov. 2011, web, 7 Apr. 2014, <http://www.kingstonist.com/2011/11/23/bill-fitsell-interview/>.

Forward to the Past

So far, the references presented in the book have been for purposes specific to the theme of each chapter. Let us now look at more of those references, in a trip forward to the past, to see just how far the study of available evidence can take us on the journey towards the origins of ice hockey.

Eton, Berkshire, 1871–1875

Lieutenant Colonel Charles à Court Repington (1858–1925), a British army officer and war correspondent, was born at Heytesbury, Wiltshire, where his father was a Conservative member of Parliament. He was educated at Eton College from 1871 to autumn 1875, at a private school in Freiburg, Baden, in 1876, and began his military career at Sandhurst in 1877.

After an untimely affair with a fellow officer's wife was made public in 1902, he had to resign his military commission. He joined *The Times* of London as a military correspondent, and later worked for the *Morning Post* and *Daily Telegraph*. He wrote several books, including two bestsellers: *The First World War* (1920) and *After the War* (1922).

In 1919, he also published his autobiography, *Vestigia: Reminiscences of Peace and War,* in which he recalled his years at Eton:

> I enjoyed every hour of it — the practice in Sixpenny, the racquets which
> I played regularly, the Fives which I never missed if I could get a game,
> the swims at Cuckoo Weir and in the main river, the beagles, the long
> cross-country jumping expeditions (where it was a point of honour, if

one could not jump over a stream, to jump into it), the rowing, and best of all, the football, which was the most popular game of all. Hockey on the ice when one could get it was also a delight...[1]

So while we know only about field hockey rules drawn up at Eton (in 1868—see chapter 7), we see that, in the 1870s, hockey on the ice was played whenever ice was available, presumably following the field hockey rules quite closely.

Crystal Palace, Bromley, London, 1870

The Crystal Palace was a cast-iron-and-glass building created by Sir Joseph Paxton and originally erected in Hyde Park to house the Great Exhibition of 1851. Following the success of the exhibition, the palace was moved and reconstructed in 1854, in a modified and enlarged form, on the grounds of the Penge Place estate at Sydenham Hill—today, a part of the London borough of Bromley. It attracted visitors for over seven decades. The palace was destroyed by fire on November 30, 1936, and the grounds the building occupied are now known as Crystal Palace Park.

The park at Sydenham Hill was built by Sir Joseph Paxton's Crystal Palace Company between 1852 and 1855, and included extensive waterways with several lakes, reservoirs and basins. The day after Christmas of 1870, according to *The Times,* huge crowds gathered to take advantage of the ice:

EXHIBITIONS, &C.

CRYSTAL PALACE

Thirty-five thousand six hundred persons visited the Crystal Palace yesterday...

The announcement that the ice in the basins of the fountains and on the lake at Sydenham was in good order and fit for skating upon attracted many...

One basin of the great lover series of fountains was appropriated to a skating club, which includes many lady members, whose graceful evolutions were watched by a large number of spectators.

The large sheet of ice on the boating lake was covered with skaters, some playing hockey, some propelling young ladies in sledges, which appeared to have been made by substituting rockers for the wheels of a perambulator, or by the simple process of mailing two straight bars of wood to the legs of an ordinary chair.[2]

Skaters were playing hockey among a crowd of 35,600—hockey was apparently a sport for the masses.

Swavesey, Cambridgeshire, 1870

We have already discovered the Fens village of Swavesey (with Over) in chapter 4, and we revisited it in chapter 8, as the perennial opponent of Bluntisham and Earith, typically designated as the Bury Fen team. The motto of Swavesey is "Steadfast in Work and Play," and its "home ice" is Mare (a. k. a. Mere) Fen.

In February of 1870, taking advantage of a generous frost, a grandiose celebration of games on ice took place on Mare Fen and was reported in the *Cambridge Independent Press* of Saturday the 19th:

> GRAND CRICKET AND SKATING MATCHES ON THE ICE
> (BY OUR OWN REPORTER)
> SWAVESEY
>
> The magnificent piece of ice, of the extent of about 80 acres, in Mere Fen, which had been flooded by the kindness of Mr. George Long, farmer, has daily during the present fortnight afforded opportunities of skating to thousands of visitors who have come from far and near. The Great Eastern Railway Company commenced on Friday last [February 11] to run special excursion trains, and enormous returns must have been made at Swavesey.
>
> On Friday sixteen skaters of Swavesey and its immediate neighbourhood, joined in a stake for money prizes...
>
> Monday was, however, the grand day, as on that day a very novel match was organized and brought off—being a cricket-match on the ice, all the players—batsmen, bowlers, and fielders—being in pattens [fen skates]...
>
> Cricket had scarcely terminated ere a skating match between sixteen of the picked men of the Cambridge Division of the county commenced...
>
> This concluded the public sports of the day. On another part of the same piece of ice, a well-contested game at hockey had been played, in which Mr. Neville Goodman, St. Peter's College, proved himself a very superior player.[3]

We recognize Neville Goodman as the "ringer" from Cambridge who would suit up for Over and Swavesey in their game played later that year

Skaters on Duddingston Loch, Near Edinburgh, *by Charles Lees,*
signed and dated (1853) on the edge of the sled in the foreground.

and would become the co-author of the 1882 *Handbook of Fen Skating*
(seen in chapter 7).

Edinburgh, Scotland, 1864

Charles Lees (1800–1880) was born in Cupar, Fifeshire, and began his
artistic career as a pupil of the eminent Edinburgh portraitist Sir Henry
Raeburn. He established a fine reputation as a portrait painter and was
elected a Royal Scottish Academician in 1830, later becoming the Academy's
treasurer.

In the 1840s, Lees began specializing in sporting and recreational subjects.
His oil painting *The Golfers,* of the grand match at St. Andrew's in 1841,
is considered the most famous golf-related work of art in the world.

Lees made several paintings with winter and skating motifs from the Edinburgh area. One of the most reproduced is *Skaters on Duddingston Loch,*
from 1853 (seen above).

The Royal Scottish Academy 1826–1916; A Complete List of the Exhibited
Works, published in 1917, mentions three of Lees's paintings that have

"shinty" or hockey in their titles (numbers attributed by the Royal Scottish Academy):

1861 — Number 381 — *Shinty: Scene on the Ice at Duddingston*
1864 — Number 213 — *"Hockey on the Ice": on St Margaret's Loch, Edinburgh*
1875 — Number 468 — *A Winter Day: "Shinty"* [4]

Unfortunately, the fate of these three paintings is unknown (the Royal Scottish Academy and the Scottish National Portrait Gallery, both in Edinburgh, and the Witt and Conway Library in London were contacted). We do have, however, a review of the second painting, published in the *Caledonian Mercury* (Edinburgh) on February 26, 1864:

The Royal Scottish Academy's Exhibition

If Mr. Charles Lees is not a great artist, he is a very delightful one, and several of his pictures in recent Exhibitions are amongst our pleasantest recollections. He has painted many a skating picture, and we confess we like them all.

Back to our memory come those wintry canvases with the 'spill' in the centre, the curiously-poised skaters all about, the orange woman in the corner, the small boy staring at her and hopelessly attempting to blow some warmth into his benumbed fingers, and high and beyond, shadowy in frosty twilight, the outline of Arthur's Seat and the Crags.

He brings winter into well ventilated apartments where we may inspect him at our leisure. Again, this artist is not only great on the ice, he is equally great in moonlight...

He has no moonlights this year; but his 'Hockey on the Ice', No. 213, is one of the most spirited winter pieces he has ever executed. After the ball comes a whole storm of uproarious urchins on their skates – every cheek and nose red with exercise, every face agrin with merriment.

In the fierce impulse of their delight they have got themselves wedged together; but in a second some lucky player will send the ball flying, and then the dense mass of fun and animal spirits will break up and stream away in far-shooting lines, the hero of the moment leading.

The picture is admirably painted; it displays great humour, character, and skill in grouping; you almost fancy you hear the laughter, the shouts, the hurtle of the skates; 'Hockey' would engrave well, we should think, and could hardly fail of popularity.[5]

The review tells us that "hockey on the ice," even in Scotland, could designate a game played on skates, and a fun one at that.

London, 1857

In December of 1857, the bitter cold inspired an anonymous author to write an essay on…the bitter cold. Published in the *Illustrated Times* on Saturday, December 19, it describes how the conditions are dealt with in London, with the Humane Society having hot brandy on hand, but it also describes the enjoyment of the cold, in the form of skating, including "figures of eight and spread-eagles." The essay concludes with a short paragraph about another activity on ice:

> Men new to the skating art are timorously making slow progress with the aid of chairs and sticks, 'all-hot' men are shouting, 'hockey' balls are flying through the air, and from the immense multitude rises one continual roar, which in any other place but London would be heard for miles.[6]

Judging by this and the 1870 Crystal Palace references, it would appear that Londoners could not see ice without starting games of hockey.

Stoke Newington, Hackney, London, 1856

It was also cold in London in January of 1856, and every available ice surface was put to good use, as described in the *Morning Chronicle* of Wednesday, January 16:

THE FROST —

The frost has been intensely severe, the last two days the ice on the Regent's Canal being so thick as considerably to impede the passage of flyboats and barges. On some of the small ponds in the northern suburbs, and on the New River Reservoir, in the Green Lanes, Stoke Newington, ice is fully an inch and a half in thickness, and numbers of persons amused themselves by skating, sliding and playing at 'hockey'. The Ornamental Water in St. James' Park, and the Serpentine, are nearly frozen over, but the ice has not sufficient stability to permit of skating. The superintendent of the Humane Society has stationed the men under his orders on the banks nearest the most dangerous spots, and extra police-constables have been placed on duty near the waters, to assist in the event of accidents.[7]

The enthusiasm for hockey is seen in all parts of London, including the district of Stoke Newington (in the London borough of Hackney) where the artificial New River was opened in 1613, and the East and West Reservoirs in 1833. We see that skateless citizens who wished to amuse themselves could always resort to "sliding" on the ice.

Exeter, Devonshire, 1855
As cold as January of 1856 was, the previous winter had seen some freezing temperatures as well—in Exeter, for example, where the *Exeter and Plymouth Gazette* reported on ice conditions:

> THE WEATHER—For a long series of years we have not experienced such a severe and continued frost as we have had during the last few weeks. The weather has been intensely cold, and at intervals there have been falls of snow. The Exe [river] has now been frozen over for more than a fortnight, and has daily been the scene of various amusements. Hundreds of persons have been continually skating on it, and on two or three days parties have played sundry games of hockey, &c., upon the ice. The river has not been frozen over to such an extent for very many years. At present the ice extends, and is safe, from Exe Bridge to Salmon Pool, a sufficient distance for the most *au fait* at skating to besport themselves.[8]

The River Exe runs about two kilometres between the Exe Bridge and the Salmon Pool, only a little over a quarter of the cleared length of Rideau Canal (Ottawa) in the winter, but still quite something for a country not recognized for its harsh winters.

Windsor, Berkshire, 1853
The royal hockey-playing episodes mentioned in earlier chapters are not the only ones known to history—far from it. We will look at four more of these, but first allow us to provide a longer version of the excerpt from Sir John Dugdale Astley's 1894 book *Fifty Years of My Life in the World of*

Sport at Home and Abroad, briefly quoted in chapter 9, in the section about goalkeepers.

> Just previous to Christmas [1853] we had a lot of hard weather, and with some first-rate ice, which gave me ample opportunity of playing my favourite game of hockey on the ice. Our other battalion was then quartered at Windsor, and it reached my ears that a match was to be played on the pond on the slopes below the Terrace of Windsor Castle, and, though I really had no business there, I felt very keen to show my powers before Royalty (the Royal family being at the Castle); so I smuggled myself down to the pond, and, as I was known to be useful at the game, Dudley de Ros of the 1st Life Guards and I tossed up for sides.
>
> The pond—as I recollect it—was an oval one with an island in the centre, on which the band of our regiment was stationed. At one end of the pond her Gracious Majesty was seated, surrounded by several of the ladies of the court, watching the game with evident interest.
>
> The Prince Consort—who was a beautiful and graceful figure-skater—kept goal for the opposite side, and Lord Listowel (father of the present earl) kept ours. I don't think that I ever enjoyed a game more, and it was that day I first had the honour of making the acquaintance of the Prince of Wales. The game waxed fast and furious and I am afraid that I was sufficiently wanting in respect to interfere once, at least, with the Prince Consort's equilibrium in my eagerness to get a goal.
>
> The edges of the pond sloped up to where Her Majesty was sitting, and in a desperate rally with De Ros I lost my balance and came down in a sitting posture, the impetus I had on carrying me right up to the Queen's feet, and the hearty laughter which greeted my unbidden arrival is still vividly impressed upon my mind.[9]

Sir Astley goes on to describe the after-game serving of "deliciously mulled port-wine" and his receiving of a "jobation" for having participated in a game "to which [he] was not asked," but the quality of his play allowed him to "not [be] cashiered on this occasion."

Windsor, Berkshire, 1849

The next episode of royal hockey is brought to us courtesy of Princess Mary

Adelaide of Cambridge (1833–1897), born in Hanover, Germany, and eventually the mother of four, including Princess Victoria Mary of Teck, who would go on to be the Queen Consort of the United Kingdom when her husband, Prince George, Duke of York, became King George V.

For several years, Princess Mary was the only English princess about the court and a constant guest at Windsor Castle. In 1849, on January 9, she wrote about the cold weather, in a letter to her friend Ellinor Napier:

> Last Wednesday we went to Windsor Castle to remain till Friday. The visit went off very well indeed. The Queen and the children are looking very well, and the latter much grown.
>
> The poor little Prince of Wales has disfigured his face by falling on an iron-barred gate, and the bridge of his nose and both his eyes are quite black and bruised, but fortunately no bones were broken. The first evening we danced till twelve o'clock.
>
> Next day [January 4], the weather being very cold, we went to see the gentlemen skate and play at Hockey; I found time to write some letters and pay a visit to the Duchess of Kent.[10]

Windsor, Berkshire, 1846

Two years earlier, a London Sunday newspaper called *John Bull* had reported on an afternoon of skating and hockey in which the Prince Consort (Albert) came out on the winning side, on the last day of 1846:

> COURT AND FASHIONABLE
>
> On Monday [December 28] the Queen, accompanied by his Royal Highness Prince Albert, walked to Frogmore, and visited her Royal Highness the Duchess of Kent. The Earl of Listowell, Colonel Seymour, Col. Bouverie, Colonel Phipps, and Captain Francis Seymour were in attendance on the Prince. The gentlemen enjoyed the exercise of skating on the lake, whilst her Majesty, attended by the Marchioness of Douro, promenaded the walks which surrounded it. After skating for upwards of an hour, the Prince returned to the Castle with Her Majesty to luncheon...
>
> On Thursday [December 31] after breakfast, Her Majesty and her distinguished visitors rode to Frogmore, where the ice on the lake was considered to be of sufficient thickness to justify the Prince and his attendants to venture on the ice. The Queen, with the Duchess of

Sutherland, the Marchioness of Douro, and the Hon. Miss Paget, in the meanwhile, promenading on the banks of the lake, while the exercise of skating was being enjoyed by the remainder of the Royal party. Afterwards a game at 'Hockey' on the lake was proposed by the Prince Consort, which was participated in by the whole of the gentlemen present. Sides were chosen; and, after an excellent trial of skill, which lasted upwards of half an hour, Prince Albert, and the players on the side of his Royal Highness, came off the victors. Her Majesty appeared to be exceedingly amused during the progress of the game. Her Majesty and the whole Court returned to the Castle to lunch between two and three o'clock.[11]

The same game was also described in *The Boyhood of a Great King, 1841–1858: An Account of the Early Years of the Life of His Majesty, Edward VII*, a 1906 book by Alexander Meyrick Broadley (1847-1916), an English lawyer, journalist, historian and collector of art and antiquities, who used the manuscripts and letters of the Royal Family:

> Christmas was commemorated with the various observances which reminded Prince Albert of old days at Rosenau, and the frost was so severe that on the last day of the year he was able to captain the victorious side in an exciting game of hockey played on the frozen surface of the lake.[12]

This passage was almost certainly written by Queen Victoria at the time of the game, and as such would be the oldest known mention of a specific captain in a game of ice hockey.

Windsor, Berkshire, 1844

In February 1842, at the age of 20, Eleanor Julian Stanley (1821-1903), eldest daughter of Edward Stanley of Cross Hall, Lancashire, and Lady Mary Maitland, began her duties as maid of honour to Queen Victoria. She kept this position for 20 years—and later returned as extra honorary maid of honour—and her extensive correspondence was preserved by the family and eventually published in 1916, in *Twenty Years at Court, from the Correspondence of the Hon. Eleanor Stanley, Maid of Honour to Her Late Majesty Queen Victoria, 1842-1862.*

On December 16, 1844, she wrote to her mother:

> DEAREST MAMA, —I am sitting with my window open and feel rather
> hot. I have no doubt the thaw was much accelerated by the Royal couple
> announcing they had fixed to-day for their first trial of their sledge, which
> you know always has the effect of dispelling the snow.
> Yesterday, as the pond at Frogmore was still frozen enough to bear
> skating upon, though in some parts the water was six inches deep over
> the ice, we all went with the Royalty to enjoy the pleasing diversion of
> standing at the edge, on the wet grass, looking at the gentlemen skating
> and playing at *Hockey;* I don't know whether it is right spelt, but it is a
> game played with a ball and crooked sticks; after this had lasted a good
> while, and it was too dark to go on playing, we all walked home through
> the grounds of the Castle, having first partaken of the Duchess of Kent's
> hospitality in the shape of mulled claret and biscuits.
> The Saxe Coburgs and Würtembergs go to-morrow...[13]

Eleanor's family name should certainly sound familiar, as she was a (distant)
relative of Frederick Arthur Stanley, 16th Earl of Derby and future donor
of the hockey cup that now bears his name and is one of the most recognizable
sports trophies in the world. Eleanor and Frederick Arthur had a common
ancestor, Sir Thomas Stanley, 2nd Baronet (1616–1651).

Windsor, Berkshire, 1841

This is the first known reference to hockey being played on ice by the royal
family. Prince Albert had married Queen Victoria in February of 1840, and
thus had been living in England for less than a year when this article in *The
Argus* (London) was published on Sunday, January 17, 1841:

> VAGARIES OF THE WEEK
> It is suggested, that, as Prince Albert has at length found an arena for
> various signal instances of domestic courage, he add to his *coat of arms*
> (or, as Pat once said, the arms of his coat) a sledge proper argent, with a
> skate volant gules, in a *field* of ice powdered.
> THE Golf Club, hearing of Prince Albert's hurling feats on the ice,
> have sent him a *gold hockey stick,* as a companion to the toy-skate, and

to be worn on the opposite button-hole. He is said to be the most elegant *Block* in the country. Frogmore Lake is in future to be called Prince Albert's Own.[14]

It is not known, but certainly intriguing, where the Prince Consort first saw— and took an interest in—ice hockey. The game must have already been relatively widespread around London and/or Windsor for him to become such a big fan in such a short time. After all, he had only been in England for less than the equivalent of one full winter when this article was written.

London, Prior to 1838

As we get to the 1830s and earlier, we find that most references to hockey on ice are from London. It is quite likely that the interest of various princes (whether Prince Consort or future king) contributed after that point to spread the interest in the game to other parts of the country, though of course the same game, albeit called "bandy," had been popular in the Fens for quite some time already (some say for centuries).

London-born Horace Mayhew (1816–1872) had a lengthy career in journalism, serving as sub-editor of *Punch* with Douglas Jerrold and William Makepeace Thackeray and as editor of the *Comic Almanac*. In 1845, he was on the staff of contributors to *George Cruikshank's Table Book,* for which he wrote the following text:

> A SCAMPER OVER THE SERPENTINE
> (A TALE OVER THE LATE FROST)
> I AM passionately fond of skating. I can cut likenesses, dance the Polka, play at football, hockey, or rounders, on the ice better than on *terra firma,* and I once challenged all England to pick up sixpences with me on any frozen river in the universe. Such is my love for skating, that even if I were to lose both my legs, I think I should have a pair of skates fastened on to my wooden substitutes, and go on skating upon crutches all the same...
> Well, with all my love for this manly pastime, I had not skated for years...At last, there came to my relief, in 1838, a good serious Russian frost. I was at that time in Lincolnshire. The papers were full of glowing accounts of skating matches on the Serpentine, of quadrille parties, and thrilling accidents every day in Regent's Park. I stood the temptation for

a long frosty week, but the thermometer having fallen one morning ten degrees, I packed my best pair of patent skates in my carpet-bag, and started in the mail for London. I took a lodging in the neighbourhood of Hyde Park, and the following morning at day-break (I could not sleep a wink all night) I was the first on the ice. Oh, how I skated! I went round and round—shrieking wildly—pirouetted, and cut an infinity of eights and sixes for very joy! must have written my initials all over the ice...[15]

One certainly does not expect "hockey" to be sandwiched between "football" (soccer) and "rounders" (a game related to baseball) in a list of games to be played on ice with skates, but Mr. Mayhew was certainly quite passionate about his skating.

London, 1835

Here is a poem published in *Leigh Hunt's London Journal* on February 4, 1835:

SLIDING

THERE's much philosophy in skating, sliding,
And playing on the ice at what's called *Hocky,* —
Rare game. I like to see a blithe young jockey,
Just out of school, o'er ponds triumphant riding; —
He's more than paid, though he should get a hiding;
He never thinks of saying "What's o'clock, eh?"
But on he speeds, light-footed as a trochee
In sede tertiâ the verse dividing.
What though he sometimes tumbles?—'tis all one;
He makes the best of what were else but gloom,
And chill, and hardship.—Reader, if your doom
In after life with ills be overrun,
That early knowledge may you wise resume, —
Make evils bend, and turn them into fun.

E. W.[16]

We see that, even spelled "Hocky," the word rhymes with *jockey.* It is possible that the author, identified only by initials, could have been Egerton Webbe (c. 1810-1840), a composer, a man of letters and friend of Charles Cowden Clarke, Leigh Hunt and Edward Holmes.

There is no certainty as to whether the "hocky" played on ice involved skates, though skating is mentioned in the previous line—but then, so is sliding, and it is the latter term that is the title of the poem. However, perhaps the strongest point to be made is the phrase "But on he speeds," something not easily done on ice without skates. A couple of months earlier, another text had been published in the same journal, which might give us an indication as to whether the game was played on skates.

London, 1834

Again, from *Leigh Hunt's London Journal,* this time dated December 3, 1834:

"NOW"

DESCRIPTIVE OF A COLD DAY

Now, the moment people wake in the morning, they perceive the coldness with their faces, though they are warm with their bodies, and exclaim, 'Here's a day'...

Now skaiters are on the alert; the cutlers' shop-windows abound with their swift shoes; and as you approach the scene of action (pond or canal) you hear the dull grinding noise of the skaits to and fro, and see tumbles, and Banbury cake-men and blackguard boys playing 'hockey', and ladies standing shivering on the banks, admiring anybody but their brother, especially the gentleman who is cutting figures of eight, who, for his part, is admiring his own figure. Beginners affect to laugh at their tumbles, but are terribly angry, and long to thump the bye-standers.

On thawing days, idlers persist to the last in skaiting or sliding amidst the slush and bending ice, making the Humane-Society-man ferocious. He feels as if he could give them the deaths from which it is his business to save them. When you have done skaiting, you come away feeling at once warm and numb in the feet, from the tight effect of the skaits; and you carry them with an ostentatious air of indifference, as if you had done wonders; whereas you have fairly had three slips, and can barely achieve the inside edge.[17]

Regarding the mention of "Banbury-cake men," a Banbury tart or cake was often triangular and filled with fruit, especially raisins. The suggestion would seem to be that pantomime makes full use of the stage hands necessary for the special effects and bakers who supply the sweets that the clown devours. *Blackguard* (pronounced blaggard) is a term for a scoundrel.

While there is again no certainty that the hockey players are wearing skates, it seems the most plausible possibility, considering the mention of the "grinding noise of the 'skaits'" and the admiration (by the ladies) or the envy (by the beginners) at the sight of the expert skaters.

Hyde Park, Westminster, London, 1829 and 1827

Another New Year's Eve, another frost, another reason to go "skaiting" and playing hockey. From the *Morning Post* of Thursday, December 31, 1829:

> THE SERPENTINE RIVER
>
> The ice yesterday presented a solid body, four inches in thickness, and transparent where the snow had been removed from the surface. The concourse of skaiters and of persons enjoying the sight from the banks were very numerous. Many Ladies were prevailed upon to trust themselves on the ice, and, after trying the experiment for a few minutes, were satisfied that there was no more cause for apprehension than on *terra firma*.
>
> Hundreds of men and boys, principally of the lowest class, were pursuing the game of hockey, namely, striking a bung with a knobbed stick. As usual, many laughable scenes arose from parties coming in contact, and some falls were the consequence. This sport, however, is a terrible nuisance to the genteel portion of the visitors.
>
> The skaiters were more numerous, by the accession of many young holiday folks; and we saw some among the performers of great tact; but the generality did not go beyond the roll on the outside edge. The same Gentlemen as on the preceding day were there, performing in circles cleanly swept, below the boat-house. the stalls and booths were more numerous.
>
> On the Lake in Kensington Gardens there were a few skaiters, principally learners, yclept 'the awkward squad'.
>
> There were few carriages; but a more than usual number of female pedestrians on the *High Parade*—the graveled walk on the south side of the River.[18]

Were the hockey players on skates? It is hard to tell, but there is a good chance that at least some of them were. The mention that "skaiters were more numerous" does not refer to hockey players on skates but, rather, to figure skaters—or, more simply, to people skating without playing hockey. The reporter makes no secret of his personal dislike of hockey.

Almost three years earlier, on January 26, 1827, the same newspaper published a somewhat more pessimistic article about a frost permitting activities on the ice, though this time skating is not mentioned explicitly:

THE SERPENTINE RIVER

Was yesterday attended by many persons, but few of fashion. The gloom which pervaded the atmosphere kept away carriage company from the favourite promenade. We saw a few Gentlemen on the ice, and there was nothing new in the retrograde movements. As usual, there were many indiscreet persons, totally regardless of the numberless notices affixed, and they suffered for their temerity. Two young men fell in, in the centre of the River; but they were speedily extricated by the new-invented flat-bottomed boat, in which was seated a man with two poles, ropes, and grappling-irons.

It may not be amiss here to mention, that if persons, instead of grasping the ice with their hands to keep their heads above water, were to turn on their backs, the legs would float, and they would escape all danger; but by resorting to the former mode to preserve life, the ice, nine times out of ten, breaks, and they sink under its surface.

The day was intensely cold, from the effects of a north-easterly wind. Although the ice was greatly increased in thickness, there were so many fissures extending across the river, that no part of the surface could be deemed perfectly safe; and around the banks there was no approach but by planks, the ice having disappeared underneath.

The *lower orders* amused themselves with the game of 'hocky', and many experienced heavy falls which produced bursts of laughter among the calm observers, who were pretty numerous on shore.[19]

As would happen again three years later in the same newspaper, the reporter makes a point of indicating that the game (of "hocky") was played by "the lower orders," another term for "the lowest class" used in the 1829 article. Here again, we do not know whether the less well-to-do could afford skates in the 1820s, but skates certainly existed and were not a luxury item, as we know that John Franklin had brought some on board with his expedition a couple of years earlier.

St. James's Park, Westminster, London, 1822

In those days, there was not much reporting of hockey games, except when some unfortunate event occurred. From *The Times* of Monday, December 30, 1822:

St. James's Park

Friday [December 27], about two o'clock, the canal being well frozen over, a great number of persons were assembled on it, some amusing themselves in skating, others sliding...

A respectable youth of the name of Leatherbarrow, was amusing himself with fetching a bung to play at hockey, on a sheet of ice in St. James's-park, which was not bearable.

It gave way, and a person from the bank of the canal rushed into the water to save the youth's life. This humane endeavour failed at the risk of his own life.

The body of the youth was taken up and conveyed to the ship, at Charing-cross, for the inspection of a coroner's jury — Verdict — 'Accidental death'.[20]

This may come as a surprise, but, as of the time of writing this book, this *Times* article is the oldest contemporary mention of the words *hockey* and *ice* together; however, the authors doubt that the hockey being described was played on skates. It is also the only known reference with those two words that is older than John Franklin's writings.

The boy's untimely death was mentioned in the same day's *Morning Post,* with more details:

An inquest was held on Saturday 28, 1822, at the Ship Tavern, Charing Cross — "on the body of Frederick Leatherbarrow, a boy about 15 years of age, who was drowned by the ice breaking under him on the canal in St. James's Park, on Friday. The deceased, it was mentioned, was an errand boy, the son of poor parents, living in Wilde-court, Drury Lane."[21]

London, c. 1818

Printmaker and caricaturist Charles Williams was active from 1797 to 1830; his date of birth and death are not known with certainty, but according to the Victoria and Albert Museum, he lived between 1775 and 1839. He was

"Skaiting—Dandies, Shewing Off" *by Charles Williams (c. 1818).*
Two differently coloured versions are known to exist. Three hockey
players, on skates, are seen in the background, just above the right
foot of the "dandy" who is falling on his back towards the left.

a prolific etcher of satirical works of his own design or of others. Much of
his early work was done for Samuel William Fores, one of the leading publishers of satirical art in the late 18th and early 19th centuries. In later years,
Williams worked for different publishers simultaneously, including Fores,
E. Walker, members of the Knight family and, from 1807, Thomas Tegg,
who published *Skaiting—Dandies, Shewing Off.*[22] A detail of that print
appeared in chapter 9, in the section of dedicated to bungs. The full work
is shown above.

While the previous (1822) reference was the oldest known of hockey and
ice mentioned together, that does not mean that hockey on ice was invented
in that year. *Skaiting—Dandies* provides evidence that hockey players, on
skates, were enjoying the game in London before then. Following is the
British Museum's description of the print, which leaves no doubt that a
bung (cork), not a ball, was used, even though it is not very clearly visible:

Ladies stand on a snow-covered bank in the middle distance watching the skaters. In the foreground are four skaters in absurd positions.

A dandy lies on his back, trying to ward off with one leg another who reels backward striking him on the chin with the point of his skate.

The former says: 'What are you at there! You'll put my wig out of Buckle.'

The other exclaims: 'O Lord! how they are laughing at us!'

A third dandy has collided with a fat man whom he clasps round the waist; both are about to fall heavily on the prostrate skater.

He says: 'Pon honor Sir I beg pardon! you must thank the Ladies!'

Men in the distance skate with ease; some play hockey with sticks and a cork.[23]

The British Museum estimates that the print was created in 1818, based both on the date of publication (1819) of the fifth volume of *The Caricature Magazine, or, Hudibrastic Mirror,* in which this print was included (the first four volumes had been published prior to 1809), and on the popularity of the dandy as the subject of caricatures, which reached a high point on that year.

Chester, Cheshire, 1816
We have now reached the oldest known newspaper account of a hockey game (here called bandy) played on ice in England. It is, in fact, the oldest newspaper account of any stick-ball game played on ice in England. It appeared in the *Chester Chronicle* on Friday, February 16, 1816:

> Monday last [February 12], that part the River this city, distinguished the name of St. John's Dee, was crowded with skaiters sliders and bandy-players; and although no serious accidents occurred, several met with very severe tumbles. Tuesday came on a rapid thaw...[24]

It is not the first time that we see a report distinguishing between "skaters" and "sliders." While there is no certainty, the likelihood that the bandy players were on skates seems quite high.

The year 1816 was known as "the year without a summer": snow fell very late, and the summer never recovered. The preceding winter of 1815/16 had been severe, and might have been linked to the eruption of Mount Tambora in the Dutch East Indies (now Indonesia) in 1815, which greatly disrupted wind patterns and temperatures. Snow is reported to have fallen "all day" in the London area on Easter Sunday, April 14, with further snow reported on May 12. Snow drifts remained on hills until late July. This "year without a summer" can be credited with creating the conditions that led to the publication of a famous novel. While Mary Godwin and her lover, Percy Bysshe Shelley, were visiting Lord Byron at his summer home, Villa Diodati, on the shores of Lake Geneva in Switzerland, Godwin was involved in a dare to write a "ghost story." One night, she had a "waking dream" that eventually became the basis for *Frankenstein, or The Modern Prometheus,* first published in 1818 (by which point she had married Shelley and taken his surname). Byron was himself an avid field hockey player, said to prefer hockey over Horace.[25]

Epsom, Surrey, 1814

Epsom is located 29 kilometres south-southwest of Charing Cross, within the Greater London Urban Area. Epsom is the same distance, to the southeast, from Eton College.

William Wilson Jr. (1800–1866) was born in Radford, Nottinghamshire. In 1833, upon the death of his father, who had served four one-year terms as mayor of Nottingham, he became a principal in the firm of W. & S. Wilson of Radford. His preserved letters were written during his time at Mr. Atkinson's boarding school at Epsom (1813–1816). They are addressed to his parents, sisters, uncle and Aunt Morley. Here is a condensed version of a letter from 1814:

To Mother at Nottingham [March?] 1814

Thanks for parcel received and obliged to father for permission;

"to learn the military exercise...get a piece when I go to town at Easter..."

Having lectures on Experimental Philosophy;

"we are attending to optics and it is both amusing and instructive to learn the wonders which this study teaches. Especially the manner in which the eye is formed for the purpose of seeing..."

Complaint about night shirts;

"they are the most beastly things that ever I wore in all my life they are as coarse and rough as a badger, I hope you will never send me more of them..."

Extracts from his journal—sermons, Latin and French exercises, map drawing etc;

"brought grass from the downs for his garden, some boys went to Box Hill 14 mile [23 km] walk, went to dancing for the first time and 'learnt my positions glisard and...steps...to make a bow', had a 'game of Hockey' on the downs, 'rose at 6 to go to skait we had a most delightful skait till breakfast'..."

Appeals for money for fireworks as promised by father;

"'as many fireworks as I like' when peace is proclaimed..."[26]

Here again, there is no certainty that the hockey was played with skates; however, the game is evoked in the same sentence as two mentions of skating, so both the ice and the skates were available.

Richmond, Richmond upon Thames, London (1814)

Dudley Costello (1803-1865) was an author and journalist born in Sussex, the youngest child of John Francis Costello (d. 1814 or 1815) and Elisabeth Tothridge (d. 1846). His father was born in the barony of Costello, county Mayo, Ireland, and served as a captain in the 1st West India Regiment under Colonel John Whyte between 1795 and 1799.

In 1838, Dudley became a foreign correspondent to the *Morning Herald,* being a very good linguist, and for some time he lived in Hanover, Germany. Paris and London later divided his time, and in 1846 he was the foreign correspondent of the *Daily News.* Costello contributed articles and fiction to a variety of other publications, and at the same time became acquainted with Charles Dickens when contributing to *Bentley's Miscellany,* which Dickens edited from 1837 to 1839. Costello also wrote book-length works.

In 1855, Costello wrote a short essay entitled "The February Winter," in which he remembers the Great Frost of 1813/14, for *Bentley's Miscellany.* That winter was the fourth-coldest in the history of the Central England Temperature record (which dated back to 1660) and was the greatest frost of the 19th century, well remembered by all people who lived through it.

War and Winter are apt to hunt in couples, at all events in the ideas of him who, not claiming to be 'the oldest inhabitant', can awake the *souvenirs* of some forty years.

In the beginning of 1814 I knew, vaguely enough, being a very juvenile school-boy, that war was going on somewhere; but there was no vagueness in my knowledge of the existence of winter. That was a tangible fact of every hour's experience.

The daily walk from Richmond-green to Kew, beside the long wall which then was decorated with chalk drawings of all the ships in the British navy, and a representation of more than all the chain and bar-shot and piles of cannon-balls than, to my apprehension, ever could have been fired off, let the war last till 'the crack of doom': that long wall above which the trees hung a canopy of rime, depending from the branches in every variety of beautiful form!

The return from Kew to Richmond, not by the road but the river, no longer a 'silent highway', but a firm and compact mass of ice on which shouting thousands were in motion, skating, sliding, playing at football and hocky.[27]

No one can be certain as to whether Costello used the term *hocky* because it was the term used during that 1814 winter, or because it was the term that his 1855 readers would recognize and understand. Either way, it would still be hockey. Was it on skates? The mention of skating and sliding makes it likely that at least some of the players were wearing them.

While we have gone pretty far back in time (or "forward to the past"), none of the accounts presented so far in this book have made mention of an actual game of hockey played prior to the alleged "hurly on the long pond on the ice" of Windsor, Nova Scotia, which could theoretically be as old as about 1805 — though, of course, that reference does not mention a specific game. For that, we'll make another trip to Scotland.

Paisley, Renfrewshire, Scotland, 1803
From the *Aberdeen Journal* of Wednesday, February 9, 1803:

On Saturday [February 5], a most melancholy accident happened in the neighbourhood of Paisley — Two boys of about 14 years of age, the one named Ritchie, and the other Macallum were playing at shinty on the ice, at that part of the Cart called the High Lin, when the ice gave way with them, and they fell in, to the depth of 10 or 12 feet. A labourer in an adjoining field, who had been alarmed with the cries of the unfortunate youths, ran immediately to the spot, but could give no assistance, as the bodies had dropped under the ice. The neighbourhood then collected, and, in about twenty minutes after they had fallen in, the bodies were taken out of the water. The means for recovery were immediately tried and persevered in for some time by the surgeons, but without effect.[28]

Another very unfortunate incident. The game here is called shinty, not hockey or bandy. Was it hockey? While in chapter 8 the authors did not extend their demonstration of the equivalence of names beyond hockey and bandy, there should have already been enough evidence presented to convince the reader that shinty was also the same game. (The first reference was discussed in chapter 7; the rest in chapter 8.)

- A quote from *The Boy's Handy Book of Sports, Pastimes, Games and Amusements* (1863) stated: "HOCKEY may be called a very simplified form of golf. It is called Shinty in Scotland, and Hurley in Ireland."[29]
- We saw that *Holiday Sports and Pastimes For Boys* (1848) had an entry that started with the following words: "HURLEY, BANDY, HOCKY, SHINTY— are synonymous for one very capital game."[30]
- The beginning of C. G. Tebbutt's article on bandy in the 1892 book *Skating* stated that the "game of bandy, otherwise known as hockey and shinney, or shinty, is doubtless one of the earliest pastimes of the kind ever known."[31]
- The "Bandy, or Ice Hockey" article by Sydney Charles King-Farlow in the book *Ice-Sports* (1901) also started with some synonyms: "Bandy, is otherwise known as Hockey on the Ice, or Shinty."[32]
- Finally, the first chapter of the book *Hockey Historical and Practical* (1899), entitled "Early History," commenced with a list of regionalisms: "Various names have been given to hockey in different parts of the British Isles, of which hurley, bandy, and shinty are the best known. Its Scotch designation is shinty, hurley its Irish, and bandy its Welsh."[33]

So here we have a game described in five different books as being the same thing as hockey (and bandy), with a contemporary newspaper article describing it as having been played on ice. It is not irrefutable proof of (ice) hockey having been played, since there is no mention of skates, but it does appear to compare advantageously to the Windsor Haliburton reference, which does not mention skates, either, is not contemporary and draws from a work of fiction.

Isleworth Ait, Hounslow, London, 1796

If the reader has been intrigued by the cover of this book, here is its story.

In 2010, an American collector discovered the earliest known print or painting depicting not only hockey on skates, but also the use of a bung on the ice. The hand-coloured stipple engraving has the inscription *"London Published by J Le Petit 22 Suffolk Street, Middlesex Hospital 1st Sep 1797"* and measures 4⅜ inches (111 mm) high by 3¹¹/₁₆ (94 mm) wide. It is on wove paper with no watermark and was found in an antique shop in Maine, though we have no information as to how it got there.

The publisher, Joseph Le Petit Jr. (c. 1770–1858) was born in the London borough of Hackney, as a member of a French immigrant family. His father, Joseph Le Petit Sr., was born in France c. 1740, and after coming to England, initially worked as a French and writing master in Upper Clapton. The family later became strongly associated with engraving, printing and print-publishing in the London area. Little is known of Joseph Le Petit Jr., but from 1797 he was the publisher of a variety of prints in London. He later continued his business, Print Publishing and Artists' Repository, in Dublin, where he also died in 1858.

Unfortunately, the lower margin of the print has been trimmed, so it cannot be used to determine the title of the work, the artist or the engraver. However, an extensive and careful research indicates that the Anglo-Dutch artist Benedictus Antonio Van Assen (1767–c. 1817) was most certainly the man behind the work.[34]

Van Assen is presumed to have been from the Netherlands, but was active in London between 1788 and 1817. He studied in the Royal Academy schools and worked as a draftsman, painter, miniaturist, engraver, etcher and copyist. A number of Van Assen's prints, which he both drew and engraved, are found in several collections. Comparing this engraving with Van Assen's other known works, regarding the use of templates, the style of drawing and the text inscriptions "in the plate," shows that they are similar enough to attribute him as the probable artist and engraver of the print, recording what was a winter sport common enough in the vicinity of London to garner the attention of the artist and the publisher.

Regarding the title of the print, there is no clue, but for sure, the term *hockey* could have been used; we have seen in Richard Johnson's *Juvenile Sports and Pastimes* that, in 1773, hockey was ready for "new improvements" and thus the term had been in use for some time already.

Considering the date of publication (September 1, 1797) and the weather conditions in London in the years preceding, it appears most likely that the captured scene took place in December of 1796, as newspapers reported skating activities throughout the entire month all over the country.

As for the location of the scene, the grey "obelisk" in the background is a great clue, and it seems almost certain that it was the Kew Observatory, west of London, putting the skaters on the tip of Isleworth Ait, an island in the Thames.

It would appear that, by quite an extraordinary twist of fate, this "hockey" print by Van Assen was very probably mentioned in a magazine in the 1890s—i.e., almost 100 years later. From *Young England—An Illustrated Magazine for Young People Throughout the English-Speaking World,* published out of London:

BANDY; OR, ICE HOCKEY—by E. T. Sachs
In the old days, and to within quite recent years, the game was played with a bung. A couple of miles from where I am writing I found a small print of a youth on the ice on skates, with a hockey stick in the hand, and a bung lying on the ice at his feet. This print is more than a hundred years old, which shows that our great-great-grandfathers knew how to enjoy themselves in the winter quite as well as we do.[35]

The exact date of the issue in which this article appeared is not known, but the content indicates that it must have been between 1892 and 1896. Edwin Thomas Sachs (1850-1910) was educated at Rugby School and lived in Holland House, Reigate, Surrey, south of London. He was a member of the editorial staff of the well-known sports-magazine *The Field* and one of the oldest members of the London Athletic Club. In his youth, Sachs was a fine half-miler and won many races and was remembered as one of the first men to take up lacrosse in London. He was also a keen hockey player, both on ice and on ground, and a member of the Molesey Hockey Club in Surrey, being its representative at the foundation of the National Bandy Association in 1891. Sachs wrote several articles about ice hockey, field hockey and the chapter about lacrosse in *Hockey and Lacrosse,* published by Routledge in 1897.

Bluntisham-cum-Earith, Huntingdonshire (Cambridgeshire), 1813/14 and Well Before

In chapter 8, we presented the beginning of C. G. Tebbutt's article on bandy in *Skating* (1892). Let us now provide the end of the article, which—after some geographical considerations explaining why Bury Fen is an ideal place for bandy—looks at the history of some of the earliest remembered (if not recorded) games:

> Concurrently with skating races, bandy matches have long been held in the fens. It is certain that during the last century the game was played and even matches were held on Bury Fen, and the local tradition that the Bury Fenners had not been defeated for a century may not be an idle boast. But it was not until the great frost of 1813-14 that tradition gives place to certainty. I propose to furnish a short account of the Bury Fen players; for, excepting a few games played on private waters in different parts of England, bandy has been confined to that district, and its history is a history of the game.
>
> When the army of Napoleon, retreating from Moscow [in the winter of 1812/13], were starved and frozen to death by thousands; when, at home, Prof. [Adam] Sedgwick [1785-1873] had to burn his gun-case and chairs to keep himself warm; when the scarcity of coal at Cambridge was so great that the trees within the grounds of St. John's College were cut down for fuel, and in all the colleges, we are told, the men sat in their rooms two and three together for warmth; then the hardy watermen, gunners, and labourers were quickening their circulation by playing bandy on Bury Fen. It was then that that fine old Fenman, William Leeland [1804-1891], at the time scarcely eleven years old, remembers watching the matches and joining in the practice of bandy. Undoubtedly matches were played before this time, and Leeland had 'heard talk' of them; but we have no records...

[From about 1825] until well into 1850 Leeland captained the Bury Fenners, and only died in the autumn of 1891, in his ninetieth year [actually in his 87th]. An interview with this fine old player was made specially interesting by his pleasant memories of matches won at bandy... [Of the players from the early part of the century,] only Mr. R. Brown (88), Jas. Searle (75), and Bill Christmas (71), still live at the time of writing (Christmas, 1891)...[36]

Thus Tebbutt squarely puts the beginnings of bandy on ice (and with skates, as this is the only sort that he has any interest in) sometime in the 1700s, and quite possibly quite early in that century, even though he acknowledges that he can only pinpoint it with certainty in the winter of 1813/14, showing his intellectual honesty as a bandy/hockey historian.

In 2013, to celebrate the 200th anniversary of this oldest recorded bandy game, a statue was erected in Earith, portraying a bandy player of old time.[37] It is believed that, at the time of this first recorded game, bandy had been played for over 100 years in the Fens.

Firth of Forth, Scotland (1607/08)

Believe or not, before Samuel de Champlain founded New France and Quebec City, Scots were already playing shinty on ice.

David Calderwood (1575–1650) was a divine (theologian) and historian said to have been born in Midlothian, Scotland. He earned a master's degree at the University of Edinburgh in 1593. From about 1604 to 1617, he was the minister in Crailing, near Jedburgh in the former county of Roxburghshire. His last years were devoted to writing *The Historie of the Kirk of Scotland,* which was published in an abridged form in 1646. The complete work was edited by Rev. Thomas Thomson (1768–1852) and published in Edinburgh by the Woodrow Society, in 8 volumes, 1842–1849. Calderwood died in Jedburgh on October 29, 1650.

A passage in the manuscript tells about the "Great Frost" in the winter of 1607/08:

A VEHEMENT FROST

A vehement frost continued from Martimesse till the 20th of Februar. The sea freized so farre as it ebbed, and sindrie went in to shippes upon yee, and played at the chamiare a myle within the sea marke. Sindrie

> **A VEHEMENT FROST.**
>
> A vehement frost continued from Martimesse till the 20th of Februar. The sea freized so farre as it ebbed, and sindrie went in to shippes upon yce, and played at the chamiare a myle within the sea marke. Sindrie passed over the Firth above Alloway and Airth, to the great admiratioun of aged men, who had never seene the like in their dayes.

passed over the Firth above Alloway and Airth, to the great admiratioun of aged men, who had never seene the like in their dayes.[38]

In modern English, this would translate to: "A vehement frost continued from Martinmas [St. Martin's Day, November 11] till the 20th of February. The sea froze so far as it ebbed, and sundry went into ships upon ice and played at the chamiare a mile [1.6 km] within the sea-mark. Sundry passed over the Firth of Forth a mile above Alloa and Airth, to the great admiration of aged men, who had never seen the like in their days."[39]

"Chamiare," or "chamie,"[40] is another word for Shinty, as attested in the *Scottish National Dictionary*.[41]

A correspondent for *The Scotsman* stated in December 1897 that in East Lothian, where he was brought up, chamie, or the chamie, was more often used than shinty as the name of the game.[42]

The severity of the cold in the winter 1607/08 is confirmed by several other sources, and was even the subject of a book: *The Great Frost: Cold Doings in London* (see opposite page).[43]

Having presented a reference older than the creation of New France, the authors are now confident that hockey has been demonstrated to have been played on ice in Great Britain earlier than in Canada—or the United States, for that matter.

Chapter 11 Notes

1. Charles à Court Repington, *Vestigia: Reminiscences of Peace and War* (Boston: Houghton Mifflin, 1919): 30.
2. *The Times* (London), 27 Dec. 1870.
3. *Cambridge Independent Press,* 19 Feb. 1870.
4. Frank Rinder, *The Royal Scottish Academy 1826–1916; A Complete*

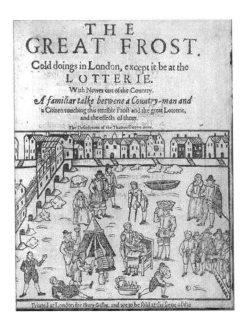

Cashing in on recent events with a quickly put-together book is nothing new. The Great Frost: Cold Doings in London, *sometimes attributed to poet and playwright Thomas Dekker (c. 1572–1632) was published in 1608.*[44]

List of the Exhibited Works. (Glasgow: James Maclehose and Sons, 1917): 210–211.

5. *Caledonian Mercury* (Edinburgh), 26 Feb. 1864.
6. *Illustrated Times* (London), 19 Dec. 1857.
7. *Morning Chronicle* (London), 16 Jan. 1856.
8. *Exeter and Plymouth Gazette* (Exeter), 24 Feb. 1855.
9. John Dugdale Astley, *Fifty Years of My Life in the World of Sport at Home and Abroad,* vol. I (London: Hurst and Blackett, 1894): 172.
10. Clement Kinloch Cooke, *A Memoir of Her Royal Highness Princess Mary Adelaide, Duchess of Teck, Based on Her Private Diaries and Letters,* vol. I (London: John Murray, 1900): 95.
11. *John Bull* (London), 2 Jan. 1847.
12. Alexander Meyrick Broadley, *The Boyhood of a Great King, 1841–1858:*

An Account of the Early Years of the Life of His Majesty, Edward VII (London: Harper and Brothers, 1906): 198.

13. Beatrice Caroline Steuart Erskine, *Twenty Years at Court, from the Correspondence of the Hon. Eleanor Stanley, Maid of Honour to Her Late Majesty Queen Victoria, 1842–1862* (London: Nisbet & Co., 1916): 93.

14. *The Argus* (London), 17 Jan. 1841.

15. Horace Mayhew, "A Scamper over the Serpentine (A Tale of the Late Frost)," *George Cruikshank's Table-book* (London: The Punch Office, 1845): 57.

16. E. W., "Sliding," *Leigh Hunt's London Journal,* 4 Feb. 1835: 36.

17. Leigh Hunt, "Now, Descriptive of a Cold Day,"*Leigh Hunt's London Journal,* 3 Dec. 1834: 1.

18. *Morning Post* (London), 31 Dec. 1829.

19. *Morning Post* (London), 26 Jan. 1827.

20. *The Times* (London), 30 Dec. 1822.

21. *Morning Post* (London), 30 Dec. 1822.

22. Charles Williams, *Skaiting-Dandies, Shewing Off,* c. 1818, British Museum, London.

23. Ibid.

24. *Chester Chronicle,* 16 Feb. 1816.

25. "Lord Byron," *The Literary Gazette, and Journal of Belles Lettres, Arts, Sciences, &c.* 22 May 1824.

26. William Wilson Jr., *Letter to Mother at Nottingham, [March?] 1814,* Letters from William Wilson Jr., DD/WR/41/24, Nottinghamshire Archives, Nottingham, England.

27. Dudley Costello, "The February Winter," *Bentley's Miscellany* 37 (1855): 312.

28. *Aberdeen Journal,* 9 Feb. 1803.

29. "Hockey," *The Boy's Handy Book of Sports, Pastimes, Games and Amusements* (London: Ward and Lock, 1863): 221.

30. Henry D. Richardson, *Holiday Sports and Pastimes for Boys* (London: William Somerville Orr & Co., 1848): 62.

31. John Moyer Heathcote, Charles Goodman Tebbutt and Thomas Maxwell Witham, *Skating* (London: Longmans, Green & Co., 1892): 429.

32. Sydney Charles King-Farlow, "Bandy, or Ice Hockey," *Ice-Sports,* (London: Ward, Lock & Co., 1901): 199.

33. J. Nicholson Smith and Philip A. Robson, *Hockey Historical and Practical* (London: A. D. Innes & Co., 1899): 1.

34. Benedictus Antonio Van Assen, untitled hand-coloured stipple engraving, 1797, Blyberg-Lefever Collection.

35. Edwin Thomas Sachs, "Bandy; or, Ice Hockey," *Young England: An Illustrated Magazine for Young People Throughout the English-Speaking World* (London: Sunday School Union, c. 1892–1896): 37.

36. Heathcote, Tebbutt and Witham, *Skating*, 430–431.

37. Julian Makey, "Villagers go bandy over fen sport diamond jubilee statue," *Cambridge News*, 16 Dec. 2013, web, 13 Apr. 2014, <http://www.cambridge-news.co.uk/Huntingdon-St-Ives-St-Neots/Villagers-go-bandy-over-fen-sport-diamond-jubilee-statue-20131216130107.htm#>.

38. David Calderwood, "A Vehement Frost," *The History of the Kirk of Scotland*, Thomas Thomson, ed., vol. VI (Edinburgh: The Wodrow Society, 1845): 688.

39. Robert Chambers, *Domestic Annals of Scotland, from the Reformation to the Revolution*, vol. I (Edinburgh: W. & R. Chambers, 1858): 405.

40. It is shown that *chamiare* and *chamie* are synonyms in Robert Craig Maclagan, *The Games & Diversions of Argyleshire* (London: David Nutt, 1901): 26.

41. "Shimmie, n. Also shammie, chamie. The game of Shinty," *Scottish National Dictionary*, n.d., web 11 Apr. 2014, <http://www.dsl.ac.uk/>.

42. Robert Craig Maclagan, *The Games & Diversions of Argyleshire*, 26.

43. *The Great Frost: Cold Doings in London* (London: Henry Gosson, 1608).

44. "Thomas Dekker," *Oxford Dictionary of National Biography*, n.d., web, 13 Apr. 2014, <http://www.oxforddnb.com/templates/article.jsp?articleid=7428&back=>.

On the Origin of "Hockey"

THE EARLIEST REFERENCES TO the game of hockey (by that name) date back to the mid-1700s, when we know it was played by schoolboys in London.[1] The authors of the Statutes of Galway (1527), which contain what is often thought to be the earliest reference to hockey, probably wrote "hockie stickes" as one might today write "hooky sticks," meaning that the sticks had a hooked appearance.[2]

Another source often mentioned as alluding to one of the earliest instances of hockey is Charles Ross's 1859 book about Charles Cornwallis, *Correspondence of Charles, First Marquis Cornwallis*. Ross writes of a "blow on the eye" during a game of hockey circa 1750; this is likely to have been speculation on Ross's part, a century after the fact.[3]

Why the game came to be known as "hockey" is disputed. The most common "modern" explanation is that the name derives from the French words *hocquet* and *hoquet* in the sense of a shepherd's crook (*bâton de berger*), alluding to the similarity with the curved stick used in the game.

This connection appears for the first time in a work by Pierre Carpentier (1697–1767), *Glossarium Novum ad Scriptores Medii Ævi, cum Latinos tum Gallicos,* published in 1766:

HOCQUET, Bâton de berger, houlette, fléau, Voy. *Hoquetus* 1. & *Picare* 3. Sup.

HOQUET, Bâton de berger, houlette. Voy. *Hoquetus* 1. Sup.[4]

The Idle Shepherd Boys *by John Pettie, 1863.*[7]

This theory regarding the word's origin appears to have cropped up towards the end of the 19th century. But although French was a dominant language in Europe in the 1700s, there is a lack of direct correlation with the term *hockey*. Indeed, earlier in the 1850s an alternate explanation was offered. From the May 1850 issue of the London magazine *Notes and Queries:* "*Hockey,* a game played by boys with a stick bent at the end, is very likely derived from *hook,* an Anglo-Saxon word too."[5]

Modern etymological dictionaries give us the following about the origin of the word *hook:*

Hook (n.)—from Old English *hoc* "hook, angle," perhaps related to Old English *haca* "bolt," from Proto-Germanic **hokaz/*hakan*—(cf. Old

Frisian *hok*, Middle Dutch *hoek*, Dutch *haak*, German *Haken* "hook"), from PIE **keg*— "hook, tooth" (cf. Russian *kogot* "claw").

Hooked (adj.)— from Old English *hoced*, "shaped like a hook, crooked, curved;" past participle adj. from hook (v.). From mid-14c. as "having hooks;" 1610s as "caught on a hook"[6]

Both of these theories are, of course, based on the premise that the game of hockey was named after the stick's appearance. But could the name have been derived from something other than the shape of the stick?

One thing that might seem curious is that an identical curved stick, called a "bandy," had already existed for centuries. A bandy (from Old French, *bander*)[8] could be used in a sport such as bandy-ball,[9] a name that at times referred to golf[10] and at other times to a game similar to hockey. It could also be used for older forms of cricket.[11]

As early as 1612, William Strachey mentioned that boys in England played a stick-and-ball game called bandy. Describing the customs of the indigenous people in the vicinity of Jamestown, Virginia, the first permanent English settlement in North America, Strachey wrote: "A kynd of exercise they have often amongst them much like that which boyes call bandy in English, and maye be an auncient game…"[12]

Such a useful stick must certainly have been one of a young boy's most valued possessions, as can be seen in *The Children's Petition* of 1669:

> It is not the boy's warm bed, or breakfast, not his meat and drink, no not his ball, his top, and his bandy, would be so delicious to him, as the time he was thus suffered to be with his Master…[13]

The last reference in London to a game called bandy is from 1749,[14] which coincides with the oldest mentions of the game of hockey.

Why would the schoolboys in London rename the bandy stick a "hockey stick"? There is no obvious reason, as the sticks had the same appearance. So perhaps it was *not* the stick that "hockey" was named after. So what else was introduced in the game that might have caused the change in nomenclature?

The answer can perhaps be found in the very earliest references to the game. Richard Johnson writes in *Juvenile Sports and Pastimes* about the game of hockey:

The materials for this sport are only of three sorts; the goals, the hockey, and the hockey-sticks...
This sport can be pursued no where with pleasure, but in a wide spacious field, where the hockey may have its full scope...
The use of the crook part is to disengage the hockey from your antagonists, when it is so surrounded by them that you cannot get at it to give it a full stroke toward their goal.
The kockey must be made of the largest cork-bung you can get. Cut the edges round, and then it is prepared for use.
The goals being fixed, the hockey prepared, and the parties agreed on, you then proceed to your sport in the following manner.
Both parties meet as nearly as possible, in the middle between the two goals, when the hockey is tossed up, and every one tries his best to beat the hockey through the goal of his antagonist...
Some boys are of such an eager, warm disposition, that they care not whom they hurt, or whose skin they break, so that they get at the kockey; but this is the mark of a bad player...
When he sees the kockey is so surrounded by both parties, that he cannot get a fair stroke at it, he makes one among them with his crook, and endeavours to get it between...
According to the rules of this game, you are never to touch the kockey with your hands...[15]

Johnson refers six times to the playing object (the cork bung) as "the hockey" and four times as "the kockey"—the latter spelling most certainly having been a typographical error by the printer.

Johnson also mentions the stick: "The bottom, however, must not be strait, but crooked, and that in the form of a shepherd's crook is valuable beyond everything." However, he makes no connection between the word *hockey* itself and the shepherd's crook. Instead, he describes the cork bung as being "the hockey," pointing out that this is the object that identifies the game.

The words "the hockey" recur in other early descriptions of the game, as in Sir Richard Phillips's *The Book of Games, or, A History of the Juvenile Sports, Practised at the Kingston Academy,* published in 1805:

The game consists in endeavouring to drive the ball (which is either made of wood or cork; and old bung cut round at the edges answers the

Old barrel bungs.

---

purpose very well, and called the hockey) through the gaol [sic] of your antagonist...

   The players next endeavour to strike the hockey, and drive it through their adversaries' goal...

   THOMAS. —Ah! look, it is over, is it not? The tall boy has driven the hockey through the sticks; the goal, I think, you call it.[16]

Similarly, George Frederick Pardon, writing in 1858, advises in *Games for All Seasons* that "the object of the game is to drive the hockey over a bound set on either side.... This alternate striking the hockey forward and backwards is the whole art of the game."[17]

   In *The Outdoor Handy Book, for Playground, Field and Forest,* published in New York in 1900, Daniel Carter Beard (1850-1941) writes:

Hockey—is practically the same as shinny, differing in immaterial points. In this game, the bung is called the 'hockey', the shinny sticks, hockey sticks; and the captains, in place of scuffling over the ball at the call of time, toss up for choice of first chance at the hockey. The winner at the call of 'play' strikes the hockey with his club...[18]

It thus seems as if the big change, compared to the old game of bandy, was that a bung made of cork was now used instead of a ball made of wood, and

Illustration of a cork cutter, from the Book of
English Trades, and Library of the Useful Arts.[23]

this bung was called "the hockey." Schoolboys might have preferred a material that was easy to shape, with the additional benefit that, if hit by one, it might not have hurt as much as the old wooden balls.

Bungs are mentioned in most of the earliest descriptions of hockey, as by William Pierre Le Cocq in 1799,[19] and are also pictured in several engravings from the late 1700s and early 1800s, as seen in chapter 9.

What might have contributed to this change of a playing object was that bungs of cork became available in large numbers during the 1700s.

Bountiful Bungs
Bungs were large stoppers for barrels, made by cork cutters.[20] The manufacturing was said to be "one of the blackest, and dirtiest of trades, and not very profitable either for the master or the journeyman."[21]

In England, cork cutting as a specialized trade seems to have appeared in the 17th century, along with the development of glass and stone bottles. Cork was pressed into square pieces and then sent to the cutters, who cut it into smaller pieces before using their knives to carve out the final—circular—product.[22] The demand for cork rose sharply in the 1700s, partly because of the novelty of using the material to seal wine bottles, and partly because of the growth of the brewing industry, spurred on by what contemporary accounts record as a tremendous increase in beer consumption during this century. César de Saussure (1705-1783), a native of Lausanne, Switzerland, made a journey to England in 1725 and spent the next five years in London. He described the conditions in the capital in a letter to his relatives written in East Sheen, in the present-day borough of Richmond upon Thames, on October 29, 1726:

> Would you believe it, though water is to be had in abundance in London, and of fairly good quality, absolutely none is drunk? The lower classes, even the paupers, do not know what it is to quench their thirst with water.
>
> In this country nothing but beer is drunk, and it is made in several qualities. Small beer is what everyone drinks when thirsty; it is used even in the best houses, and costs only a penny the pot. Another kind of beer is called porter, meaning carrier, because the greater quantity of this beer is consumed by the working classes. It is a thick and strong beverage, and the effect it produces, if drunk in excess, is the same as that of wine; this porter costs threepence the pot.
>
> In London there are a number of ale-houses, where nothing but this sort of beer is sold. There are again other clear beers, called ale, some of these being as transparent as fine old wine, foreigners often mistaking them at first sight for the latter. The prices of ales differ, some costing one shilling the bottle, and others as much as eighteenpence.
>
> It is said that more grain is consumed in England for making beer than for making bread.[24]

Similar observations were made by Charles Henry Cook (1858-1933), writing under the pen name John Bickerdyke, in *The Curiosities of Ale & Beer: An Entertaining History,* published in 1886. Cook quotes John Taylor (1578-1653), a Thames waterman, who dubbed himself "The Water Poet."

Image of a brewer from the Book of English Trades. *Notice the large bung-holes in the barrels.*

The stronger *Beere* is divided into two parts (viz.), mild and stale; the first may ease a man of a drought, but the latter is like water cast into a Smith's forge, and breeds more heart-burnings, and as rust eates into Iron, so overstale Beere gnawes aulet holes in the entrales, or else my skill failes, and what I have written of it is to be held as a Jest.[25]

Cook then describes the emergence of porter in the early 1700s:

It appears that in the early years of last century the lovers of malt liquors in London were accustomed to regale themselves upon three classes of these beverages; they had ale, beer and twopenny...

It seems to be to some extent a moot point among the learned how porter obtained its present name, for no record seems to have been kept of its christening...[26]

The brewing of porter grew into an enormous industry during the 18th century.

> Pennant gives a list of the chief porter brewers of London at the end of last century, with the number of barrels of strong beer they brewed from Midsummer, 1786, to Midsummer, 1787. Samuel Whitbread heads the list with 150,280 barrels... The total amount produced by some twenty-four of the chief London brewers was considerably over one million barrels...[27]

So it was seemingly not hard for a group of schoolboys to get hold of a large cork bung from a brewery.

Of course, what we have seen so far does not tell us why the bung was called "the hockey." The explanation may lie in what was in the barrels. There exists a connection between the word *hock* and Rhenish wine, which until the mid-1700s was exported from Germany to England in barrels before being bottled. The *Dictionarium Britannicum* by Nathan Bailey (c. 1691–1742), published in 1736, provides one definition:

> Hock, or *Old Hock, Rhenish* Wine; so called from the Village of *Hock-heim* [sic] *on the Mayne,* where is supposed to be the best Growth."[28]

John Ash (c. 1724–1779), in his *New and Complete Dictionary of the English Language,* (1775), defined *hock* thus:

> Hock (s. *from* Hockheim) Rhenish wine, old strong Rhenish wine.
> Hock'amore (s. *from* hock) Hock, old strong Rhenish wine.
> Hock'heim (s.) A village in Germany famous for the best growth of Rhenish wine.[29]

Besides wine, was something else stored in barrels for which cork bungs were used? It appears that a connection between the word *hock* and various sorts of beer is even stronger and goes back much farther in time.

Hocktide, or *Hock tide,* was a medieval term used to denote the Monday and Tuesday (Hock Monday and Hock Tuesday) in the week following the second Tuesday after Easter. At Hocktide in pre-Reformation time, people took part in various festive and sports activities that raised money for the local parish. After the Reformation, it was kept as a festive season with various traditional customs.[30]

Hock ale, or *Hocking ale,* was the beer brewed for the festivals at Hocktide. The earliest known reference to hock ale comes from Hertfordshire, from the accounts of the church warden of St. Michael's Parish in the town of Bishop's Stortford for the year 1484:[31]

Item pd for ix b² malte to the hoke ale	vj *s.* iiij *d.*
Item pd for iiij b² whete to the hoke ale	iij *s.* iiij *d.*
Item pd for brewyng of the hokyng ale xvj b²	xvj *d.*

Murray informs us: *"Hockey, hawkey,* or *horkey* (also, hocky, hooky, hoacky, hoky, hoaky, hockey, hawkie) was also the name for the feast at *Harvest-home.* The Hock-cart was the wagon which carried home the last load of the harvest."[32]

The feast at Harvest-home was associated with much drinking, as Robert Herrick (1591–1674) noted in his 1648 poem "The Hock-cart, or Harvest Home":

> And for to make the merry cheere,
> If smirking wine be wanting here,
> There's that, which drowns all care, stout beere;
> Which freely drink to your Lord's health,
> Then to the plough, the commonwealth,
> Next to your flailes, your fanes, your fatts;
> Then to the maids with wheaten hats:
> To the rough sickle and crookt sythe,
> Drink, frollick, boyes, till all be blythe.[33]

In "The Horkey, a Provincial Ballad," published in 1806, the poet Robert Bloomfield (1766–1823) mentions the "horkey-beer," a brew specially prepared for the occasion:

> And Farmer Cheerum went, good man,
> And broach'd the *Horkey beer;*
> And *sitch a mort* [such a number] of folks began
> To eat up our good cheer[34]

Illustration by George Cruikshank, prepared for an 1882 edition of Bloomfield's poem "The Horkey, a Provincial Ballad."[35]

The old name "hook ale," or similar, seems to have survived into the 18th century as a term for various types of beer. In 1715, just after George I assumed the British throne, the satirist, poet and London tavernkeeper Edward "Ned" Ward (1667–1731) published *A Vade Mecum for Malt-Worms; Or, A Guide to Good Fellows,* which bore the (extremely) informative subtitle:

> Being a Description of the Manners and Customs of the Most Eminent Publick Houses, in and about the Cities of London and Westminster, with a Hint on the Props (or Principal Customers) of Each House, In a Method so Plain that Any Thirsty Person (of the Meanest Capacity) May Easily find the Nearest Way from One House to Another. Dedicated to the Brewers.[36]

The second edition, entitled *A Guide for Malt-Worms,* was published in 1720.[37] The guides, written in verse, offer a rare contemporary record of the beers drunk in London's taverns in the early 1700s. In this edition, Ward writes about the tavern in St. Ann's Lane, Aldersgate:

> O Thou! that tak'st thy Christian Name from Saint,
> Who's Tutelary to the men that Paint,

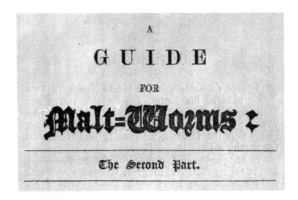

And wear'st a Sirname, that can ne'er be right,
Since, though thy Name is LUKE, no colour's White;
Give ear, and hearken to the great Renown
Of thy pale Hocky, and Two-peny brown...

But, above all thy Customers, TOM Sly,
Good Mrs. LUKER'S servant, by the by,
Is careful, with his Handsel, to salute you,
And with half Pint of Hocky pay his Duty...[38]

The most frequently mentioned drinks in the two books are mild and stale (sometimes paired together, suggesting they were indeed drunk together) and twopenny. But as we can see, one of the popular drinks was called "the Hocky."

Later in the 1700s, the name appears to have been used as a term for porter. Michael Combrune describes the making of "Old Hock" in his *Theory and Practice of Brewing*, published in 1762:

OF THE NATURE AND PROPERTIES OF HOPS

Old hock requires the same proportion of hops, as are used in keeping pale strong or keeping pale small beer; but more or less according to the time it is intended to be kept before it becomes fit for use. The length is about two barrels, from a quarter of the palest and best malt. As spontaneous pellucidity is required, its whole medium must not exceed 138 degrees, for the drying and extracting heat. The management of it, when fermenting, is under the same rules with the liquor just now mentioned, or those which are allowed a due time to become of themselves pellucid.[39]

Writing 46 years later, Duncan MacDonald provides a similar explanation in *The New London Family Cook; or, Town and Country Housekeeper's Guide:*

OLD HOCK

This is nothing more than white or pale porter; made with pale malt, in quantity equal to that of amber, or high dried malt for brown stout, and without any of those ingredients which gave colour. Sometimes brown stout is even made by simply adding from two to three pounds of essentia bina to a barrel of old hock.[40]

As it happens, the good supply of these types of beers led to the word *hockey* becoming associated with drunkenness. In December 1770, a Mr. T. Norworth writes in *The Gentleman's Magazine, and Historical Chronicle:*

OBSERVATIONS OF DRUNKENNESS

... We have therefore contrived a great variety of names and phrases, most of them whimsical and ludicrous, to veil the turpitude of what is pleasing in itself, and generally connected with reciprocations, if not of friendship, yet of the lesser duties and endearments of society.

I believe few people are aware how far this has been carried, or have any notion that the simple idea of having drunk too much liquor, is expressed in near FOURSCORE different ways. I send you a list of them for the amusement of your readers in your Christmas Magazine.

I am Sir, your humble Servant,

T. NORWORTH

To express the Condition of an Honest Fellow, *and no* Flincher, *under the Effects of* good Fellowship, it is said *that he is:*

1. Drunk...
15. Hockey[41]

Some years later, the same expression appeared in the second edition of the well-known book by Francis Grose (1731-1791), *A Classical Dictionary of the Vulgar Tongue,* published in 1788:

HOCKEY. Drunk with strong stale beer, called old hock.
See HICKSIUS DOXIUS, and HICKEY.[42]

Grose's definition for *hicksius doxius* is "drunk." For *hickey*, "Tipsey quasi, hickuping."

"Stale" was beer that had been matured, possibly for up to two years, a habit that grew during the early 1700s; the term originates from the word *stall*, which meant "held."[43]

The Great Vats *by Gustave Doré (1872) depicts the fermentation tanks in the Barclay, Perkins and Company brewery, Southwark, London.*[44]

Conclusion?

There is no doubt from the above that the word *hockey* was associated with a common beer or wine, as well as with the consumption of those beverages. It may therefore be that the cork bung used in schoolboys' games was termed "the hockey" because it was taken from barrels in which drinks with similar names were stored.

The smoking gun would be an 18th-century text including wording like "the hockey, which can be taken from a barrel." This has not surfaced yet. There are few contemporary references to hockey prior to the early 1800s, but the existing ones always describe the game as being played with a bung. It is quite possible that, during the years that had passed since the mid-1700s, people became unaware of, or forgot, the origin of the word *hockey*, but that from the beginning it was associated with a bung made of cork.

Another interesting aspect is that the bungs were flat, so it appears that hockey in the beginning was played with an object similar to a puck, while in later years it was found that it could be played just as well with a ball— especially from the mid-1800s, when the India-rubber ball came into vogue and mostly replaced the bung, both on ice and on the ground.

Still, it was the flat bung that was used to play hockey on the ice in London and its surroundings up to 1891, when the Fen style of playing with a ball took over. The bung was later and definitively replaced by the Canadian invention made of rubber.

Of interest is the fact that a brewery in London, dating back to 1701, still manufactures a seasonal cask ale by the name of Hock. The brewery's well-known Hock Cellar is a 200-year-old storage room that is now a tasting and reception area.[45]

While the authors don't pretend that this theory on the origin of the word *hockey* has been proven beyond a reasonable doubt, they do believe it appears more plausible than the other currently existing theories. The link with beer, if correct, would certainly represent a strange connection from the past that came full circle two centuries later, as major breweries became the primary sponsors of hockey in the authors' home countries of Canada and Sweden.

Chapter 12 Notes

1. Master Michel Angelo (Richard Johnson), *Juvenile Sports and Pastimes, to Which are Prefixed, Memoirs of the Author: Including a New Mode of Infant Education* (London: Thomas Carnan, 1773): 91–96. Also Richard Phillips, *The Book of Games, or, A History of the Juvenile Sports, Practised at the Kingston Academy; Illustrated with Twenty-four Copper Plates* (London: Tabart & Co., 1805): 7–16.

2. *The Galway Corporation Statute Book (or Liber A) of 1527,* folio 033,
    James Hardiman Library, National University of Ireland, Galway.
    The Statutes of Galway (written in English) are often described as
    making the earliest reference to "hockey sticks." The Statutes banned
    hurling and handball, but allowed "the great football": "...at no tyme
    the use ne ocupye the horlinge of the litill balle with hockie stickes
    or staves, nor use no hande ball to playe without the walles, but onely
    the great foote balle, on payn of the paynis above lymittid." Or, in
    modern English: "...at no time the use nor occupy the hurling of the
    little ball with hooked sticks or staves, nor use a handball to play outside
    the walls, but only the great football on pain of the pains above limited
    [a fine of eight pence]."

    Notice that the word *hockie* most certainly has nothing to do with
    the term *hockey*—it is meant to describe the stick as being "hooky"
    (i.e., "hooked" or "curved"). It should therefore be read as "hooked
    sticks" and not "hockey sticks." It is also worth mentioning that John
    Lydgate used the same way of describing a curved stick 100 years ear-
    lier—"Wyth a Staff mad lyk an hook"—in *The Pilgrimage of the Life
    of Man,* published in 1426.

3. Charles Ross, *Correspondence of Charles, First Marquis Cornwallis,*
    vol. I (London: John Murray, 1859): 3. An often-used "proof" that
    hockey was played at Eton College in the mid-1700s comes from Ross's
    book: "During his Eton career he received, while playing at hockey, a
    blow on the eye, which produced a slight but permanent obliquity of
    vision. The boy who accidentally caused this injury was Shute Barring-
    ton, afterwards the highly esteemed Bishop of Durham."

    In editing this work, Ross had access to a more than 400 letters be-
    tween Cornwallis and his own father, General Alexander Ross, written
    during the period 1782–1805. It is, however, not known whether the
    word *hockey* was ever mentioned in the letters.

    Unlike the schools in Central London—including Charterhouse,
    Christ's Hospital and Westminster—there exists no other record of
    the game at Eton until 50 years after Cornwallis attended the college,
    around 1750. The statement, therefore, has to be met with some skep-
    ticism—especially since it is a secondhand reference from Charles Ross.
    It may be that the injury referred to was caused by the crooked stick,

or bandy, used in cricket up to about 1760, and that this stick might later — incorrectly — have been remembered as a "hockey stick."

4. Pierre Carpentier, *Glossarium Novum ad Scriptores Medii Ævi, cum Latinos tum Gallicos, seu Supplementum ad Auctiorem Glossarii Cangiani Editionem,* vol. 4 (Paris: André-François Le Breton, 1766): 358-359.

5. "Minor Queries, Howkey or Horkey," *Notes and Queries,* no. 28 (May 11, 1850): 457.

6. Douglas Harper, *Online Etymology Dictionary 2001–2014,* web, <http://www.etymonline.com/index.php?l=h&p=25&allowed_in_fra me=0>.

7. John Pettie, *The Idle Shepherd Boys,* from *Wordsworth's Poems for the Young* (London: Alexander Strahan & Co., 1863): 17.

8. *Encyclopaedia Perthensis; or Universal Dictionary of the Arts, Sciences, Literature, &c. Intended to Supersede the Use of All Other Books of Reference,* vol. III (Edinburgh: The Royal Physical Society, 1816): 234.

9. David Cram, Jeffrey L. Forgeng and Dorothy Johnston, *Francis Willughby's Book of Games: A Seventeenth-Century Treatise on Sports, Games, and Pastimes* (Aldershot, U. K.: Ashgate Publishing, 2003): 179.

10. Joseph Strutt, *Glig-Gamena Angel-Ðeod, or, The Sports and Pastimes of the People of England* (London: John White, 1801) and Delabere Pritchett Blaine, *An Encyclopaedia of Rural Sports; or A Complete Account, Historical, Practical, and Descriptive, of Hunting, Shooting, Fishing, Racing, and Other Field Sports and Athletic Amusements of the Present Day* (London: Longman, Orme, Brown, Green and Long-mans, 1840): 131-132.

11. Blaine, *An Encyclopaedia of Rural Sports,* and Robert Forby, *The Vocabulary of East Anglia; An Attempt to Record the Vulgar Tongue of the Twin Sister Counties, Norfolk and Suffolk, as It Existed in the Last Twenty Years of the Eighteenth Century, and Still Exists; with Proof of Its Antiquity from Etymology and Authority,* vol. I (London: John Bowyer Nichols and Son, 1830): 14-15.

12. William Strachey, *The Historie of Travaile into Virginia Britannia,* Richard Henry Major, ed. (London: The Hakluyt Society, 1849): 77–78. This is the first known use of the term *bandy* for a stick-and ball game similar to hockey. It is well documented that a great number of the North American Indian tribes traditionally played stick-and ball

games. Some of them used sticks similar to those in field hockey; others used sticks resembling the ones used for lacrosse.

Strachey, who visited Jamestown, Virginia, between 1610 and 1611, here uses the term *bandy* to describe the natives' game—indicating that this term also was used in England around 1600 for a stick-and ball game corresponding to hockey. Strachey's manuscript about the Jamestown colony was written after his return to England in 1612, but was not published until 1849.

13. Richard Chiswell, *The Children's Petition, or A Modest Remonstrance of that Intolerable Grievance Our Youth Lie Under, in the Accustomed Severities of the School Discipline of This Nation: Humbly Presented to the Consideration of the Parliament* (London: Richard Chiswell, November 10, 1669). The campaign to persuade Parliament to end corporal punishment in schools began in 1669 with this publication, which suggests that a teacher who "is not able to awe and keep a company of youth in obedience without violence and stripes should judge himself no more fit for that function."

14. The *Daily Advertiser* (London) of August 9, 1749, carried an advertisement with this message: "ON Thursday next, a Match at BANDY will be play'd, at Tottenham Court, ten on each Side, for a Guinea a Head. To begin playing at Two o'Clock in the Afternoon p.r dely [?] Note. The Players are to meet at Mr. Hands's, the Two Brewers in Broad St. Giles's."

This might have been an advertisement for a match of Irish hurling without "air-play"—an ancient version of the game resembling Scottish shinty that was common in the northern parts of Ireland. The old English term *bandy* was sometimes used by the English for Irish hurling—and the parish of St. Giles was at this time inhabited by a great number of Irish immigrants.

15. Master Michel Angelo (Johnson), *Juvenile Sports and Pastimes,* 91–96.

16. Richard Phillips, *The Book of Games,* 12–13.

17. G. F. P. (George Frederick Pardon), *Games for All Seasons* (London: James Blackwood, 1858): 20.

18. Daniel Carter Beard, *The Outdoor Handy Book, for Playground, Field and Forest* (New York: Charles Scribner's Sons, 1900): 451.

19. William Pierre Le Cocq, *Letter to Parents,* 17 Dec. 1799, Priaulx Library, Island of Guernsey.

20. John Mason Good, Olinthus Gregory and Newton Bosworth, *Pantologia. A New Cyclopaedia, Comprehending a Complete Series of Essays, Treatises, and Systems, Alphabetically Arranged, with a General Dictionary of Arts, Sciences, and Words*, vols. II and III (London: 1813).

21. Richard Phillips, *Book of English Trades, and Library of the Useful Arts* (London: J. Souter, 1818): 124–126.

22. Good, Gregory and Bosworth, *Pantologia.*

23. Phillips, *Book of English Trades,*

24. Madame Van Muyden, ed., *A Foreign View of England in the Reigns of George I and George II: The Letters of Monsieur César de Saussure to His Family* (London: John Murray, 1902): 157–158.

25. John Bickerdyke (Charles Henry Cook), *The Curiosities of Ale & Beer: An Entertaining History* (London: Swan Sonnenschein & Co., 1886): 158.

26. Ibid., 365–366.

27. Ibid, 368.

28. Bailey, Nathan, *Dictionarium Britannicum: Or a More Compleat Universal Etymological English Dictionary Than Any Extant,* 2nd ed. (London: T. Cox) 1736.

29. John Ash, *The New and Complete Dictionary of the English Language* (London: Edward and Charles Dilly, and R. Baldwin), 1775.

30. James A. H. Murray, *A New English Dictionary on Historical Principles, Founded Mainly on the Materials Collected by the Philological Society,* vol. V, part 1 (London: Clarendon Press, 1901): 319–320.

31. J. L. Glasscock Jr., *The Records of St. Michael's Parish Church, Bishop's Stortford* (London: Elliot Stock, 1882): 26.

32. Murray, *A New English Dictionary,* vol. V, part 1: 319–320.

33. Maitland, Thomas (Editor), The Works of Robert Herrick. Edinburgh: Reprinted for W. and C. Tait, 1823, Volume I: 140.

34. Robert Bloomfield, "The Horkey, a Provincial Ballad," *Wild Flowers; or, Pastoral and Local Poetry* (London: Longman, Hurst, Rees and Orme, 1806): 38.

35. Robert Bloomfield, *The Horkey* (London: Macmillan and Co., 1882): 20.

36. Edward Ward, *A Vade Mecum for Malt-Worms; Or, A Guide to Good Fellows, Being a Description of the Manners and Customs of the Most Eminent Publick Houses, in and about the Cities of London and West-*

minster, with a Hint on the Props (or Principal Customers) of Each House, In a Method so Plain that Any Thirsty Person (of the Meanest Capacity) May Easily find the Nearest Way from One House to Another. Dedicated to the Brewers (London: Thomas Bickerton, 1715.)

37. Edward Ward, *A Guide for Malt-Worms: The Second Part, Being a Description of the Manners and Customs of the Most Eminent Publick Houses, in and about the Cities of London and Westminster, with a Hint on the Props (or Principal Customers) of Each House, in a Method so Plain that Any Thirsty Person (of the Meanest Capacity) May Easily Find the Nearest Way from One House to Another. Done by Several Hands* (London: Thomas Bickerton, 1720): 27.

38. Ibid.

39. Michael Combrune, *The Theory and Practice of Brewing* (London: R. and J. Dodsley; T. Becket and P.A. de Hondt; and T. Longman, 1762): 163.

40. Duncan MacDonald, *The New London Family Cook; or, Town and Country Housekeeper's Guide* (London: James Cundee, 1808): 394.

41. T. Norworth, "Observations of Drunkenness," *The Gentleman's Magazine, and Historical Chronicle* 40 (December 1770): 559.

42. Francis Grose, *A Classical Dictionary of the Vulgar Tongue: The Second Edition, Corrected and Enlarged* (London: S. Hooper, 1788).

43. Martyn Cornell, *Beer: The Story of the Pint—The History of Britain's Most Popular Drink* (London: Headline Book Publishing, 2003).

44. Gustave Doré, "The Great Vats," *London: A Pilgrimage* (London: Grant & Co., 1872).

45. "Other Seasonals Not Currently Available," *Fuller, Smith & Turner*, n.d., web, 14 Apr. 2014, <http://www.fullers.co.uk/rte.asp?id=175>.

The Expansion Years

Sɪᴛᴜᴀᴛɪɴɢ ᴛʜᴇ ᴏʀɪɢɪɴs ᴏꜰ ɪᴄᴇ hockey in England poses a brand new question: How did it *get* to Canada?

Up until now, the question was: Where was hockey invented? Or more specifically, what was its birthplace within Canada? But unless we believe that hockey was "reinvented" in Canada after having been played in England under that name for over half a century—and under various other names for more than a century—the question no longer involves which pond the game was first played on, but how it crossed The Pond.

There is an easy—though perhaps not entirely satisfactory—answer: hockey came to Canada the same way that cricket (once very popular), rugby (which evolved over time into Canadian football) and other sports came to Canada.

Unfortunately, we don't exactly know how those sports came to Canada, either. We know that they all came from England, and we know that the majority of English-speaking settlers in Canada in the 19th century were from the United Kingdom, so it should certainly come as no surprise that games and sports commonly played in England became popular in Canada too. Settlers brought with them their language, their religion, their allegiance to the monarch, much of their toponymy (there are, in England, more than 15 Kingstons, three Windsors, one Halifax and one Dartmouth) and their favourite games. It's what settlers do.

As far as the games are concerned, in the case being studied here, it is mostly the folk games that the settlers brought with them. It is no coincidence that the older accounts in Canada written by Canadians (see the summary table at the end of chapter 1) use words other than hockey: *hurly, hurley on the ice* or *hurl, break-shins* or *shinny,* and *ricket.* And only two (pre-1875) references written by Canadians use the term *hockey:* the articles in the 1864 *Halifax Reporter* and the 1867 *Halifax Evening Reporter,* though the latter also uses the term *ricket.*

Immigrants

We saw in chapter 1 that Nova Scotia has, by far, more pre-1875 references to hockey or hockey-like games, written by Canadians, than all other claims combined. That province—or, at the time, colony—had immigrants of many origins. Irish immigrants mostly came to Nova Scotia in the mid-1700s or between 1815 and 1845.[1] They would have brought the hurling (or hurley/hurly) mentioned in the Windsor and Pictou references and in a couple of the Halifax-Dartmouth references.

Despite the colony's name, which is Latin for "New Scotland," there were not that many Scots among the early settlers;[2] significant numbers began arriving starting in 1773, when the ship *Hector* famously brought to Pictou a group of 189 Highlanders (though only 171 survived the voyage), mostly from Lochbroom in Ross-shire.[3] There are surprisingly few mentions from Nova Scotia of the Scottish term *shinny,* but one Pictou reference uses *break-shins,* which is etymologically much the same.

Another group of immigrants to Nova Scotia were loyalists who fled the United States following the American Revolution (1775-1783). A subgroup, called the Maritime Loyalists, emigrated to Nova Scotia, though their large numbers and suspicion towards the Halifax establishment led to the creation of the separate colony of New Brunswick.[4] It was likely they who brought the game (and name) of ricket,[5] found throughout the Nova Scotia references—from the very earliest[6] to the most recent known pre-1875 mention.[7]

There is also the 1906 "shinty" reference from Kingston, a recollection of games played c. 1846-47. The history of the Scottish presence in Kingston is well known; most notably, Queen's University (originally Queen's College) was created and funded by the Presbyterian Church in collaboration with the Church of Scotland.[8]

"Visitors"

On the other hand, all six references from European "visitors" (as opposed to people born in Europe who immigrated in Canada) that actually name the activity, call it "hockey," "ice hockey" or "hockey on the ice." Five of the six are from officers of the military—one Irish and three English. John Franklin provided two of them; at the time, he was acting as an explorer, but he was also a Royal Navy officer.[9]

Besides Franklin's Deline correspondence, there are, of course, the Niagara Falls reference (from Sir Richard George Augustus Levinge of the 43rd Regiment) and the Kingston mention (from Sir Arthur Henry Freeling of the Corps of Royal Engineers).

There is also the 1864 reference from Halifax-Dartmouth, via Irish-born Vice-Admiral Charles Cooper Penrose Fitzgerald, who uses the term *hockey* as well. English Lieutenant Henry Buckton Laurence, who created the *Curling on the Lakes* print in 1867, did not designate the game played in the background, but he almost certainly would also have used *hockey* had he needed to name it.

Halifax has pretty much always been a garrison city; the list of nearly 200 British regiments stationed in Halifax at one point or another between 1749 and 1906 is rather impressive.[10]

These reports of hockey in places where the British military was present seem consistent with a progression that now looks quite natural, as far as hockey—by that name and played on the ice—is concerned:

SCHOOLS AROUND LONDON
↓
MILITARY ACADEMIES CLOSE TO LONDON
↓
BRITISH TROOPS
↓
NORTH AMERICA

The other mention of hockey played on ice in Canada prior to 1875 is the only one that did not come from a member of the military, but rather a priest—later the bishop of Norwich. In his 1906 book *A Bishop in the Rough*, Englishman John Sheepshanks (1834-1912) wrote about hockey played (on ice) in New Westminster, British Columbia, in 1862.[11]

In Montreal, we know that the instigator of the first documented games is James George Aylwin Creighton, who not coincidentally hailed from Nova Scotia. He brought with him knowledge of the game, and may well have obtained other tips about it from English (or possibly other British) sources while in Montreal. After all, just 10 years before, the first "proper" game of rugby was played in Montreal, between officers of a British garrison and a civilian team composed mainly of McGill students.[12]

By 1875, British troops were gone, but news still travelled relatively quickly from the "mother country" (as seen from the English-speaking population's point of view, of course)—witness the 1876 use of the Hockey Association rules in Montreal just a year after they were promulgated in England.

Meanwhile...

Obviously, ice hockey did not come to a halt in England in 1875—far from it. As mentioned in chapter 7, NSA rules (two coexisting sets) were officialized in 1883 and the game's popularity did not diminish, although it remained at the mercy of unpredictable weather conditions—the frosts that were necessary for the game to be played— rendering the creation of tournaments or leagues an act of faith not undertaken before 1897, with the New Niagara Hockey Tournament.[13]

In January of 1887, for example, a game of hockey between "an Odiham team and a team under the captaincy of Mr. Hargreaves, of Maiden Erlegh, near Reading" saw the home team prevail, but the "return match, however, did not come off owing to the sudden change in the weather."[14]

A legitimate question that could be asked is whether those frosts were frequent enough for hockey to have been regularly played on ice in England in the 19th century and earlier, and not just on a handful of occasions. The authors have compiled the list of all winters during which skating or stick-ball games on ice were reported (as opposed to just freezing temperatures, which give little indication on the thickness of the ice), and it was found that, between the years 1800 and 1875, there were reports of skating in 72 of 76 winters.[15] In the 18th century, the number of newspapers was limited, so the picture obtained is almost certainly not a full one; yet it was still possible to find skating reports for 26 of the 50 winters of the second half-century, and 12 in the first half.[16]

The oldest retrieved mention of the use of iron skates (as "skeates," "scates" and "scheets," all spellings derived from the Dutch *schaats*)[17] in England is from December of 1662, where they were worn in St. James's Park in Westminster (London), as noted in two different published diaries. The first is that of Samuel Pepys (1633-1703), deciphered by the Rev. John

Smith of St. John's College, Cambridge, more than a century after Pepys's death and published in 1825. On three consecutive Mondays, Pepys noted skating activities:

> [December 1, 1662] To my Lord Sandwich's, to Mr. Moore; and then over the Parke, (where I first in my life, it being a great frost, did see people sliding with their skeates, which is a very pretty art,)...
> [December 8, 1662] Then to my Lord Sandwich's, and there spent the rest of the morning in making up my Lord's accounts with Mr. Moore, and then dined with Mr. Moore and Battersby his friend, very well and merry, and good discourse. Then into the Parke, to see them slide with their skeates, which is very pretty.
> [December 15, 1662] To the Duke, and followed him into the Parke, where, though the ice was broken and dangerous, yet he would go slide upon his scates, which I did not like, but he slides very well.[18]

Similar to Pepys's diary, the second was also published more than a century after the event. John Evelyn (1620-1706) was an English writer and gardener whose diaries spanned more than 60 years (1641-1706) of English history. They were found by chance, in 1817, hidden in an old clothes basket. They were first published in 1818, but it was the second, expanded, edition of 1827 that contained the reference to the skating of 1662 (the spelling from the 1827 edition has been preserved, although later editions made some alterations):

> Having seene the strange and wonderful dexterity of the sliders on the new canal in St. James's Park, perform'd before their Majesties by divers gentlemen and others with scheets, after the manner of the Hollanders, with what swiftness they passe, how suddainely they stop in full carriere upon the ice, I went home by water, but not without exceeding difficultie, the Thames being frozen, greate flakes of ice incompassing our boate.[19]

London would finally get its first indoor (artificial) ice rinks late in the century. The year 1896 saw the opening of the National Skating Palace, which was not the first indoor rink, but the site of the first hockey game to be played indoors.[20] The first two games played there were, at least nominally, the first ice hockey games between teams representing their countries, as

HOCKEY ON THE ICE.

A capital match took place at the National Skating Palace on Saturday evening, between two teams representing England and Canada. A large number of spectators thoroughly enjoyed the spirited contest, displaying much interest in the principal combatants. It was generally expected that Canada, led by Mr. Meagher, would have won, but the result was exactly the reverse, England making three goals to nil, two of them due to Mr. Davidson, and one to Mr. Tyler. The players were: England—Hebert, W. B. Cooper, Tyler, White, Davidson, and Hick; Canada — Hancock, Meager, S. B. Cooper, Stanton, Owen, and Hon. Algernon Grosvenor.

Newspaper account of the game at the National Skating Palace on February 1, 1896.

"England" and "Canada" met on Saturday, February 1[21] and Thursday, February 6.[22] "England" won both games, by scores of 3-0 and 4-2. Coverage of the second game included an illustration (seen on page 252.).

It is not known whether "Team Canada" actually featured more than one Canadian, but we have seen previously that Algernon Grosvenor was English. It *is* known that at least one Canadian played for the team designated as Canada in those games.

George (Alfred) Meagher (1866-1930), born in Kingston, took an interest in ice skating and hockey at an early age. The second-youngest of 15 siblings, he was the younger brother of Daniel (1845-1912), a doctor who played in the first Montreal game (on the Torrance team—in the game reports, he was the first-named player on the team, after the captain).[23] George was also the uncle of Arthur Farrell (1877-1909), who won the Stanley Cup in 1899 with the Montreal Shamrocks, and successfully defended its possession in two challenges in 1900. Farrell wrote the first Canadian book on hockey in 1899[24] and was inducted into the Hockey Hall of Fame in 1965.

Meagher was also an excellent figure skater, earning both the amateur and professional world figure skating championship titles. He was inducted

An artist's representation of the action in the game played on February 6, 1896.

into the Skate Canada Hall of Fame in 2010. In the 1890s, he made several trips to Europe, where he performed as a figure skater, but he was also always happy to arrange ice hockey games, introducing the game to Paris (in 1894),[25] Glasgow (in 1896)[26] and Brussels (in 1899).[27] He is considered the founder of Belgian ice hockey.[28] In 1898, he organized and participated in games between Davos and St. Moritz in Switzerland.[29]

Canada had been playing ice hockey formally for less than a quarter of a century, and already it was exporting it back to Europe!

Chapter 13 Notes

1.   "The Irish in Nova Scotia," *Nova Scotia Blogs,* 17 Mar. 2011, web, 19 Apr. 2014, <http://www.novascotia.com/about-nova-scotia/blogs /irish-nova-scotia>.

A hockey game between Virginia Water and Palace Bandy Club, played a few months after the opening of the National Skating Palace (a.k.a. Hengler's Grand Cirque) in London.[30]

2. "Arrival of the English and the Scottish Settlers," *Sectarianism in Ireland*, n.d., web, 19 Apr. 2014, <http://sectarianisminireland.weebly.com/arrival-of-scottishenglish-settlers.html>.

3. "The Hector Passenger List, Arrived in Pictou 1773," *Pictou County, Nova Scotia GenWeb*, 15 Mar. 1998, web, 19 Apr. 2014, <http://www.rootsweb.ancestry.com/~nspictou/pass_ships/hector.html>.

4. Bruce G. Wilson, "Loyalists," *The Canadian Encyclopedia*, 2 Apr. 2009, web, 19 Apr. 2014, <http://www.thecanadianencyclopedia.ca/en/article/loyalists/>.

5. *The Diary of William Bentley, D. D., Pastor of the East Church, Salem, Massachusetts, Volume 1: 1784-1792* (Salem: The Essex Institute, 1905): 253–254.

6. Tim Fashion, "Winter. —Now," *Acadian Magazine; or Literary Mirror* (Halifax, N. S.), January 1827.

7. *Acadian Recorder* (Halifax), 3 Dec. 1869.

8. J. M. Bumsted, "Scots," *The Canadian Encyclopedia*, 27 Aug. 2013,

web, 19 Apr. 2014, <http://www.thecanadianencyclopedia.ca/en/article/scots/>.

9. John Franklin, *Narrative of a Second Expedition to the Shores of the Polar Sea, in the Years 1825, 1826, and 1827* (London: John Murray, 1828).

10. John Cordes, *British Regiments in Halifax—by Date*, 30 Jun. 2006, web, 19 Apr. 2014, <http://www.johncordes.ca/genealogy2/regiments/britishregiments_halifax.html>.

11. John Sheepshanks, *A Bishop in the Rough* (New York: E. P. Dutton & Co., 1906): 57.

12. Tim Burke, "Montreal Rich in Grid History but Could Bring Down the CFL," *The Gazette* (Montreal), 24 Jul. 1986.

13. *Pall Mall Gazette* (London), 8 Mar. 1897.

14. *Reading Mercury, Oxford Gazette* (Reading, U. K.), 22 Jan. 1887.

15. British newspapers reported on skating activities in all 76 winters between 1799–1800 and 1874–75, except for four. The only winters when skating seems not to have been possible were: 1800–01, 1821–22, 1827–28 and 1833–34.

16. The "Little Ice Age" has been conventionally defined as a period extending from the 16th to the 19th centuries. The period between 1750 and 1840 was extraordinary for the frequency of explosive volcanic eruptions, which maintained dust veils high in the atmosphere and may have contributed (perhaps significantly) to the reversal of what otherwise would have been a noted climatic recovery from the late 1600s onwards.
    "History of Weather," *The Champion* (London), 30 Aug. 1818: 549–550; "Historical Weather Events," *Meteorology@West Moors*, web, 19 Apr. 2014, <http://booty.org.uk/booty.weather/climate/wxevents.htm>; James A. Marusek, "A Chronological Listing of Early Weather Events," *Breadandbutterscience.com*, 3 Jun. 2011, web, 19 Apr. 2014, <http://www.breadandbutterscience.com/Weather.htm>.

17. Douglas Harper, *Online Etymology Dictionary, 2001–2014*, web, 1 Apr. 2014, <http://www.etymonline.com/index.php?term=skate>: "**skate** (n.2): 'ice skate,' 1660s, *skeates* 'ice skates,' from Dutch *schaats* (plural *schaatsen*), a singular mistaken in English for plural, from Middle Dutch *schaetse*. The word and the custom were brought to England after the Restoration by exiled followers of Charles II who had taken refuge in Holland."

18. The entries for December 1 and 15 are quoted from Baron Richard Griffin Braybrooke, ed., *Memoirs of Samuel Pepys, Esq., F. R. S., Secretary to the Admiralty in the Reigns of Charles II and James II, Comprising His Diary from 1659 to 1669,* vol. I (London: Henry Colburn, 1825): 183, 185. The December 8 entry is quoted from Baron Richard Griffin Braybrooke, ed., *Diary and Correspondence of Samuel Pepys, F. R. S., Secretary to the Admiralty in the Reigns of Charles II and James II,* 4th ed., vol. I (London: Henry Colburn, 1854): 357.

19. William Bray, ed., *Memoirs of John Evelyn, Esq. F. R. S., Comprising His Diary, from 1641–1705-6, and a Selection of His Familiar Letters,* vol. II (London: Henry Colburn, 1827): 204.

20. From an advertisement in *The Times* (London), 23 Jan. 1896: "NATIONAL SKATING PALACE (HENGLER'S GRANDE CIRQUE): Mr. MEAGHER (Champion Skater of the World) is now organizing the PALACE HOCKEY-MATCHES and other NOVEL EFFECTS."

21. The story from the London *Echo* of February 3, 1896, read as follows:

HOCKEY ON THE ICE

A capital match took place at the National Skating Palace on Saturday evening [February 1], between two teams representing England and Canada. A large number of spectators thoroughly enjoyed the spirited contest, displaying much interest in the principal combatants. It was generally expected that Canada, led by Mr. Meagher, would have won, but the result was exactly the reverse, England making three goals to nil, two of them due to Mr. Davidson, and one to Mr. Tyler. The players were: England — Hebert, W. B. Cooper, Tyler, White, Davidson, and Hick; Canada — Hancock, Meag[h]er, S. B. Cooper, Stanton, Owen, and Hon. Algernon Grosvenor.

22. The report of the second match, played on February 6, 1896, appeared in the *Penny Illustrated Paper and Illustrated Times,* 22 Feb. 1896, together with a drawing depicting the game:

The Hockey Match Played on the Ice Between England and Canada at the National Skating Palace produced play of a very high order indeed, the result being in the nature of a surprise, for few could have anticipated that the Canadians, reared as they are half their lives on ice-fields, would have succumbed. Yet our countrymen by very excellent play managed to score a sensational victory, the result standing four goals to two. A few words anent the new Recreation Hall of London. A marvellous transformation strikes the visitor on entering the old Hengler's Cirque. In the place of the old cirque one finds a perfect fairy palace, the illusion being enhanced by dainty electric lights peeping out from every conceivable form of flower and plant. The ice is the most perfect of its kind ever produced artificially.

23. Susanna McLeod, "Spirits, Skates and Hockey," *Kingston Whig-Standard,* 23 Mar. 2011, web, 19 Apr. 2014, <http://www.thewhig.com/2011/03/23/spirits-skates-and-hockey>.
24. Arthur Farrell, *Hockey: Canada's Royal Winter Game* (Montreal: C. R. Corneil, 1899).
25. *Brooklyn (N. Y.) Eagle,* 13. Dec. 1896.
26. Ibid.
27. Jan Casteels, *90 Jaar IJshockey in Belgie* (Itegem, Belgium: Jan Casteels, 1995).
28. Ibid.
29. *The Field* (London), 21 Jan. 1898, and *Davoser Zeitung,* 14 Jan. 1899.
30. *Black and White Magazine* (London), 4 Apr. 1896: 420. The drawing was made by Ernest Prater (1864–1950), a noted English artist and book illustrator, known also for his work as a war correspondent and reportage artist during the Anglo-Boer War.

The drawing was accompanied by the following text: "Hockey on the ice has always been a favourite sport with good skaters, and of late, thanks to the ice rink at Hengler's, a pastime nature has this year denied to southern skaters can be enjoyed by performers and witnessed in complete comfort by spectators. Virginia Water has long boasted a crack team of hockey players, and few other organisations have lived with them at their special sport. These gentlemen met a Palace team recently [March 26] at Hengler's, and after a grand and protracted struggle suffered defeat by four goals to two."

The Original Six

A<small>S WE REACH THE CONCLUSION</small> of this book, the authors acknowledge that not all questions have been answered. However, at least a few facts have been established.

1. Ice hockey, fitting the six-point definition set out in the Society for International Hockey Research's 2002 report on the Windsor, Nova Scotia, claim, and often *called* hockey (sometimes "hockey on the ice"), was played in England for several decades before it was played in Canada.
Even using the narrowest interpretation of the SIHR report—one that requires a report of a specific game, published in a contemporary publication—a game called hockey was played as early as February 3, 1838, on Croxby Pond, Lincolnshire, and a game called bandy (the same game, but with a different name) was played as early as January 28, 1831, in Colne, Huntingdonshire.

Applying a definition of hockey that does not require the reporting of a specific game, hockey was played on ice, with skates, and was called hockey as far back as the early 1820s, in Shrewsbury, Shropshire, as evidenced by the Charles Darwin letter.

The tradition of hockey (called bandy) being played on ice with skates in the Fens goes back to the mid-1700s, and the illustration on the cover of this book, clearly showing ice hockey players, dates from 1796 or 1797.

2. There were several instances of organized hockey games played in England before the one played on March 3, 1875, in Montreal.
We consider a game to correspond to the definition of "organized" if it was arranged in advance between identified teams and played at a specific place, date and time (though the time may not have been mentioned in the game reports), with a recorded outcome. Several reports fulfilled all these criteria, in particular:

- Two reports (Spetchley, Worcestershire, 1870, and Moor Park, Hertfordshire, 1871) also had the names of every goal scorer—a feature not available for the first Montreal game—as well as the names of all players.
- Another report (Elsham, Lincolnshire, 1871) also gave the times of the goals (information not available for the first Montreal game), but not the names of all players.
- A fourth (Swavesey, Cambridgeshire, 1857) identified all players, as well as which team won the game, but not the exact score. In this case, the game was called bandy.

3. No reasonable definition of hockey could be imagined that would include all games played in Montreal since March 3, 1875, but exclude all games played in England prior to that date.
The statement is also true if "Montreal" is replaced by any of the other Canadian towns or cities that have a birthplace claim.

4. Prior to the 1890s (and even later in many regions), bandy and hockey were exactly the same activity, called by different names depending on the region.
Any observed differences were due to local variations of the game, not to the fact that the game was called by one name or the other. In particular, while the game in the Fens was called bandy and was played according to slightly different rules than the game called hockey that was played in London, it does not mean that the former was not hockey. Separate sets of rules were established by the NSA in 1883, one for the game "as played in the Fens" and the other "as played in Metropolitan District." This situation can be compared to organizations such as the International Ice Hockey Federation or the American Hockey League, which have slightly different rules from

the National Hockey League—and yet, the game played in all leagues is considered hockey. The Pacific Coast Hockey Association also played under different rules than the National Hockey Association (and later, the NHL)—for a time, the PCHA game even required a different number of players to take the ice. That did not prevent these leagues from meeting each year and determining the Stanley Cup champion—both were playing hockey.

5. The activity in which children and adults engaged on ice with skates in England in the 19th century—and even before—was not merely a variety of "stick and ball games." It was hockey.
It was not "hockey as we know it today," but then, neither were the games played in Montreal in the 19th century.

And most importantly:

6. Ice hockey does not have mysterious origins. It came very naturally to English (and other British) field hockey players who took their game to the ice and put on skates when the weather provided such ice, which occurred almost every winter.
Early versions of ice hockey came to Canada from British settlers and immigrants—via the United States, in the case of the United Empire Loyalists—while the more modern forms usually came from British (mostly English) military personnel stationed in Canada. In the 1870s, hockey rules probably arrived through "regular" communication channels of the times—the same ones that brought information about the royal family, for example.

Let us now revisit the "main" Canadian birthplace claims—the six principal claims from among the ones considered in chapter 1. One common element among all of these claims is that they are both strengthened and weakened by the information provided in this book. They are strengthened—save, perhaps, for the Montreal claim, where there is no doubt that hockey was played in Montreal—because we now know it is entirely plausible that ice hockey could have been played in those places, considering that the game had been played previously throughout Great Britain by the people who populated much of Canada or who later were sent as military reinforcements. However, the claims are also all weakened, because it is now clear that no Canadian town or city could be considered the "birthplace" of ice hockey, since for every reference to hockey played in Canada, there is an earlier, more conclusive reference to hockey played in Great Britain.

Windsor, Nova Scotia
Whichever way one looks at it, the Windsor claim will always suffer from relying chiefly on a fictitious character in a novel imagining a conversation that involves "hurly... on the ice" (no skates mentioned) in a book written a few decades after the activity is alleged to have taken place. The proponents of the Windsor claim do have a non-fictitious reference—not a great one, as it describes events 60 years after the fact, but it's a start—and it may be a good idea to give this reference more prominence, in particular by making a facsimile of the original clipping available to other researchers.

Deline, Northwest Territories
The Deline claim, if it hews to the "first hockey on ice in Canada" line, is actually quite strong. We know with certainty that, in 1825, hockey was played there on ice and that skates were available. We also know that there is a very good chance that Sir John Franklin, from his military training, could have experienced ice hockey earlier in his life, so the likelihood that the game played on the ice actually involved skates seems quite high. And in fact, the Deline references, dating from 1825, are the second-oldest con-temporary references to a game called hockey played on the ice; only the drowning report of a hockey player in St. James's Park in 1822—where the use of skates is far from certain—is older. Of course, we know that hockey, under that name, was played on the ice with skates prior to these references, thanks to non-contemporary, but reliable, references such as the Darwin letter.

On the other hand, Deline should really abandon the term *birthplace,* which hurts its credibility. After Franklin's informal games, played to pass the time, no hockey was played in Deline for over a century and a half, which does not bode well for any kind of birthplace pretence.

Niagara Falls, Ontario
As with Deline, there is no doubt that hockey was played on the ice in Niagara Falls (in this case, in 1839), and here we have an absolute certainty that they were playing on skates. However, these games occurred a year later than the Croxby Pond game mentioned at the beginning of this chapter (and described

in detail in chapter 3). And with their "forty or fifty being ranged on each side," those Niagara Falls games must not have been pretty sights.

The Niagara claim is also similar to Deline in that there is no evidence that the game continued to be played in the area once the British military left, though it did not take quite as long for the game to return, as Niagara Falls was home to a team in the Southern Ontario Hockey Association before the end of the 19th century.[1]

Kingston, Ontario

The Kingston claim is, to the outside observer, nearly identical to that of Niagara Falls, except that it is better known. While it is not certain that the hockey played there in 1843 was on skates, the authors are quite convinced that, as with Niagara Falls, it actually was. However, the Kingston hockey, which might have taken the form of some games, or could have been just informal practices, took place four years later than the Niagara Falls games, and five years later than the Croxby Pond game. And as in Niagara Falls, when the troops left, it would appear that they took their game with them, as the only other Kingston reference uses the term "shinny" and provides little reliable information. However, hockey did return to Kingston, and probably somewhat sooner than to Niagara Falls: the rivalry between Queen's University and Royal Military College started with a game played on March 10, 1886.[2]

Halifax-Dartmouth, Nova Scotia

This is certainly the most interesting birthplace claim to re-examine. First, we need to explain why three references advanced the proponents of the Halifax-Dartmouth claim were excluded from our enumeration in chapter 1.

First among these is an article in the *Novascotian* on Thursday, February 24, 1831:

> There has been excellent skating upon the head of the North West Arm, and large parties of our Townsfolks and the Military, have enjoyed, during several afternoons of this and the past week, the healthy and spirit stirring game of Wicket.[3]

The term *wicket* is assumed to refer to an early form of hockey on the ice. This is, however, the only account using that name that can be found in any contemporary report describing a game on the ice.

A game called wicket was, however played in New England from the early 1700s onward—and was understood there to be a primitive form of cricket, played in England up to the middle of the 18th century. In England, cricket was occasionally played on the ice—and in some cases, even on skates.[4]

The second overlooked reference is an 1863 poem entitled "Frost." It appeared in the *Halifax Reporter* on January 20, 1863, and some stanzas include evocations of skating and games on the ice, such as:

> Hurra! the lake is a league of grass!
> Buckle and strap on the stiff white glass.
> Off we shoot, and poise and wheel;
> And swiftly turn upon scoring heel;
> And our flying sandals chirp and sing
> Like a flock of swallows upon the wing.[5]

According to Martin Jones, this describes a hockey game, possibly played indoors at the newly built private indoor rink.[6]

However, this poem was already a relatively old one, having first been published in 1850 under its full title, "Frost in the Holidays."[7] However, the poem's age is not as important as the fact that it was written by the Irish-born poet William Allingham (1824–1889), who spent most of his adult life in England and never visited Canada.[8] So the poem could not possibly have been describing hockey—or any other activity—played in Nova Scotia.

Finally, on January 25, 1864, the *Halifax Morning Sun* published an article under the headline "A Few Hints on Skating!" The 1,000-word article takes a stand against hockey played on the ice, stating that the activity "ought to be sternly forbidden, as it is not only annoying, but dangerous." It goes on to advocate playing the game only on the ground: "In its right place, hockey is a noble game, and deserving of every encouragement, but on the ice it is in its wrong place, and should be prohibited. Any weak place in the ice is sure to give way if the ball should happen to pass over or near it; for the concourse of fifty or a hundred persons all converging upon the same point is a test which no ice, save the very strongest, is able to bear."[9]

However, this article had originally been published (with no author credited) a year earlier, in the January 1863 issue of *London Society: An Illustrated*

Magazine of Light and Amusing Literature for the Hours of Relaxation, where it was titled "On the Ice."[10] It had also been reproduced in the February 1863 issue of *The Eclectic Magazine of Foreign Literature, Science, and Art,* under the title "Skating on the Ice."[11]

It is possible that Martin Jones has become aware of this, as the reference does not appear on the "Hockey's Home" website.

Even without these three references, Halifax still has many others to put forward, some of them quite good, though the authors are reluctant to place too much credence in the "silhouette" image. If an outline of a child carrying what looks vaguely like a hockey stick, but without a ball, a puck or skates, can be considered as evidence of ice hockey being played in Halifax, then what should be made of a gravestone, from the 15th or 16th century, found at the Clonca church in Inishowen, County Donegal, Ireland?

The Scots-Gaelic inscription on this gravestone reads FERGUS MAK ALLAN DO RINI IN CLACH SA—MAGNUS MEC ORRISTIN IA FO TRI SEO, *which translates to "Fergus Mac Allan made this stone—Magnus Mac Orristin of the Isles under this covering." Mr. Mac Orristin is the most ancient person known by name who, we know with certainty, played a stick-and-ball game similar to hockey in the British Isles—in this case, apparently an early form of hurling.*[12]

(A detail of the gravestone, made from a cast held at the Gaelic Athletic Association Museum at Croke Park Stadium in Dublin, can be seen at left.)

Yet, with all its other references, Halifax does appear to have had a long, uninterrupted tradition of playing hockey (under a few different names) since at least the second quarter of the 19th century. It was certainly not the birthplace of hockey, and it was also not necessarily the first place in Canada where it was played (it has no supporting documents older than the Franklin references from Deline), but it is possible that there is enough evidence to consider Halifax-Dartmouth the "cradle" of hockey in Canada, from where James George Aylwin Creighton took the game to Montreal. SIHR's committee on the Origins of Hockey may wish to give it due consideration.

As an aside, it is not clear where the term *ricket* originated, but one source, from Salem, Massachusetts in 1791, describes ricket as "played double," possibly meaning that it was played between two teams and using two goals.[13]

Montreal, Quebec

The Montreal claim is already strong, as mentioned before, in the sense that nobody doubts that hockey was played there in 1875 and in every year since.

But is it the birthplace of organized hockey? Probably not; at least unless a very narrow definition of "organized" is used, one requiring that the game be played indoors and have been announced in newspapers (not just through word of mouth) ahead of time, with the exact time being mentioned, and admission being charged (though "subscribers could present their tickets").[14]

But the strength of the Montreal claim is that, from that first game, hockey became increasingly structured, at an accelerated pace, thanks in large part to the early work, enthusiasm and "marketing" know-how of James

Creighton, the organizer and promoter of nearly all games played in Montreal between 1875 and 1879 and the person who "got the ball rolling" (although perhaps a metaphor involving a puck should be used instead).

In Montreal, from this first game in 1875:

- Most games were advertised in advance and reported on, along with the scores and the names of the players.
- The following year, rules (from the Hockey Association, the English national field hockey organization) were used.
- In the third year, the Hockey Association rules were adapted for play on an indoor ice rink and published.
- The ninth year saw the inauguration of an annual tournament, the Montreal Winter Carnival Hockey Tournament.
- In the 12th year, a five-team league was established, the Amateur Hockey Association of Canada (AHAC), with improved rules. Today, the AHAC is considered the ancestor of all North American hockey leagues and, to a large extent, of all ice hockey leagues in the world.

The first Montreal game was the launching pad for the rapid transformation of the game, with Canada making the sport its own, reinventing it, and, in the process, becoming the world's dominant hockey force, a position it has never relinquished.

The precursor to the IIHF, the Ligue Internationale de Hockey sur Glace (LIHG), was founded in May of 1908, and to a large extent adopted the Canadian rules (descended from the Montreal rules),[15] many of which were already in use in various places in Europe. Great Britain, which early on had begun using some of the Canadian rules, joined the LIHG in November of the same year[16] and, as a consequence, "formalized" its adoption of rules largely inspired by the Canadian ones—while, in parallel, the more "traditional" rules continued to be used for the game that kept the name *bandy* and evolved into a distinct sport.

In just 33 years, Canada had taken ownership of hockey to such an extent that it had (in part via the LIHG) imposed many of its own rules upon the country from which it had inherited the game.

Canada won the first six Ice Hockey World Championships (including Olympic tournaments), starting in 1920, and won 19 of the first 28, up

James George Aylwin Creighton, the father of organized hockey in Canada.

until 1961. In the following eight years, against the top players of the strongest European nations, Canada won four more medals while icing players who, for the most part, would not have been considered to be in the top 100 of their own country.

In all the history of men's ice hockey, there have been just 12 "best on best" tournaments. These include all editions of the Canada Cup (first held in 1976) and the World Cup (first held in 1996), as well as the Olympic tournaments since 1998. Canada has won eight of those 12 tournaments, while no other country has yet won more than once.

In women's hockey, Canada has won 10 of 15 world championships, earning the silver medal in the other five, and has won four of five Olympic tournaments since 1998. (Note: In women's hockey, unlike men's, the IIHF World Championships do feature "best on best" competition.)

Today, regardless of where it is played, hockey is a truly Canadian game. *That* is the legacy of the first Montreal game, thanks in large part to the leadership of James Creighton, who recognized how ideally suited to Canada's climate and people the game of ice hockey was, and who masterfully gave it the impulse it needed to become the greatest winter sport that exists. In the authors' humble opinion, Creighton deserves a place among the honoured members of the Hockey Hall of Fame.

Chapter 14 Notes

1. *Daily Mail and Empire* (Toronto), 6 Jan. 1898.
2. Erin Flegg, "FebFest Honours First Hockey Game," *Queen's Journal*, 13 Feb. 2007, web, 20 Apr. 2014, <http://queensjournal.ca/story/2007-02-13/sports/febfest-honours-first-hockey-game/>.
3. *Novascotian* (Halifax), 24 Feb. 1831.
4. "Bandy-wicket" is defined as "the game of cricket" in Robert Forby, *The Vocabulary of East Anglia: An Attempt to Record the Vulgar Tongue of the Twin Sister Counties, Norfolk and Suffolk, as It Existed in the Last Twenty Years of the Eighteenth Century, and Still Exists; with Proof of Its Antiquity from Etymology and Authority*, vol. I (London: John Bowyer Nichols and Son, 1830): 14–15.

   In his blog, *Our Game*, John Thorn, the official historian of Major League Baseball, writes: "Wicket is a vanished game that for more than a century was the dominant game of parts of New England, notably Connecticut, and the Western Reserve, extending to Ohio and what is now termed the Midwest. Not baseball and not cricket, it may be understood as a primitive form of cricket, one no longer played in England by the middle of the 18th century." (John Thorn, "The Old-Time Game of Wicket," *Our Game*, 13 Jul. 2012, web, 19 Apr. 2014, <http://ourgame.mlblogs.com/2012/07/17/the-old-time-game-of-wicket/>).

   See also John Thorn, "The Oldest Wicket Game, Newly Found," *Our Game*, February 5, 2012, web, 19 Apr. 2014, <http://ourgame.mlblogs.com/2013/02/05/the-oldest-wicket-game-newly-found/>; Ray Hardman, "Before There Was Baseball, There Was Wicket," *WNPR News*, 31 Oct. 2013, web, 19 Apr. 2014, <http://wnpr.org/post/there-was-baseball-there-was-wicket>; "Wicket," *Protoball*, 14 May 2013, web, 19 Apr. 2014, <http://beta.protoball.org/Wicket>; "A Cricket March in Skates," *The New Times* (London), 4 Feb 1826; "Cricket Match on the Ice [in skates]," *Bell's Life in London, and Sporting Chronicle,* 28 Jan. 1838; "Cricket in Skates," *Windsor and Eton Express,* 29 Jan. 1842; "Cricket Match on the Ice [in skates]" *The Guardian* (London), 23 Jan. 1850.

5. *Halifax Reporter,* 20 Jan. 1863, as reproduced in Martin W. Jones, *Hockey's Home — Halifax-Dartmouth: The Origin of Canada's Game* (Halifax, N. S.: Nimbus, 2002): 36.

6. Jones, ix, 35.

7. William Allingham, "Frost in the Holidays," *Poems* (London: Chapman and Hall, 1850). It should be noted that the version reproduced in Jones's book, assumed to correspond accurately to the version published in the *Halifax Reporter,* bears some differences from the original version published in *Poems.* Only three stanzas are quoted (there are nine in the original), some words and much of the punctuation differs, and the last stanza was not included in the original version.

8. William Allingham, *Dictionary of National Biography,* vol. I suppl. (London: Smith, Edler & Co., 1901): 38-40.

9. "A Few Hints on Skating!," *Halifax Morning Sun,* 25 Jan. 1864.

10. "On the Ice," *London Society: An Illustrated Magazine of Light and Amusing Literature for the Hours of Relaxation,* January 1863: 11-18.

11. "Skating on the Ice," *The Eclectic Magazine of Foreign Literature, Science, and Art,* February 1863: 252-258.

12. Flintan O'Toole, "Gallowglass gravestone," *A History of Ireland in 100 Objects,* 30 Apr. 2013, web, 19 Apr. 2014, <http://www.scribd.com/doc/138658050/History-of-Ireland-in-100-Objects> and <http://www.100objects.ie/portfolio-items/galloglass-gravestone/>.

13. *The Diary of William Bentley, D. D., Pastor of the East Church, Salem, Massachusetts, Volume I: 1784-1792* (Salem: The Essex Institute, 1905): 253-254.

    Bentley's diary entry for April 28, 1791, reads: "Puerile Sports usual in these parts of New England. To begin with the Calendar month of January. The youth of the male sex are busy on their Skates... Then comes the Shuttlecock & lasts through May. The action required in this diversion is continued but easy, & the females in proper apartments enjoy it as well as the males. Afterwards the Bat & Ball and the Game at Rickets. The Ball is made of rags covered with leather in quarters & covered with double twine, sewed in Knots over the whole. The Bat is from 2 to 3 feet long, round on the back side but flatted considerably on the face, & round at the end, for a better stroke. The Ricket is played double, & is full of violent exercise of running."

14. *The Gazette* (Montreal), 3 Mar. 1875.

15. Horst Eckert and Ernst Martini, *90 Years IIHF 1908–1998* (Zurich: International Ice Hockey Federation, 1998): 7.

16. *The Times* (London), 2 Dec. 1908.

Shinty

Ricketts

46173143R00159

Made in the USA
Lexington, KY
31 October 2015